# LIFE AFTER PRIVACY

Privacy is gravely endangered in the digital age, and we, the digital citizens, are its principal threat, willingly surrendering it to avail ourselves of new technology, and granting the government and corporations immense power over us. In this highly original work, Firmin DeBrabander begins with this premise and asks how we can ensure and protect our freedom in the absence of privacy. Can – and should – we rally anew to support this institution? Is privacy so important to political liberty after all? DeBrabander makes the case that privacy is a poor foundation for democracy, that it is a relatively new value that has been rarely enjoyed throughout history – but constantly persecuted – and politically and philosophically suspect. The vitality of the public realm, he argues, is far more significant to the health of our democracy, but is equally endangered – and often overlooked – in the digital age.

Firmin DeBrabander is Professor of Philosophy, Maryland Institute College of Art. He has written commentary pieces for a number of national publications, including the *New York Times, Washington Post, The Atlantic, LA Times, Salon, Aeon, Chicago Tribune,* and *The New Republic.* Professor DeBrabander is the author of *Do Guns Make us Free?* (2015), a philosophical and political critique of the guns rights movement.

# Life after Privacy

## RECLAIMING DEMOCRACY IN A SURVEILLANCE SOCIETY

**FIRMIN DEBRABANDER**

Maryland Institute College of Art

# CAMBRIDGE
## UNIVERSITY PRESS

University Printing House, Cambridge CB2 8BS, United Kingdom

One Liberty Plaza, 20th Floor, New York, NY 10006, USA

477 Williamstown Road, Port Melbourne, VIC 3207, Australia

314–321, 3rd Floor, Plot 3, Splendor Forum, Jasola District Centre, New Delhi – 110025, India

79 Anson Road, #06–04/06, Singapore 079906

Cambridge University Press is part of the University of Cambridge.

It furthers the University's mission by disseminating knowledge in the pursuit of education, learning, and research at the highest international levels of excellence.

www.cambridge.org
Information on this title: www.cambridge.org/9781108491365
DOI: 10.1017/9781108868280

© Firmin DeBrabander 2020

First published 2020

Printed in the United Kingdom by TJ International Ltd, Padstow Cornwall

A catalogue record for this publication is available from the British Library.

Library of Congress Cataloging-in-Publication Data
NAMES: DeBrabander, Firmin, author.
TITLE: Life after privacy : reclaiming democracy in a surveillance society / Firmin DeBrabander, Maryland Institute College of Art.
DESCRIPTION: Cambridge, United Kingdom ; New York, NY, USA : Cambridge University Press, 2020 | Includes bibliographical references and index.
IDENTIFIERS: LCCN 2019058605 (print) | LCCN 2019058606 (ebook) | ISBN 9781108491365 (hardback) | ISBN 9781108868280 (ebook)
SUBJECTS: LCSH: Privacy, Right of – Philosophy.
CLASSIFICATION: LCC K3263 .D43 2020 (print) | LCC K3263 (ebook) | DDC 342.08/58 – dc23
LC record available at https://lccn.loc.gov/2019058605
LC ebook record available at https://lccn.loc.gov/2019058606

ISBN 978-1-108-49136-5 Hardback
ISBN 978-1-108-81191-0 Paperback

# Contents

# Preface

Twenty-first century democratic citizens have a paradoxical, increasingly contradictory relationship to privacy. Americans, for example, know, or are taught that privacy is important to the nation's history. Some say there would be no United States if the colonists did not stand up for their privacy against the British crown. And civil rights gains achieved in the latter twentieth century imply robust privacy claims. But ours is become a confessional culture, where people instinctively share the most intimate, sometimes embarrassing, or even offensive comments, images, and opinions. This is practically the norm, and it is facilitated – and encouraged – by digital technology, for which public sharing is the default action.

If you hope to take part in the expansive and all-encompassing digital economy, with its many wonders and remarkable conveniences, you have little choice but to expose many aspects of your personal life. Or your data is simply harvested by corporate and government entities, eager to learn every iota of information about you; they are busy concocting ingenious ways to extract this data, and infer key details about your life – which they then use in ways we can hardly fathom.

There is good reason to worry about those who harvest our data. There is reason to worry about what they might do with it all. Many of these agents are immensely powerful. They include some of the largest corporations on earth, and some of the largest governments. Their intentions for this surveillance are often worrying, if not downright ominous. And yet, it is a striking feature of the digital economy that we, the subjects of a massive onslaught of surveillance, are also central agents of said surveillance. Which is to say: we happily enable it.

We expose our lives as a matter of course; we offer up intimate details, and broadcast them widely and indiscriminately on social media. Or, we ignore pervasive surveillance, and manage our personal information nonchalantly, if irresponsibly, oblivious to the possible consequences of a life lived in the public eye. Of course, we are largely unclear what those consequences might be, or we put little thought to them. Because, it turns out, despite our democratic heritage – and the historical import of privacy in America – most of us are at a loss to say *why* privacy is important, *why* we ought to protect it, *what* is lost when privacy is invaded or obliterated.

This is a perhaps galling state of affairs, given the fact that privacy figures so prominently in our national story – and the fact that privacy is crucial for democracy as such, according to philosophers and political theorists. The United States is of course not alone in forsaking privacy. Democratic citizens the world over are busy forking it over for the sake of digital conveniences.

European democracies have enacted regulations, widely hailed by privacy advocates, to strengthen consumers' hand in protecting their private information from large tech firms and digital retailers. The United States has been lax in this regard, due in no small part to the power of corporate lobbies, which have prevailed upon Congress to avoid similar regulations. As a result, the American consumer is practically colonized by digital interests and agents that want to know every little detail, and monetize it all. To date, the American consumer has not put up much of a fight; and consumer behavior suggests that might not be in the offing. Many are too happy for Amazon to tell us what we should buy next – what we will desire, what will suit our lifestyle, without our even realizing it. Many are thrilled when retailers know our location at any given moment, assist our shopping ventures, and sate our appetites.

In recent years, several important political and commercial controversies have highlighted how tech firms and their customers disregard our privacy interests – such as they are – and collect sensitive information at will, and in some cases seek to manipulate us. Each new controversy reveals more that is known about us, how little privacy we enjoy, and the ravenous appetite and ingenious methods of our many spies. Each incident prompts a flurry of calls for stronger regulations to help consumers protect and preserve their privacy. But it is unclear what those regulations might accomplish, given our entrenched culture of sharing.

If consumers are given greater powers to protect individual privacy, can we count on them to do so, now that they seem content, inured, or wholly disposed to exposing themselves on a regular basis, just to conduct daily business and socialize? What about the fact that prospects for preserving privacy are constantly worse, thanks to the frightening speed at which digital technology advances and evolves? Researchers envision bold new frontiers for surveillance and data extraction – some within our own bodies – and it will be hard to resist these advances, and the remarkable innovations they bring.

A crisis of privacy may also be a crisis of democracy, which, many political theorists contend, requires the inviolate privacy of its citizens. For this reason, and despite the digital tidal wave that crashes upon us, we have no choice but to press ahead, some argue, with whatever privacy regulations and protections we can muster, no matter how modest, or incomplete. We must do whatever we can to help citizens defend privacy, and appreciate it, because that is the ultimate redoubt of freedom. Privacy is necessary, its advocates argue, to produce willful and self-determining citizens. When we lack privacy, and everything is known about us, we can be manipulated by spies – to such an extent, perhaps, that we are ultimately reduced to automatons who can be easily cowed, coerced, and directed by powerful agents. Twentieth-century totalitarian regimes engaged in such efforts, and produced paranoid citizens who were no longer recognizably human, political theorists warned – citizens who would comply with or carry out atrocities. Democracy – liberty – is unthinkable without privacy.

The task of this book is to think it. My aim is to understand the prospects and future of democracy without privacy, or very little of it – and with a citizenry that cares little about privacy, and does not know why to appreciate it, or protect it. I do not take on this task happily, mind you. I enjoy my privacy (again, such as it is) – I am the first to admit it. If I had my druthers, my personal data would be sacrosanct. At least, that sounds good in theory; in practice, it's another matter. Like everyone else, I am steadily sucked into the digital economy, and carry out tasks and chores enabled by surveillance.

For the longest time, I resisted inscribing appointments in my Google calendar, and used an old-fashioned pocket diary instead. After forgetting a few important meetings, however, I gave in, and resorted to the digital calendar, which is synchronized with my cell phone and email, and alerts me to looming appointments anytime, anywhere. This has become a convenience I can scarcely live without. But now my professional calendar – and increasingly, my personal schedule, too – resides somewhere in the public eye, and can be accessed by, well, who knows? Shall I trust that Google will take good care of this information, which, according to some incisive minds, gives deep insights into my habits and preferences? Shall I trust that this information will not get into the hands of perhaps insidious agents who wish to influence me, coerce or control me? By taking advantage of digital technology, and exposing myself in the process, I make myself vulnerable in ways I cannot fully understand or predict – even while said technology sells itself on the promise of liberating me and empowering me.

As I signed off on the final proofs of this book in the Spring of 2020, the world faced an unprecedented crisis that has accelerated and deepened our reliance on digital networks that endanger privacy. The coronavirus pandemic shut down the global economy, causing massive upheaval and distress: people were marooned in their homes, forced to work via online platforms; they had to rely increasingly on internet retailers, while brick-and-mortar shops closed their doors or suffered shortages. Schools and colleges transitioned curricula online in a matter of days, and students had to conduct their learning before a computer screen – if they were lucky enough to have classes still. It was, some said, a taste of things to come, when more, if not most of our economic and social life will be engaged online.

Governments, often aided by powerful corporations, have chosen to combat the pandemic by unleashing massive surveillance programs, taking full advantage of the promise and potential of digital networks. Governments have collected data from networked thermometers (i.e., 'smart thermometers') to identify infection hotspots in certain communities. They have monitored people's movements through cellphone location data, to evaluate or enforce quarantines. Those nations that best contained the disease have carried out thorough contact tracing, which involves collecting and analyzing a host of data points, from cell phone usage, to credit card transactions, and surveillance camera footage, in order to recreate a detailed picture of people's movements and interactions with one another. Contact tracing enables governments to effectively carve out the disease – or literally, people potentially infected with the disease – from society, so that society may continue to function. As the globe has teetered on the brink of depression, and leaders struggled to restart the economy, the prospect of contact tracing – and its extensive surveillance – is hard to resist.

In some cases, governments have sought to allay civil rights concerns by saying that surveillance measures can be retracted when the crisis subsides. But that is unlikely. Soon after 9 – 11, the last cataclysm to similarly shock social life in the US, the government ramped up vast surveillance measures to combat a shadowy enemy. A fearful populace largely went along, and accepted expanded surveillance powers, which were soon normalized. Surveillance methods from the war on terror were repurposed for other uses, especially law enforcement. We should expect a similar result from the coronavirus pandemic. The pandemic has revealed our terrifying vulnerability, racing across the globe, infecting millions in a matter of months. The global response – quarantine, social distancing – has been devastating as well, ruining businesses, bankrupting families, isolating people, and inducing anxiety. Eager, even desperate to escape two fearsome options—disease or societal shutdown – people will tolerate expansive surveillance, and governments will happily double down.

Given the future of the digital economy that rapidly engulfs us, we have little choice but to consider that surveillance is here to stay, and likely expand. We must plan accordingly, and see how democracy is manageable under such circumstances. What are the prospects for freedom as privacy is diminished? How can we be, and act as, potent citizens? How can we hold government and corporations accountable, and make them serve us – as opposed to themselves only? How can we continue to be self-determining citizens when the withering glare of surveillance pierces us thoroughly and completely?

Perhaps privacy is not so necessary to democracy after all. Perhaps there are other essential elements – another wellspring of vibrancy. While many bemoan the loss of privacy, it turns out that the public realm has been greatly diminished in recent decades, and this, I will argue, is more harmful to democracy. Political freedom can be bolstered if we reconvene a vibrant and, yes, messy public life in liberal democracies, which, of their nature, tend to hamper the public realm. What's more, it turns out that privacy is a varied and often confused, even ill-founded notion, which has rarely been achieved or enjoyed throughout history. Protecting privacy, even if that were possible, is not our best hope for ensuring a democratic future. Isn't it conceivable that people have known freedom and political power in the absence of inviolate and certain privacy? Isn't it conceivable that we can do so again – soon?

# Acknowledgements

This book could not have been written without the gracious, timely, and continuous assistance and inspiration of many people. First and foremost, I must thank my wife, Yara Cheikh, for planting many of the concerns in this book, regarding digital society. Her inquisitions, furthermore, forced me to hone my arguments, and her political activism was inspirational, and instructive. I am greatly indebted to my father: our morning conversations about ethics and politics helped me shape my critique of privacy. My mother was always an eager and willing proofreader, providing helpful feedback and first impressions – and keeping me up to date on the hot topics of interest on National Public Radio (NPR). Thanks to my children for their love and support, and for being fascinating case studies in our fast-evolving digital culture. I am also grateful to my colleagues at the Maryland Institute College of Art for supporting my various endeavors, and in many ways. Finally, I must thank my wonderful students at MICA; the idea for this book came out of many classroom discussions and debates over the nature and importance of privacy.

# 1

# Confessional Culture

The current crisis of privacy is, or ought to be, especially surprising in the United States, because privacy concerns, historians and legal scholars attest, were a prime driver in the creation of the nation, and the erection and expansion of our basic freedoms. Our disregard for privacy is surprising for another reason: it defies predictions and expectations of how we are supposed to act under surveillance. Why, if we know we are watched – and we admit as much – is online behavior so shameless, seemingly open and free? Why do so many of us feel compelled to blare intimate details, and share mundane and embarrassing events with the whole world? What does that say about us? Is human nature changing before our very eyes, in the digital age, such that we show no compunction about living an utterly public life, in most all respects? How can we retain any enduring or grudging respect for privacy in this brave new world? Some people muster objections; some admit there is something wrong in privacy invasions – but what? We have a vocabulary of privacy, and a deep historical relationship to it (or so we are told), but hardly know what it means anymore, why it is of value, and worthy of defense. And in the digital age, privacy requires no modest or ordinary defense, but a monumental call to arms, to beat back the tidal wave of surveillance – which we invite, and facilitate.

Privacy is not mentioned in the US Constitution. Nevertheless, scholars have argued that privacy protections stem from the values and experiences of the nation's founders, and are clearly implied in the Bill of Rights. In one respect, "the history of America is the history of the right to privacy."[1] From the inception of this nation, immigrants were driven here by privacy concerns of a kind. The Pilgrims departed England, for example, because they wanted to

---

[1] Frederick S. Lane, *American Privacy* (Boston: Beacon Press, 2009), 1.

be left alone in peace to practice their faith. And the colonial struggle with England was galvanized by controversies over privacy invasions.

The seeds of the Revolutionary War were sown in the dispute over who would bear the cost of the French Indian War, and the ongoing efforts to protect the American frontier and the empire at large. Britain claimed that the colonists needed to bear a greater burden of the costs of such defenses. The colonists objected, and sought to avoid taxation by concealing the fruits of their trade. In Massachusetts in 1755, the English government tried to raise funds by issuing "writs of assistance," which authorized custom house officers to "randomly search sailing ships, dockside warehouses and even private homes for untaxed property."[2] The colonists chafed under this policy, and opposed efforts to renew the writs upon the death of King George II in 1760. In the hearing for their renewal, colonial lawyer James Otis eloquently articulated the opposition. "One of the most essential branches of English liberty is the freedom of one's house," Otis claimed. "A man's house is his castle; and whilst he is quiet, he is well guarded as a prince in his castle. This writ [of assistance], if it should be declared legal, would totally annihilate this privilege."[3] Otis cites a long-standing element of English Common Law known as Castle Doctrine – "one's home is his castle," a sacrosanct space where he is most perfectly free. Castle Doctrine is still prominently invoked in US law today, in, among other things, self-defense and gun rights concerns. Courts have recognized a robust right of self-defense for individuals wielding guns in the home, against unwanted strangers.

The concern for privacy became a major driver of the Revolutionary War, and though the term does not appear in our founding documents, its influence can be detected – and privacy protections inferred. In the Bill of Rights, for example, the Third Amendment, which prohibits soldiers being quartered in one's home, is a clear reaction against British efforts to do the same, invading and occupying colonists' private dwellings. The First Amendment protects our right to make up our minds privately, regarding political and religious affiliation. The Fourth Amendment, which protects against "unreasonable searches and seizures" of the citizenry, such as the British soldiers perpetrated, prominently articulates privacy concerns. In the 1960s, Fourth Amendment jurisprudence becomes the bedrock of a constitutional right to privacy recognized by the Supreme Court.

Prior to that, however, privacy makes a notable appearance on the US legal scene in the 1890s thanks to an influential article written by Samuel Warren

[2] Lane, 10–11.
[3] Lane, 12.

and the future Supreme Court Justice Louis Brandeis. Attempting to express an explicit right to privacy, which they felt was lacking, Brandeis and Warren claim that it amounts to or consists in a "right to be left alone." The US Constitution and English Common Law (which is our Constitution's forbear and foundation) recognize a citizen's right to be protected from intrusion in his person and property. But, Brandeis and Warren explain, times had changed; new technology had emerged, and advanced civilization revealed a new realm in need of defense beyond the merely physical, namely, "man's spiritual nature … his feelings and his intellect."[4] US law had evolved to offer protection for intellectual property, the men point out. But this was insufficient to combat attacks on our emotional well-being, which privacy invasions constituted.

Brandeis and Warren are concerned primarily with gossip, and how technological innovations embolden and empower the gossip mongers, and stoke the general appetite for their wares. A more immediate motivation for their article, it seems, was Warren's annoyance at the exuberant media coverage of his daughter's wedding. The men single out "instantaneous photographs," a new invention at the time, and the "newspaper enterprise" that disseminates them to a hungry public. The latter spurred journalists to pry more deeply into private lives, recording intimate details for posterity. "The press is overstepping in every direction the obvious bonds of propriety and of decency," Brandeis and Warren complain. "To satisfy a prurient taste, the details of sexual relations are spread broadcast in the columns of daily papers. To occupy the indolent, column upon column is filled with idle gossip, which can only be procured by intrusion upon the domestic circle."[5]

They feel they are dealing with a new breed of offense, which is somewhat abstract – the feelings of hurt, or anger, or irritation that emerge when insight into one's private life and emotions are disseminated to the curious, simply for curiosity's sake. And when people hungrily absorb the details of private lives, this media indulgence promotes immoral behavior – prurience and indolence. This seems to be the focus of Brandeis and Warren's ire, as opposed to the offense in privacy invasions, for those whose privacy is invaded. They are more confident in articulating, and more intent in highlighting, the ill that is media gossip, which "both belittles and perverts men," than explaining exactly why and how privacy invasions hurt those whose lives are invaded.[6] This is a recurring theme

---

4   Louis Brandeis and Samuel Warren, "The Right to Privacy," *Harvard Law Review IV*, 5 (1890). http://groups.csail.mit.edu/mac/classes/6.805/articles/privacy/Privacy_brand_warr2.html.
5   Brandeis and Warren.
6   Brandeis and Warren.

going forward: while the hurt from invaded privacy is *felt*, the offense – to those whose lives are exposed – is difficult to pinpoint or spell out. As a result, privacy protections become hard to justify, and easy to surrender.

Law evolves to offer protection for more abstract aspects of our lives, Brandeis and Warren maintain. Such is its natural progression, and it is the result of advancing civilization. Civilization satisfies our basic physical needs, and teaches that happiness consists in more than the satisfaction of those needs. Rather, happiness has a significant emotional and spiritual component. Intellectual property rights are one such creation of advanced civilization and mature jurisprudence, protecting intangible goods – prosecuting people who steal our ideas, for example, preserving ownership and authorship. To that extent, intellectual property protection might seem like a good jumping off point for defending against privacy invasions. But Brandeis and Warren argue it's the other way around. The foundation of intellectual property protections is not private property, but "inviolate personality," that is, the notion of a sacrosanct personal space that ought not be invaded or robbed or exposed under any circumstances.[7] The right to be let alone is a foundational right, a precedent right in common law, which then infuses our Constitution. Until Brandeis and Warren put pen to paper, it was only in need of being pronounced; its growing and newfound significance was made clear by evolving technology and evolving culture.

Only in the 1960s, when the US Supreme Court was presided over by Justice Earl Warren, did the right to privacy receive the full legal recognition and sanction that Brandeis and Warren anticipated. The term "privacy" is pronounced in only 88 Supreme Court cases prior to the 1960s, but in 107 cases under Earl Warren's tenure, suggesting that "the Warren Court made privacy a central legal concept in American law."[8] Justice William O. Douglas was its chief evangelizer. In one notable case, *Griswold* v. *Connecticut*, Douglas wrote the majority opinion, and explained that while certain rights are not explicitly mentioned in the Constitution or under any single provision of the document, they become evident if we would hope to fully enact the provisions of the Bill of Rights.[9] The right to privacy is one such right – and is implied by the First Amendment. We cannot exercise freedom of speech, assembly, or religion without an antecedent right to privacy, which creates an inviolate zone that government, or other powers and interests, dare not trespass. Of itself, the First

---

[7]  Brandeis and Warren.
[8]  Lane, 153–4.
[9]  *Griswold* v. *Connecticut*, 381 US 479 (1965).

Amendment implies a right to privacy, but other provisions combine to carve out a space where we must be let alone, in order to fully enjoy the freedoms spelled out in the Constitution.

Strikingly, Douglas aims to lend privacy an air of longevity, declaring that the institution is "older than the Bill of Rights – older than our political parties, older than our school system."[10] Privacy is as old as the institution of marriage, too, he claims, which is at issue in the case at hand, concerning the state of Connecticut's right to prohibit married couples from learning about contraception. Marriage is a sacred institution, Douglas maintains, and privacy is essential for protecting the intimacy of this bond. This claim is dubious on a few fronts. For one thing, as we will see in Chapter 5, the notion of privacy is hardly monolithic or eternal, but has changed over the centuries. What's more, marriage has changed, too; the institution that Douglas hails was not in fact the repository of sacred intimacy in times past.

In a later case, *Papachristou v. City of Jacksonville*, Douglas invokes the right to be let alone in the case of those accused of loitering and wandering where they are not wanted or permitted. We have a right to meander, uninterrupted and uninterfered because it is one of those private activities "responsible for giving our people the feeling of independence and self-confidence, the feeling of creativity," which is the lifeblood of democracy.[11] Democracy requires that privacy be protected, because it nurtures an independent spirit, and emboldens citizens to experiment, with their travels as with their thoughts. People in a democracy should feel free to speak out, unconstrained by social pressure, perhaps liable to uttering what is wild and offensive on occasion, because this is the ground of dissent, which expands the frontier of liberty in unexpected ways. Douglas leveled this argument against the backdrop of the civil rights movement, whose proponents had to persevere amidst immense social pressure, and outright oppression. It was clear to him, as to many, that privacy is a necessary protection for the expansion of rights that we soon take for granted. Individuals must be allowed to consider, cultivate and express potentially dangerous ideas, free from the intrusion and coercion of social forces intent on maintaining stability, and the status quo.

Privacy and personal independence are inseparable, according to Douglas, and, tellingly, he invokes Thoreau in this regard. Thoreau and his mentor Emerson eloquently and memorably celebrate a strong brand of American individualism, perhaps the quintessential expression thereof. And their account presumes no small degree of privacy, protecting the individual from

---

[10]  *Griswold v. Connecticut*, 381 US 479 (1965).
[11]  *Papachristou v. City of Jacksonville*, 405 US 156 (1972).

the corrupting influence of society, secluding him as far as possible, so that he might hear the authentic voice of his conscience – and more. It is an account that clearly resonates in later iterations and defenses of privacy.

Douglas admires Thoreau's "Walking," which endorses an individual's free and unplanned departure into nature, sauntering in the fields with no prescribed agenda or plan. One is purified in this venture, Thoreau maintains, liberated and opened to hear the voice of truth, which a person can only detect when alone with his thoughts. Society compels us to focus on economic gain, and the lures of wealth and class, none of which truly fulfills us. To the contrary, society infects us with a kind of madness. Unfortunately, we are born into its bondage, which is why so many people take for granted the economic and social demands placed on us, and mindlessly heed them. But real freedom beckons nearby. We only need to stride out into the fields and woods – alone.

In a famous ode to our rightful independence, Thoreau declares that society has us "study the laws of matter at and for our convenience, but a successful life knows no law. It is an unfortunate discovery . . . that of a law which binds us where we did not know before that we were bound. Live free child of the mist!"[12] To discover authentic existence, and live fully, we must detach ourselves from the laws of men. In so doing, we find favor with God, and emulate how He also transcends law – the law of Nature. On one hand, alone in the wilds, we may finally enjoy the peace and quiet to hear the voice of God, and discern his will. In liberating ourselves from human law in this manner, furthermore, we emulate God, the creator of the laws of Nature, who also transcends them.

Thoreau engages in a more elaborate and insistent exercise in self-purification at Walden Pond, where he holes up in a cabin on land owned by his friend Emerson. Embarking on this two-year experiment, Thoreau declares that he will learn how to live deliberately, that is, simply, thoughtfully, consciously. He will isolate and identify his real needs, which he suspects are few. Society dictates that our needs are many, and then sends us endlessly chasing their fulfillment – creating new needs all the while. This is a lie, an unnecessary complication. Authentic living, *real* living, can only be achieved through a kind of separation and isolation – privacy, if you will. Thoreau constructs the cabin himself, bereft of creature comforts; he grows and forages for food, drinks from the stream, and bathes in the pond. He sits on his doorstep listening to the birds, contemplating the sights and sounds around him, straining to detect the immanent wisdom of nature. Most of all, however,

---

[12]   Henry David Thoreau, "Walking," in *Nature/Walking* (Boston: Beacon Press, 1991), 113–14.

Thoreau quiets the din of outside voices, voices that issue demands, fears, worries, and concerns, which, when immersed in the workaday world, seem utterly normal. From his perch, aloof and apart from the common worries of men, their ridiculous nature is readily apparent. Everyone would do well to enjoy this kind of privacy, even for a while, and box out all the chatter. "Let us settle ourselves and work and wedge our feet downward through the mud and slush of opinion and prejudice and tradition and delusion and appearance . . . till we come to a hard bottom and rocks in their place, which we call reality."[13]

Thoreau is moved to compassion at the sight of his peers, weighed down with needless concerns, driven by insatiable and nonsensical social pressures. But Emerson, his intellectual ally, depicts society as nothing less than an adversary; one must be utterly insulated against its assaults and corruptions. A person is properly "Self-Reliant," Emerson argues in his famous essay celebrating individualism. If you would attain the truth and discover the sacred kernel of life, you must ruthlessly block off outside influence and look within. Thoreau relishes his time at Walden Pond, for it reveals the eternal wisdom of the philosophers he has read – it makes clear the truths others have taught for generations. For Emerson, however, you must strike out on a radically new and independent path to attain wisdom. "When good is near you, when you have life in yourself, it is not by any known or accustomed way; *you should not discern the footprints of any other*; you shall not see the face of man; you shall not hear any name—the way, the thought, the good shall be wholly strange and new."[14] Society has nothing to recommend you – nor does history, or tradition, it seems.

Nature is a conduit to authenticity, by this account. Or better yet, nature is the purifying force or milieu that makes each of *us* a conduit for the truth – an empty vessel for the divine. "In the woods," alone, Emerson writes, "all mean egoism vanishes. I become a transparent eyeball; I am nothing; I see all; the currents of the Universal Being circulate through me; I am part or particle of God."[15] I need not physically remove myself from society to enjoy this vision. I can learn to commune with nature in quiet moments when it offers itself to me – which can be anywhere. I must practice the art of solitude, and embrace sacred loneliness whenever possible. Emerson describes doing so while crossing the town commons in the snow, enveloped in silence, and stopping to gaze up at the stars; suddenly, he is one with them.

---

[13]  Henry David Thoreau, *Walden* (New York: Dover Publications, 1995), 16.
[14]  Ralph Waldo Emerson, "Self-Reliance," in *Nature and Selected Essays* (New York: Penguin Books, 1982), 181.
[15]  Ralph Waldo Emerson, "Nature," in *Nature/Walking* (Boston: Beacon Press, 1991), 8.

Emerson and Thoreau offer an account of individualism that will be essential for privacy advocates: if I am to be a proper individual, robust and self-determining, authentic and in touch with "reality," I must filter out external influences and prejudices. I must heed only the voice that wells up within – provided I am able and allowed to hear it. This will prove to be a high bar for privacy, indeed.

The legal, cultural and political forces elevating privacy arguably culminated in the twentieth century, such that privacy became a "fixation ... of US public culture," where it has been "foundational to [our] sense of personhood and national identity."[16] Indeed, the language of privacy is very familiar to us, ingrained as it is in our national narrative and legal system. We instinctively know that privacy matters, and thus find it perfectly normal, or at least unremarkable, when privacy is invoked in public commentary or political speeches. And as I will soon argue, the concern for privacy is still operative or manifest in certain quarters of our lives, in some form or fashion. For the most part, however, in our daily behavior – in cases where privacy concerns should figure prominently – we tend to forsake it with little thought or compunction. Which suggests that, in practice, privacy rings hollow. Few people seem to know what it really means, what it consists in, why it ought to be defended – nor do they seem to care. It attests to a stark disconnect in our culture. Some may retort (or complain) that we hear about privacy incessantly; it is hardly a lost value or norm, but something that still reverberates in our society – the media is littered with its mention. I would contend that the people who matter are not the ones raising the issue, bandying it about, championing it – cherishing it. Increasingly privacy concerns emanate from a select population of scholars, advocates, journalists, and policy makers. And their arguments and warnings do not seem to resonate with the general population. An effective defense of privacy, such as we would require in the digital age, demands a deeper, broader foundation.

For digital technology has made privacy so much more vulnerable, and, in 2013, Edward Snowden exposed an expansive spying program, carried out by the US government, to collect copious amounts of information about its own citizen population, from the digital trails we leave behind in our daily business. Unique to this age and economy is how we, who know that our digital behavior exposes intimate details of our private lives, largely assist our monitors, readily and continuously offering up personal information. To be specific, Snowden, a former contractor for the National Security Agency (NSA), uncovered its PRISM program, which collects data on our digital interactions from major

---

[16] Sarah Igo, *The Known Citizen* (Cambridge, MA: Harvard University Press, 2018), 2, 4.

internet companies, with their compliance. The budget for this program was relatively small ($20 million), suggesting how easy it is for government spies to gather the desired information.[17] We practically volunteer the information. Political philosophers and theorists have long warned that privacy is a prime target of ruling powers, who would happily invade it in order to subdue or control us. What's new today is that we the citizens join in its destruction – actually, we are the principal agents of its demise. The NSA, and anyone else interested in monitoring us (and they are legion) only has to sit back; the intimate details of our lives fall into their laps.

Snowden's revelations were not, nor should have been, terribly surprising to most, upon minimal reflection. Since the War on Terror ramped up last decade, it was well known that the US government was interested in spying on its citizens, and anyone else. Almost immediately after the 9–11 attacks, the Bush administration authorized the NSA to eavesdrop on US citizens and residents, searching for evidence of new terrorist plots.[18] It was revealed at the time that the government had pressured communications companies to enable said eavesdropping, and the government seemed to back off – temporarily. Thus, the American population knew that widespread surveillance of the home population was a likely temptation for our ruling parties, and a perennial threat. And when Snowden revealed the NSA spying operations, there was a profound outcry – at least publicly, and in the press. Scholars, politicians, and civil rights advocates bemoaned the news, and still do for the most part. But average citizens were not impressed, it seems. One study noted that only about a third of those familiar with Snowden's revelations were motivated to improve privacy measures as a result.[19] And in fact, according to another study released soon after Snowden's leak, a majority favored NSA efforts to "[track] the telephone records of millions of Americans," and felt "it is important for the federal government to investigate possible terrorist threats, even if it intrudes on personal privacy."[20]

A summary report three years later suggested that Snowden's revelations were perhaps even less impactful. Subsequent terror attacks prompted people

---

[17]   Leo Kelion, "Q&A: NSA's Prism Internet Surveillance Scheme," *BBC.com*, July 1, 2013, www .bbc.com/news/technology–23051248.

[18]   Eric Lichtblau and James Risen, "Bush lets U.S. spy on callers without courts," *New York Times*, December 16, 2005, www.nytimes.com/2005/12/16/politics/bush-lets-us-spy-on-callers-without-courts.html.

[19]   "CIGI-IPSOS Global Survey on Internet Security and Trust," Centre for International Governance Innovation and IPSOS, November 24, 2014, www.cigionline.org/sites/default/files/documents/internet-survey-2014-slides.pdf.

[20]   "Majority views NSA phone tracking as acceptable anti-terror tactic," Pew Research Center, June 10, 2013, www.people-press.org/2013/06/10/majority-views-nsa-phone-tracking-as-acceptable-anti-terror-tactic/.

to worry more that national security programs did not go far enough in fighting terror, and were less concerned about civil rights protections, in comparison.[21] Most people have taken modest measures to protect privacy online, but the Snowden affair did not inspire widespread adoption of anything more sophisticated which might prove a greater obstacle for NSA spying.[22] Of course, many plead ignorance about sophisticated programs to protect their privacy. They say they would like to do more to protect their data, but are not aware of the best, most effective options. And many remain cynical that they could still elude government surveillance, even after enacting available privacy protection measures. What's more – and what is perhaps especially frustrating for privacy advocates and Snowden doomsayers – most people report that they are not principally worried to block out government spying. Among those who took measures to maintain anonymity online, they indicate that they sought to "avoid 'social surveillance' by friends and colleagues rather than the government or law enforcement."[23] In fact, government and police are dead last among potential monitors that internet users wish to elude.[24]

Political theorists will find this troubling because governments have proven to be a serious threat when they have access to and collect our sensitive personal information. This lends government immense power, which is too easy to abuse, and often leads to and assists oppression. Some argue that the destruction of privacy was essential to twentieth-century totalitarian regimes that aimed at nothing less than total domination of the citizen population. And there is something almost obscene in the fact that Americans of all people are so little concerned with government surveillance, and more worried about snooping family and friends. Protecting our privacy is a central lesson of our nation's history. If we learn anything from the birth of our nation and its founding documents, it's that privacy – from government intrusion – is a supreme virtue and must be jealously defended.

I suspect most Americans know this one way or another; or they should, if they paid attention to their history. Most of us instinctively affirm that privacy is an important value, worthy of protection, if not reverence. As I have argued, we are steeped in a tradition of privacy, from accounts of our history, to essential legal arguments, and our very notion of individualism. Perhaps this is why we will *say* we care about privacy, and would *like* to do a better job

[21] Lee Rainie, "The state of privacy in America," *Pew Research Center*, September 21, 2016, www .pewresearch.org/fact-tank/2016/09/21/the-state-of-privacy-in-america/.
[22] Rainie, "The state of privacy in America."
[23] Rainie, "The state of privacy in America."
[24] "The state of privacy in post-Snowden America," *Pew Research Center*, September 21, 2016, www.pewresearch.org/fact-tank/2016/09/21/the-state-of-privacy-in-america/.

protecting it – and we are uncomfortable with expansive and invasive government surveillance programs. But our behavior indicates something else.

Most consumers say that they are eager to receive discounts and promotions from retailers, but not at the cost of divulging personal information.[25] However, they quickly dispense with their purported trepidation when the rubber hits the road. Retailers know this, and justify their snooping on the basis of tradeoffs: so long as customers receive ample benefits in exchange for divulging personal information – and personalized advertising is the most effective – they will submit to pervasive surveillance. Researchers confirm this. When asked in the abstract, consumers reject the idea of tradeoffs; but when presented with a "real-life tradeoff case – asking . . . whether they would take discounts in exchange for allowing their supermarket to collect information about their grocery purchases" – a very common practice, I might add – "more than twice as many . . . say yes to tradeoffs."[26]

A striking feature of the digital age is that we, individual citizens – eager consumers and avid social media users – hand over personal information to those who watch us. We subscribe to tradeoffs with retailers and social media giants, even when the rewards for exposure are minimal. We do this willingly, in some cases happily, and are not so timid or careful or concerned about displaying our most intimate details, eccentric whims, or caustic opinions. This is a surprising turn of events for many political thinkers, who have long warned that mass surveillance strips us of a feeling of personal freedom, and makes us less liable to speak out and express individual differences, unique opinions, whims, tastes.

In short, a confessional culture is ascendant in the digital age, and this flies in the face of dire predictions about panopticism. Panopticism refers to the surveillance scheme designed by eighteenth-century social reformer Jeremy Bentham, and which he first intended for a prison. His panoptic prison was to be a circular structure with inmates housed in cells around a central tower, whose occupant is obscured, his watchful eye unseen. This structure was revelatory, and widely inspirational, because it illustrates a highly efficient use of power. Consider: you don't need someone literally occupying the tower; if obscured, the inmates never know for sure if or when they are watched – but will behave as if they always are. In this way, "visibility is a trap," as the philosopher Michel Foucault puts it.[27] The

---

[25] Joseph Turow, *The Aisles Have Eyes* (New Haven, CT: Yale University Press, 2017), 158.

[26] Nora Draper, Michael Hennessy and Joseph Turow, "The Tradeoff Fallacy," A Report from the Annenberg School for Communication, University of Pennsylvania, www.asc.upenn.edu /sites/default/files/TradeoffFallacy_1.pdf.

[27] Michel Foucault, *Discipline and Punish*, trans. Alan Sheridan (New York: Vintage Books, 1995), 200.

intention is that inmates might internalize the spectral watchman, and discipline themselves.

And Bentham had high hopes for the impact and influence of the panoptic schema outside the prison walls. If implemented in a variety of venues across society, people would be motivated to behave morally, work diligently, and become better persons and citizens all around. Widespread, perhaps even pervasive panopticism would keep everyone "on the up and up," so to speak, invigorate the economy, improve general well-being, diminish the social welfare state, and lighten the load on government, police, and church, tasked with keeping us all in line. Indeed, Bentham's bold prediction proved tantalizing, and Foucault details how this political revelation was applied throughout the state and society, from schools to factories to hospitals.

From a political perspective, physical force is inefficient in exerting control. It is often expensive, and it can also backfire: extreme force exerted by those in charge might cause people to lash out and revolt. This is most clearly the case for people who are accustomed to freedom, as Machiavelli would say – or people who fancy themselves free, as in a democracy. Surveillance provides an elegant and devastatingly effective solution for powers intent on ruling, and perhaps oppressing, in a democratic age. The architecture of surveillance is "so light," Foucault liked to say; it is subtle, hardly noticeable. It only requires open spaces, through which people can be watched – and watch one another. In this respect – and perversely – methods of surveillance can be easily commingled with or couched within euphemistic calls for openness, transparency, letting in the light. And, in another perversion, Foucault says, we start to see panoptic schemas used to enhance growing disciplinary power that imbues incipient democracies in the nineteenth century, stymying the personal freedoms they promised.

Actually, if we consider its relation to democracy, this gets to the heart of what makes panopticism so powerful and insidious. Panoptic surveillance also fits nicely with the rhetoric and ideology of individualism, because, well, it succeeds so well at individualizing – but not in a good, empowering way. Rather, individuals wither under the spotlight. And in their loneliness, and growing paranoia, they turn into agents of their spies. Consider again Bentham's plan: at the heart of his prison is a spectral watchman – a vague, ominous presence. This vagueness is key, and essential to the supposed efficiency of his system. We, the spied upon, may not know who our spies are exactly, what they want, what they are on the lookout for – what they are soon to punish us for, perhaps. Much is left to the imagination, where it does its critical damage. The spied upon are only supposed to see one another, and in their lateral relations, through their own watchful, worried eyes, compel one another to keep in line – whatever that might mean, exactly. It's better if we are left guessing about that too, to some extent. The result will be that we the watched are reduced to a kind of paranoia, where we are less than free.

Surveillance makes power anonymous, also automatic.[28] Power will not be exerted top-down or from without, in rough imperious fashion, sure to rankle the democratic masses. In panoptic schema, rather, power operates from within each individual – at his or her own behest. Because I do not know precisely who I am curtailing my behavior for, and how, this will largely seem self-directed. And I will seem free and self-determining throughout. With this, we arrive at the full genius of panopticism: it leaves us feeling autonomous and independent, but compliant and chastened instead. And we are the primary agents of social conformity and political obedience, which, depending on the nature and extent of the panoptic scheme employed, Foucault argued, can be stifling indeed.

In many ways, the modern surveillance state has far surpassed Bentham's aspirations – so much so that the title "surveillance state" hardly fits the bill. Retailers, for example, are deeply invested in monitoring us, too, and throughout our daily lives, in a host of hidden ways – shadowing our every move, tracking our every want and whim. The immensity, complexity, and immanence of contemporary surveillance systems has prompted critics to come up with titles that capture it better, like "tenticular oligarcy," or "Big Other," as opposed to Big Brother – conveying the ominous anonymity of our current spies.[29]

Networked digital technology seems the ideal tool to achieve the power dynamic Foucault says is so devastatingly effective in keeping people underfoot in democracies. In terms of the architecture of surveillance, one can hardly imagine anything so "light" or subtle as digital media. I may steer clear of certain websites, forums, or chat groups, and watch what I say and do online, for fear of who is watching me, and what their agenda is. And my censorship will seem self-directed. Thus, we are all silently, covertly – obligingly and automatically – urged towards conformity and quiescence.

Except that this is not how things have turned out. Or so it seems. By and large, the digital generation does not appear to behave online as if some disapproving Big Brother (or Big Other) were watching our every move, influencing our every decision, paralyzing us with fear, and demanding self-

---

[28] Foucault, 176.
[29] See respectively Bernard Harcourt, *Exposed* (Cambridge, MA: Harvard University Press, 2015), 79; and Shoshana Zuboff, *The Age of Surveillance Capitalism* (New York: Public Affairs, 2019), 20.

censorship. Quite to the contrary, on social media, people are prone to divulging all manner of mundane, intimate, or unsavory details of their personal lives, with little evident concern for the shadowy agents listening in – or even what their friends, family, and co-workers (or bosses) might think.

Facebook users issue "status updates" reporting where they are at any given moment, no matter how ordinary or insignificant – or embarrassing. Social media platforms offer people the opportunity to report how they feel on a near-constant basis, declaring emotional highs and lows, relating caustic social and political views, sharing lascivious desires. I think of former (and beloved) students I had to block on Facebook, lest their political tirades became too wrathful and foul-mouthed, if my children should spy them over my shoulder – or their sexual confessions became too frank, bawdy, and detailed. Oftentimes, their stories and rants made me wonder, do they even think about their audience, witness to these emissions? Do they forget that I – or their grand-parents, or professional contacts, or bosses – might be party to them? Do they just ignore who will see their posts? Or if they do recognize their audience, do they simply not care about embarrassing themselves or others? This confessional culture is not limited to millennials and former students, of course. I am routinely shocked by gushing or careless posts from older peers on social media, who say things they should know better than to share, if they hewed to older, pre-internet rules of etiquette. I think in particular of one forty-plus Facebook friend who is an exultant new mother, and divulges every thought about her child, and shares every momentous detail of his existence – and who can begrudge her excitement, really? But then she broaches a new frontier, and posts close-up pictures of her breastfeeding, which leaves little to the imagina-tion. Some have dubbed these "brelfies," and apparently this is a widespread phenomenon in the digital age.[30] While this phenomenon may have admirable intentions, normalizing breastfeeding, or celebrating motherhood and the female form, it defies anticipations for surveillance, which should prompt us to hide ourselves, or curtail eccentric, highly personal behavior.

Our confessional culture has arguably been brewing for some time now, and before the emergence of social media – perhaps even as far back as the social and political revolutions of the 1960s, when people came to embrace their sexual identities and predilections, and speak about them openly and frankly.[31] The 1990s boom in memoir writing, and the popularity of Reality TV

[30]  See, for example, Lucy Waterlow, "Rise of the Brelfie," *Daily Mail Online*, February 25, 2015, www.dailymail.co.uk/femail/article-2968246/Mums-head-head-brelfie-Morning-breastfeed ing-selfies-list-parenting-trends-thanks-stars-like-Miranda-Kerr.html.
[31]  Igo, 268.

shows shone a bright light on otherwise mundane and unsavory details of private lives.[32] But none of this approaches the level of routine sharing and deep exposure we now expect on social media. The sexual liberation movement, the memoirs, and Reality TV made it acceptable for personal, shameful details to be revealed; they made the prospect of exposure less fearsome, or horrifying, and even a bit therapeutic. With social media, however, confession is pervasive: people share routinely, and as a matter of fact – unprompted, and often unconcerned for norms transgressed or defied. Indeed, this has become so common, and people so nonchalant about sharing details that would have been embarrassing in an earlier age, that universities and employers regularly scour applicants' social media platforms in search of troubling behavior and opinions. And though this is widely known and reported, many persist in baring their souls and lives nonetheless.

We know we are watched online and in social media; we know we are monitored by our government, and, increasingly, commercial interests, too. When prompted, many of us will say we disapprove, but, by and large, we do not behave like we knew or cared about the spying, or reckoned with its implications. We do not behave as if we inhabited a digital panopticon, or tentacular oligarchy, or what have you. Why?

Philosophers have long argued that human consciousness is inherently narrative: this is a major way we seek to understand and give meaning to reality, and human existence. Specifically, we aim to project a narrative structure onto our lives – give them a beginning, climax, and hopefully a fitting conclusion – and also situate them within a greater narrative, be it social, historical, or cosmic. Thanks to social media, we get to curate the stories of our lives – in real time – and, if need be, change characters, dominant plot lines, or background themes how and when we like. Or, in documenting everyday events and occurrences, we may elevate them and memorialize them for posterity. Suddenly our chores, the many stops we make throughout the workday, gain special significance in being shared – and, of course, connections are made, satisfying our inherent need to socialize and build bonds. And in this respect, our digitally curated lives fit into another great American tradition: entrepreneurship.[33] We are busy constructing an identity and life story – a brand – that we then champion and market, like everyone else selling something in this country.

This implies that there is also a competitive element to the social media sharing. It is increasingly common for people to boast about their romantic

[32]  Igo, 338–44.
[33]  Harcourt has made a similar argument. Cf. *Exposed*, 99.

relationships in digital platforms, for example, and post substantiating pictures and gushing proclamations and confessions, complete with "weekiversary posts" diligently marking the duration of the relationship.[34] This has the unintended (or perhaps intended) consequence of shaming people who are not in love, or people who may now doubt the intensity of their own romance, and then wonder why they or their partner are not similarly bragging about it online. Apparently, this phenomenon has goaded some people to stay in relationships longer than they should have, just for the sake of "keeping up with the Joneses" online.[35] They make their romances seem more devoted and titillating than they are, and persist in the fantasy – which comes to supplant the real thing. Consider the title of a recent article documenting this trend: "Are you really in love if it's not on Instagram?" Romance is not real if it's not announced and performed on social media.

We might pay special attention to millennials, in this regard, since they are the generation growing up with, and on, social media – and they seem to be the most egregious sharers online. In one respect, they are not really doing anything too exceptional for young people – they are only taking advantage of new technology to do what previous generations have always done: socialize with a fury, and in ways that may seem strange, uncomfortable, or even dangerous to parents and elders, publicizing details they should otherwise conceal, or at least not flaunt. We should see millennials as "digital flâneurs," one social media critic argues, who share in order to catch the attention of their peers, which they long for ardently.[36] And in doing so – paradoxically – they betray concern for privacy. For, by issuing forth a mass of information, aren't they diverting our attention from other details, in the process?[37] Aren't they hiding, in some fashion, behind the flood of data? This may be one way of achieving a degree of privacy in this data-ridden age. In all their sharing, millennials have simply figured out new ways to control the social situation, with the tools available to them.

While these are all compelling accounts behind digital sharing, I am generally dubious that it is so strategic and premeditated as some think, or contend. So much of it seems perfunctory and routine, and the revealed information so mundane and insignificant. Alternately, and as mentioned, people are so often prone to leaving posts that are unintentionally rude,

[34]  Krista Burton, "Are you really in love if it's not on Instagram?" *New York Times*, March 24, 2018: www.nytimes.com/2018/03/24/opinion/sunday/relationships-love-instagram.html.
[35]  Burton, "Are you really in love?"
[36]  danah boyd, *It's Complicated: The Social Lives of Networked Teens* (New Haven, CT: Yale University Press, 2014), 203.
[37]  See boyd, 75.

unthinkingly offensive – directed at wide audiences, to which they have put little apparent consideration. It's hard to see it as being much more than instinctual and reflexive, at this point.

Perhaps there is a simpler explanation to the phenomenon of online shamelessness that defies predictions for surveillance: people forget or ignore that they are watched. Thanks to the digital medium, which can be accessed and employed alone in one's room, behind four walls, it sustains the semblance of privacy. When I share online, I certainly seem to do so privately, or behind the protective layer of this medium. Or perhaps I may share anonymously, which means my identity seems even more secure. Digital communication is mediated communication, after all, where the mediation figures prominently – it is the computer or smartphone screen before me. This serves to remove me somehow from the target(s) of my emissions, and my audience. As a result, I feel I am at a remove when I divulge, or surveil others in turn. I might put it otherwise: there is a kind of epistemological disconnect at work here. To people who behave shamelessly online, they will affirm that they know someone is watching them – they will affirm that their actions are not concealed, but public in some fashion. Indeed, their emissions reach a broader population than if they had been shouted aloud in a public square. But it doesn't feel like this. It feels like their emissions are controlled, curated, and their author at safe remove from people he might hurt or offend or embarrass. Or as we see in the phenomenon of online trolling, people are emboldened by the perceived anonymity to wage destruction.

Technology writer Christine Rosen relays a story that illustrates the epistemological disconnect I have in mind. A college student reported to her a surprising encounter with a Facebook acquaintance: the acquaintance in question was of the opposite sex, and the student hardly knew her at all; she was one of countless friends party to his social media feed, and he had never spoken to her in person. But one day on campus, he bumped into her, and they struck up a conversation. He was shocked to find that he was sweating profusely, though it was not a hot day. "It wasn't until much later that I realized maybe I was sweating because I kind of liked her," he told Rosen, "and was off my game because she was right in front of me."[38] Rosen goes on to argue that digital communication allows us to forget the kind of emotional signals – both those from our own bodies, and from others – that typically punctuate and guide everyday public conversation.[39] This example also points out how differently we view the digital medium, which causes us to

---

[38] Christine Rosen, "Expose Thyself! On the Digitally Revealed Life," *Hedgehog Review*, 20/1 (2016), https://iasc-culture.org/THR/THR_article_2018_Spring_Rosen.php.

[39] Rosen, "Expose Thyself!"

behave differently than when we are out in public – because digital communications seem private or safe – or safer. It is easy for me to feel "on my game," as the
student puts it, when I am alone in my room composing clever comments online,
behind the veil of a constructed personality perhaps, and feel little pressure to
respond to anyone in front of me, in the moment. What's more, I may discover
likeminded or sympathetic audiences online, and speak only to them – people for
whom it's always easy to be "on my game."

   In any case, the phenomenon of online sharing and shamelessness, our
newfound culture of exposition, is a testament to how little we are concerned
for privacy. Evidence of surveillance abounds; its presence is not hard to detect
or infer in our daily lives. But it hardly deters anyone from divulging private
details – habitually. To the contrary, this phenomenon suggests we may be
immune to surveillance. Which is a fascinating prospect in itself. What would
that mean for governments who harbor vast plans to spy on their people – as in
China, which I will take up shortly? Why aim to monitor people if coercion is
not the goal or anticipated result? Perhaps governments are happy to let us
share and expose ourselves, and they will sit and watch and take it all in.
Perhaps they don't want us to hide our true feelings and eccentricities at all,
but live freely and openly, for all to see.

   Despite this confessional culture, and the epistemological disconnect of digital
communications, some of us do feel compelled to object when emissions are
monitored, and private information collected and analyzed. The problem is, this
compulsion is largely visceral. We may know when to object, but increasingly, we
don't know *how* – we don't know what to say, how to articulate or express the harm
that is inflicted by widespread government and commercial surveillance. And this
is strange of course, because, again, we are steeped in a culture and tradition that
supposedly prizes privacy – which is founded on it, we are told. Our difficulty in
expressing the problem is evident in, among other things, a word that recurs in
protests against surveillance schemes, which are dubbed "creepy."

   The data broker Axciom engineered an extensive program to collect information on individuals, which it then sells to retailers who wish to know more
about customers, actual and prospective. The program gathers information
"continuously on approximately seven hundred million identifiable individuals," drawn from a few sources, including "Fortune 100 companies' records
of people who 'purchased something or signed up for a mailing list or some
kind of offer,'" and "every data attribute you could gather publicly about
consumers from public records."[40] The breadth of this program spooked

---

[40]   Turow, 156.

even a leading publication from the data brokerage industry itself, which fretted over the company's "aggressive quantification of individuals" that it deemed "creepy."[41]

Retailers are increasingly interested in knowing where you are at any given moment. Thanks to beacon technology, they can outfit aisles with digital devices that communicate with your mobile phone, alerting where you are in the store, before which product, and then merchants can barrage you with pertinent and alluring promotions and discounts.[42] Retailers will soon communicate with you in similar fashion whether you are in the parking lot about to enter the store, or simply driving by.[43] They aim to deliver personalized messaging and marketing drawn from our detailed purchase history, or other available personal information amassed by data brokers and catalogued by retailers. The corporate entities engaged in this massive data collection recognize a "creepy factor" in what they do, but are ultimately confident that we can grow accustomed to it all, and be placated by the benefits we receive in turn.[44]

A privacy scholar ascribes a similar "creepiness factor" to the imminent networking of major devices and appliances in our homes, such as when "your heater or clothes dryer monitor how much power you're using, or ... your fridge [alerts] you that you're low on milk."[45] And the journalist covering a new startup deems it "creepy" for helping "landlords, employers and online dates strip-mine intimate data from your Facebook page."[46] The company in question produces tenant reports for landlords, culled from social media sites of prospective tenants. The journalist composed her own tenant report, and was dismayed to find that it included a "list of my closest friends and interests, a percentage breakdown of my personality traits, a list of every time I've tweeted the words 'loan' and 'pregnant,' and the algorithm's confidence that I'll pay rent consistently."[47]

Why is this kind of deep spying considered "creepy"? It suggests we are uncomfortable with it, of course, but to call it creepy is not to say it is wrong

---

[41] Turow, 157.
[42] Turow, 1.
[43] Turow, 213.
[44] Turow, 217.
[45] David Lazarus, "Our privacy is losing out to Internet-connected household devices," *LA Times*, January 15, 2016, www.latimes.com/business/la-fi-lazarus-20160115-column.html.
[46] Caitlin Dewey, "Creepy startup will help landlords, employers and online dates strip-mine intimate data from your Facebook page," *Washington Post*, June 9, 2016, www.washingtonpost.com/news/the-intersect/wp/2016/06/09/creepy-startup-will-help-landlords-employers-and-online-dates-strip-mine-intimate-data-from-your-facebook-page/?utm_term=.8e0d97e8fadc.
[47] Dewey, "Creepy startup."

per se; it is to register worry, concern, doubt. When we say something is creepy, we mean to say we suspect it is wrong, or there is something potentially damaging or dangerous about it, but we are unsure what it is, and certainly cannot specify it. It is a feeling – a sense of being ill at ease.

We are uncomfortable – or at least, some of us are – with the prospect of constant and pervasive monitoring, of the most intimate and seemingly random details of our lives. But we do not know how to object any longer. Increasingly, many do not feel the need or urge to object at all. As I will soon show, objecting, or taking a harder stand on surveillance seems unlikely, and perhaps impossible given our dependence on digital technology – which will only grow. Facing this immense expansion of digital technology, which threatens our privacy at every turn, surveillance seems normal. If or when people do manage to object, they may do so out of a sense of obligation, a sense that this is what we as Americans are supposed to do. But in truth, the value of privacy seems lost on us.

This must be fixed if we would muster a defense of privacy. Attempts to impose regulations that give individuals more power over whether they can share private information are intolerably tenuous and, I fear, ultimately doomed so long as the majority no longer understands and appreciates privacy – clearly, convincingly, and self-consciously.

**2**

# Defending Privacy

In Plato's dialogue "Meno," the eponymous speaker, after much frustration, declares that Socrates, his insistent interviewer, is like a "broad torpedo fish" – better known to us as an electric ray – which stuns and paralyzes those who approach it.[1] The two men had conversed at length on the topic of virtue, something Meno professed to know much about, and he readily produced several definitions. After Socrates debunked each in turn, Meno was at a loss. Like the torpedo fish, he tells Socrates, "you now seem to have had that effect on me, for both my mind and my tongue are numb, and I have no answer to give you. Yet I have made many speeches about virtue before large audiences on a thousand occasions, very good speeches I thought but now I cannot even say what it is!"[2]

Meno is not the only one tormented by Socrates, of course. The philosopher has a habit of subjecting purportedly wise people to withering inquiry, and, ultimately, shame. It is not surprising that the Athenians tired of his ways and sought to silence him. They couldn't tolerate his pestering and humiliation any more. But behind Meno's complaint, Plato wishes to convey an important point about the human condition: we often lack a clear understanding of the most crucial terms and values in our lives, even those we repeatedly invoke, and believe we know well. In truth, our relationship to those guiding values, like piety, or justice, or beauty, is merely reflexive, or prompted by convention, but is essentially hollow. And under those conditions, Plato contends, we are morally led astray.

Our relationship to privacy is similarly fraught. It's a value we generally *say* we appreciate, a value we *think* we understand well – a value we often invoke,

---

[1] Plato, "Meno," in *Five Dialogues*, trans. G. M. A. Grube (Indianapolis, IN: Hackett Publishing Co., 2002), 70.
[2] Plato, "Meno," 70.

or at least utter, and which is deeply inscribed in American thought and culture. But many can no longer say *why* it is important. This disconnect is increasingly evident in our daily behavior, I have argued: we abandon it en masse in the digital age; we happily, eagerly surrender it, to avail ourselves of digital conveniences, even when they are trivial.

Accordingly, privacy is a topic of natural interest for philosophers, who, like Plato, seek to articulate guiding values, explain why we esteem them – or ought to – and deepen, or rekindle our appreciation. And indeed, because privacy is a presumed and touted value, but increasingly ignored, disrespected, and forgotten, some have felt the need to step up and ring the alarm, define privacy again, specify the underlying danger of its loss, or accommodate and update it in light of our new digital reality. Anything less, and we are sleep-walking into a state of total exposure where we are subject to manipulation, abuse, or domination.

I will consider a few notable approaches to define privacy, to see if any are clear and compelling enough to inspire deep and widespread respect for the institution – respect that can withstand the growing onslaught from digital technologies.

Why do invasions of privacy upset or disconcert us? Or rather, why ought they? Because we value our autonomy, which demands that our privacy be protected. Surveillance undermines our ability to think for ourselves, to live our lives in a unique fashion, as we see fit. Surveillance supplies a covert pressure that compromises individual freedom. As such, some claim, it is nothing less than an attack on personhood itself – for where is personhood if we may not be unique, self-determining individuals? This is a recurring and important argument for privacy, which we will have to consider at length. It is already implicit in Foucault's admiration for panopticism: the latter works so well precisely because it stifles personal freedom – and effectively hijacks autonomy.

To better grasp the harm done in acts of surveillance, consider the following example offered by philosopher Michael Lynch: suppose someone were to break into your house, read your diary, and then photocopy it for other people.[3] Many will say this is wrong – but what is the wrong committed? How to put it? Is it just that someone did what you did not authorize or approve? Is it because someone stole your property? As if this were just a form of theft? No, that's not it – that does not seem to capture the nature of the offense. There is something more. Even if you never found out that someone read your diary and circulated it to others – even if you never got to register

---

[3]   Michael Lynch, *The Internet of Us* (New York: W. W. Norton and Co., 2016), 103.

outrage or shame, you have been harmed by this act. But how? Isn't it because your autonomy has been violated at its core – cut off at the root, in some way? A primal and basic form of self-control is lost: the ability to control how or if your personal information is disseminated at all. Someone has taken over that decision – robbed you of it, even if you don't know it.[4]

At first glance, this argument may seem unsatisfying. Why are you harmed if someone accesses your private information without your permission? Because you expect to be the one who controls such access. OK, but so what? The real harm would seem to lie beneath – it is something deeper than just your presumption of control, which has been rudely, if secretly, taken away. Lynch proceeds to specify:

> Part of what makes your individual mind your mind is that you have a degree of privileged access to your mental states, and that includes the ability to access the content of those thoughts and feelings. Part of the reason we value having this control is because it is a necessary condition for being in a position to make autonomy decisions, for our ability to determine who and what we are as persons.[5]

Privileged access to a selection of mental states, this is the condition of a person's autonomy, more broadly speaking. It is what enables you to strike a unique path in this world, go where you want, make decisions for yourself, decisions that suit your particular needs, setting, and place in history.

This privileged access is a highly sensitive part of the soul – in a way, the essence of "you." And when others invade it, and peer inside, you are at risk of no longer being viewed as a unique person, a human individual; you are now some kind of object, liable to manipulation and abuse. Your inner workings are glimpsed, so to speak, and your spy may learn how to push your buttons. In the eyes of your spy, who took your diary for example, "your existence as a distinct person will begin to shrink. [Your relationship with him] will be so lopsided that [he] may well cease to regard you as a full subject, as a master of your own destiny."[6] A power imbalance emerges when your spy knows much about you – and not the reverse. You are essentially dehumanized before him; you are less mysterious, reduced to a bundle of stimuli, perhaps.

There is much to commend this argument. It would seem to be sufficiently alarming: with privacy threatened, nothing less than personhood is at stake. Part of being a self-respecting human individual is the presumption that we control access to a selection of mental states – and it is an affront to our dignity

4  Lynch, 103.
5  Lynch, 103–4.
6  Lynch, 104–5.

when we learn otherwise. And even before we make this discovery, we are objectified in the eyes of our spies. Regarding this latter contention, I might offer one quibble, in light of the example above. Is it not equally or somewhat plausible that, upon inspecting your diary, your spy might be impressed? He might marvel at your inner workings, the subtlety and ambiguity of your thoughts; perhaps a glimpse will not deliver what he needs to read you like an open book. Rather, he might appreciate your complexity. I must insert an important caveat here: as we will soon see, a lot rides on the intent, mind-set, or plans of those who peer into your life. What do they hope to do with the information? They might find what they need, and ignore the rest; they might choose to objectify you, and proceed as long as it works – prepared to revisit your soul at a later date for more data. Of course, there is also a troubling middle ground: is said spying temptation enough to view you in this manner – that is, objectify you? Is spying necessarily a temptation to power – and control?

We should be offended to lose presumed control over access to our mental states – we will feel disrespected, less human before those who know so much about us. Surveying the digital landscape, I am not sure this argument will resonate much, or that it is relevant any longer. Indeed, on social media, people are tripping over themselves to surrender this privileged access, in a way, offering an intimate view into personal feelings and fleeting emotional states. As mentioned, digital citizens seem to operate as if their feelings are not real unless publicly validated, online. Some do not feel they are properly in love, for example, unless they blare it to the world, and share candid insight into intimate events, and emotional highs and lows – on a daily (sometimes hourly) basis. Is this merely a trend? Or the new norm, which we will all soon emulate online? Better yet: does all the social media sharing really provide deep, or near complete personal insight? Is there more that remains hidden, out of view – more that is essential to a person's well-being and uniqueness? That may well be the case; but, as I will soon argue, it turns out there is much to my identity and personality that eludes my self-consciousness. I do not know all that goes into the making of me, nor will I ever. The roots of my autonomy, to the extent that I have it and exercise it, are vague and tangled.

Of itself, I am not sure how much the argument from autonomy may motivate people to care about their privacy in this day and age, especially when we speak abstractly in terms of personhood, dignity – "privileged access to mental states." It might be more effective to raise the specter of tyrannical government.

A trademark of the fearsome totalitarian regimes of the twentieth century was their wanton destruction of privacy. They aimed to so invade and conquer and dispel the private lives of their citizens, Hannah Arendt argues, in order to dominate them fully, and effectively preclude the possibility or need for politics at all. That is, in so denuding the citizens, totalitarian governments hoped to erase distinguishing marks, features, hopes, and desires, and render them one individual – a mass that can be prodded this way and that, with no questioning, feedback, or complaint. This is possible "only if each and every person can be reduced to a never changing identity of reactions, so that each of these bundles can be exchanged at random for any other."[7] This invokes the dynamic described above, that in exposing a person's inner workings, they might be objectified, and manipulated. But intense personal exposure is also intimidating. Destroying privacy was an act of violence, and meant to coerce, if not terrify, the citizens. In Stalinist Russia, the severe surveillance – carried out by terrified citizens themselves, in many cases, spying on their neighbors – was supplemented and enhanced by overt and literal violence, and millions died in the Gulag. To this extent, surveillance became a self-fulfilling prophecy: in viewing people objectively – in seeking to view them as, and turn them into, objects – it did so: people were reduced to an animalistic state where their "only freedom would consist in preserving the species."[8]

Earlier authoritarian states did not have such ambitions and devastating plans for their populations. Or if they did, they were not able to pull them off so expansively and devastatingly as their twentieth-century counterparts. Premodern monarchs, for example, were largely content to leave the people be, and enrich and glorify themselves. Many kings, especially of the "enlightened" sort, could tolerate or even underwrite a rich public life for their subjects. Greedier monarchs could squeeze the public realm, curtailing the sphere in which people could behave as free and expressive citizens. Totalitarian regimes, by contrast, aimed to destroy the public realm, sever people from one another, and leave them in a state of mass loneliness. Arendt distinguishes loneliness from isolation and solitude: isolation is a temporary feature of public life, which I require to do my work, to make things that are then brought into the public sphere, and offer my contribution to the common world.[9] When isolated, I live in expectation of a public life, I operate with it in view, or in mind, and it continues to motivate me positively. Or I take part in it vicariously, even when I am not literally in it, immersed in the public realm. Solitude is restorative; I require it to draw on reserves of energy to then

---

[7] Hannah Arendt, *Origins of Totalitarianism* (New York: Houghton Miflin Harcourt Publishing Co., 1994), 438.
[8] Arendt, *Origins*, 438.
[9] Arendt, *Origins*, 475.

immerse myself again in work and public life. In loneliness, however, "I am actually one, deserted by all others."[10] Totalitarian regimes seek to produce the latter, where citizens are marooned in a state of mutual desertion, and cannot live in hope of a sustaining and unifying public life. The "common world" of men is destroyed under totalitarianism, and each stands alone before a mammoth government. "For the confirmation of my identity I depend entirely upon other people, and it is the great saving grace of companionship for solitary men that it makes them 'whole' again."[11] But totalitarianism persecutes companionship, because it renders everyone suspect, and suspicious of one another. Trust is a rare commodity. Once these regimes destroy the public realm, they turn their withering glare on isolated citizens. Then, the restorative promise of solitude is gone as well.

For totalitarian regimes, it is not enough to eradicate the public realm and consign citizens to the safety of their private lives. In that case, they may retain some degree of political potency and independence. Totalitarianism aims to hobble the people politically, and turn them into predictable and submissive tools of the state. Isolated and watched, divided and conquered, citizens are at the mercy of those in power; their dignity is destroyed, and they must live as paranoid creatures, in a twitching, fearful state, where satisfying physical needs is their highest goal, their remaining aspiration. Then also, citizens may tolerate any number of atrocities – or help carry them out.

Whether Americans are attuned to signs of authoritarianism (or incipient totalitarianism), or even worried about it at all, are pertinent questions with the rise of President Trump, and the broader threat to global democracy that shadowed his rise. Previously, critics, scholars, and pundits pointed to surreptitious or otherwise ordinary actions of government, and indicated patterns of behavior that amounted to authoritarian moves, or betrayed authoritarian ambitions. But with President Trump, there was no longer any guesswork. He exulted in blatant authoritarian claims, complaints, and alliances. He professed admiration for several autocrats, saying, among other things, that he liked how the North Korean people listen to and respect their leader, Kim Jong-un – who sends his political prisoners to concentration camps, or worse. Trump appreciated how similar leaders fashion themselves strongmen, and galvanize public support in the process – or at least command public awe, and fear. Accordingly, Trump touted himself a strongman, albeit one mixed with a canny, ruthless Wall Street boss. He

[10] Arendt, *Origins*, 476.
[11] Arendt, *Origins*, 476.

scorned rule of law, even before he took office, and faced an FBI inquiry into Russian ties to his campaign – an inquiry he tried to shut down immediately – and obviously. Trump cast doubt on the US electoral system, both before and after his victory. He derided the nation's intelligence community, threatened the free press, attacked judicial independence, and urged the Senate to do away with long-standing rules and traditions (like the filibuster) so that he might advance his agenda.

For his efforts, his base, and conservatives more broadly, rallied around him. Trump's presidency revealed that a plurality of Americans tolerates, if not welcomes, autocracy, and is tired of politics – the democratic process – which is suspected of being "rigged." Instead of being instinctively vigilant and resisting authoritarian rule, many Americans like a strongman plenty, such as Trump purports to be. Ironically, those Americans who have claimed to be uniquely wary of tyranny – gun rights supporters who say they need assault rifles to prevent said tyranny – are among Trump's most ardent fans. Apparently, they are fine with the right kind of tyrant.

Many worry about the enduring impact of the Trump presidency on US democracy. Will it make for cruder discourse and hardened partisan divides? Will it accustom us to boorish behavior and wanton lies, in the highest reaches of government? Will this experience render us more tolerant of or oblivious to continuing, and perhaps more serious, authoritarian tendencies in our leaders? Since the 9–11 attacks, and in order to wage the War on Terror, the American people have allowed the government to violate our civil rights and expand executive powers – just the kinds of things authoritarian regimes like to do. They want to engage in mass surveillance of the home population, many claim, and as Edward Snowden revealed. Our tolerance of these affronts suggests that Americans are not impressed by, and perhaps are already inured to the advance of authoritarian government that might slide into totalitarianism. With Trump – and a humming economy – the nation may sink deeper into apathy and nonchalance, or an outright love affair with his brand of authoritarianism.

The United States is not alone in this regard. Some Eastern European nations have dispensed with democratic institutions in favor of authoritarianism – with voter support. One explanation for this troubling trend is that we are now two generations removed from the demise of totalitarian regimes, and, thus, it is easy to forget the dangers. A recent study found that "over two-thirds of older Americans believed that it was absolutely important to live in a democracy; among millennials, less than one third did. Twenty years ago, one in sixteen thought that 'army rule' was a good system of government. A few years ago one in six did."[12]

In sum, it is unlikely that Americans will become suddenly jealous of their privacy thanks to fear of tyranny. Too many people are not fazed by such a threat; it is too remote or outlandish. And many people welcome it.

Perhaps changing behavior in the digital age suggests that we ought to conceive privacy, and privacy concerns, differently, and not so dramatically. A recurring theme in privacy theory is control: I ought to have control over my personal information – when I lose such control, I lose what is essential to my personhood and inner freedom. And when the spies are given free access to my inner realm, this is the invitation to, or first step in, emergent oppression. But this may not be what concerns people most when it comes to privacy. People may not care principally about "restricting the flow of information but ensuring that it flows properly."[13] When we navigate society and the economy, we enter into information exchanges with norms that vary according to the context and demands of the situation. We are fine when details about our lives are revealed or exchanged or exposed, so long as contextual norms about informational flow are met, we achieve our personal goals, and social welfare more broadly is seemingly advanced. This disputes the notion that privacy is an immutable, eternal right and expectation that is the same in all times, societies, and cultures. Rather, privacy changes as cultural and economic systems demand. Such as now, in the digital revolution. This is not to say that privacy is gone; it is variable, and we must speak of it accordingly.

People get upset over privacy invasions not because some inner citadel has been breached – as if that were an offense in itself – but when contextual norms over information flow are broken, defied, or ignored. We see outcry over privacy today because new technologies often do just that. Different relational contexts have different norms guiding the exchange of information – what and how much personal information you accept is revealed is very different in a doctor's office as opposed to the workplace, the voting booth, or the classroom. Put simply, the amount of information revealed about you in a given setting is a function of contextual integrity.[14] Privacy standards depend on the goals of a given context, and what permits these goals to be achieved. Employers may need to know certain personal details about you, given the goals of the workplace. They may decide you cannot conceal certain facts, lest

[12]   Yascha Mounk, interviewed by David Frum, "If America's Democracy Fails, Can Other Ones Survive," in *The Atlantic*, March 4, 2018, www.theatlantic.com/international/archive/2018/03/yascha-mounk-democracy/554786/.

[13]   Helen Nissenbaum, *Privacy in Context* (Stanford, CA: Stanford University Press, 2010), 2.

[14]   Nissenbaum, 132.

this undermines the professional task at hand, and endangers the company as a whole. That may vary according to the case because, for different employers and workplaces, certain employee secrets will never be a liability. In the medical context, some health professionals will need to know many intimate or embarrassing details about you; others will not. There may be considerable variation even within similar settings.

Though the digital age has proven disruptive, this does not mean it has totally upended expectations for our economic and social relationships. Don't we still navigate them with an immanent handbook of norms – an unspoken understanding of when and how much personal information we should and may divulge? In a way, society acts as an anchor, securing our varying privacy norms in an overall respect for the institution – which, on the whole, is not being lost, though its character and appearance are changing. Society dictates the nature of the various power relationships we enter into in any given context, and they in turn dictate privacy norms in no haphazard, fleeting way. These contexts, we must remember, are "structured social settings characterized by canonical activities, roles, relationships, power structures, norms (or rules) and internal values (goals, ends, purposes)."[15]

Norms governing informational exchange may shift, but when they do, it will not be entirely surprising or disconcerting. Change will be accepted, if not expected or welcomed, because such norms are rooted in larger social systems that evolve slowly, and often – at least in democracies – with popular support or recognition. What's more, we inhabit a consumer economy, and consumers enter into economic relationships willingly, consciously, and rationally for the most part; thus, we may presume that they accept the new terms of the power relationship with their retail spies, and recognize a benefit. Privacy becomes an issue when informational norms governing any task, transaction, or relationship are defied, and in such a way that the goals of the task are not achieved, fully or in part. Because the underlying social structure, which anchors informational norms, is solid, privacy infractions that are troubling or problematic, and contrary to our interests – or even subversive of society itself – clearly announce themselves as such, and then we will object or resist accordingly. However, recent social media history suggests that might not be the case.

Privacy advocates were outraged when Mark Zuckerberg, founder of Facebook, said that "people have really gotten comfortable not only sharing more information and different kinds, but more openly and with more people ... [That] social norm is just something that has evolved over time.

---

[15] Nissenbaum, 132.

We view it as our role in the system to constantly be innovating and be updating what our system is to reflect what the current social norms are."[16] This was one of Zuckerberg's early defenses of his company, accused of exploiting people's sensitive information. Facebook merely happened upon the scene and discovered that norms had changed – "evolved" – regarding public exposure. The social media company is thus innocently following changing social norms and taking advantage of them when it scoops up and monetizes our personal information – to help us get what we want, and better achieve personal, social, and professional goals. Critics contend that this ignores the role – the *seminal* role – social media companies play, and have played, in changing our norms on sharing, prodding us to be more forthcoming with personal information. To avail yourself of the medium of communication Facebook offers, where you can stay in touch with family and friends from across the years and many continents, find countless hours of diversion, and even curate a new identity to market to the world (but especially to old high school acquaintances who never found you terribly hip or interesting), you only need to expose numerous details of your personal life.

Social media companies are not what they seem and often pretend to be. To its billions of members, Facebook's primary business seems to be helping people connect with one another, and communicate more often, consistently, genuinely, openly. And the company is happy to play up that image. Social media platforms enable a host of virtual communities. In suburban America, where the physical infrastructure of community is largely non-existent, and we are isolated amidst the sprawl, digital community has become a crucial stand-in. But helping people connect, this is not the raison d'être of these companies. As Facebook has become embroiled in controversies about how it shares or leaks the private information of its members, the company's real business model becomes increasingly apparent. If consumers choose to pay attention. Or care.

Many were up in arms when it was revealed that the political consulting firm Cambridge Analytica had harvested the private information of 50 million Facebook members, which it may have used to manipulate the 2016 presidential election. The company had paid American Facebook users to "download and use a personality quiz app" on the social media platform, and subsequently "scraped the information from [users'] Facebook profiles as well as detailed information from their friends' profiles."[17] There were rumblings that

[16] Bobbie Johnson, "Privacy no longer a social norm, says Facebook founder," *The Guardian*, January 10, 2010, www.theguardian.com/technology/2010/jan/11/facebook-privacy.
[17] Zeynep Tufekci, "Facebook's surveillance machine," *New York Times*, March 19, 2018, www.nytimes.com/2018/03/19/opinion/facebook-cambridge-analytica.html.

this had been an unprecedented data breach, but Facebook sternly denied it. And indeed, Cambridge Analytica may have done little that was wrong beyond holding on to user data after Facebook insisted the company delete it. Laid bare in this incident was Facebook's business model, which Cambridge Analytica simply took advantage of. Facebook touts itself as a platform "for social interaction," but makes money "by profiling us and then selling our attention to advertisers, political actors and others. These are Facebook's true customers, whom it works hard to please."[18] The social media company composes profiles of its users (and shadow profiles on non-users) by drawing inferences from every single click and "like" on our Facebook feeds, also our browsing histories, and even "external data like financial information."[19] And the company has learned too well how to coax this information out of us – urging us to click on and "like" stories and posts – compounding the information it uses to profile us.

In 2014, critics were horrified to learn that Facebook had "manipulated the news feeds of over half a million randomly selected users to change the number of positive and negative posts they saw," as part of a "psychological study to examine how emotions can be spread on social media."[20] One might immediately wonder, why is this company engaging in a so-called "psychological study"? For its own edification? So that it can learn more about its members, and serve them better? Hardly. Facebook learned that its platform was surprisingly, or insidiously, effective at influencing users' emotional states, and, in turn, their eagerness to take part in social media, and share – that is, divulge information that can be monetized. Naturally, the company sought to downplay the impact of this "study." "The reason we did this research is because we care about the emotional impact of Facebook and the people that use our product," the lead researcher explained at the time – and in the same breath admitted that "we were concerned that exposure to friends' negativity might lead people to avoid visiting Facebook."[21] In other words, the company's researchers were primarily concerned with keeping people's business, and drumming up more. When users are exposed to negative stories or posts, or God forbid a host of them, they are less enthusiastic sharers, Facebook discovered. Users who encounter positive or affirming stories on their Facebook feed, by contrast, will be excellent, forthcoming members.

---

[18]  Tufekci, "Surveillance machine."
[19]  Tufekci, "Surveillance machine."
[20]  Vindu Goel, "Facebook tinkers with users' emotions in newsfeed experiment, stirring outcry," *New York Times*, June 29, 2014, www.nytimes.com/2014/06/30/technology/facebook-tinkers-with-users-emotions-in-news-feed-experiment-stirring-outcry.html.
[21]  Goel, "Facebook tinkers."

The positive posts that populate a Facebook page can be selected algorithmi-
cally, drawing on user profiles. "Ultimately, we're just providing a layer of
technology that helps people get what they want," Facebook's chief product
officer said. "That's the master we serve at the end of the day."[22]

After the 2016 election, we learned that "what people want" includes fake
news. Leading up to the vote, many noted how users' Facebook pages were
getting "bluer" or "redder" depending on the political allegiances they
betrayed. The social media company was putting its algorithm to work,
selecting posts – and ignoring their veracity or legitimacy, apparently – that
populated Facebook members' feeds. Liberal users were given a heavy dose of
left leaning posts and news stories; the reverse was true for conservatives. This
served to pull the political camps further apart, make discourse nastier, and the
campaign acrimonious. "Rather than connecting people – as Facebook's
euphoric mission statement claims," one critic quipped, "the bitter polarization of the social network ... suggests Facebook is actually doing more to
divide the world."[23] A prominent player in the polarization, exploiting the rift
and making it worse, was the phenomenon of fake news stories, fictitious
accounts generated by enterprising authors and outlets all over the world
(but especially in Russia and Eastern Europe), which incriminated one
candidate over another – but favored Donald Trump, on the whole. A prime
example was the case of the fictitious newspaper "The Denver Guardian,"
which suggested in one headline that Hillary Clinton was behind the death of
an FBI agent.[24] Many conservative Facebook users were buoyed by the story,
and happily circulated it – clicked on it, liked it, etc. If they got wind of another
story, alleging that the Pope endorsed Trump, a sufficient number might have
been motivated to hit the polls, tipping a close election.[25] In case this seems
improbable, consider that in the 2010 US election, "340,000 extra people
turned out to vote ... because of a single election day Facebook message."[26]
The 2016 presidential race was decided by a mere 70,000 voters in 3 rustbelt
states. With its ability to influence users' emotional states, Facebook revealed

[22]  Goel, "Facebook tinkers."
[23]  Olivia Solon, "Facebook's failure: Did fake news and polarized politics get Trump elected?"
      *The Guardian*, November 10, 2016, www.theguardian.com/technology/2016/nov/10/facebook-
      fake-news-election-conspiracy-theories.
[24]  Eric Lubbers, "There is no such thing as the Denver Guardian, despite that Facebook post you
      saw," *Denver Post*, November 5, 2016, www.denverpost.com/2016/11/05/there-is-no-such-thing-
      as-the-denver-guardian/.
[25]  "Read all about it: The biggest fake news stories of 2016," CNBC, December 30, 2016, www
      .cnbc.com/2016/12/30/read-all-about-it-the-biggest-fake-news-stories-of-2016.html.
[26]  Zoe Corbyn, "Facebook experiment boosts US voter turnout," *Nature*, September 12, 2012,
      www.nature.com/news/facebook-experiment-boosts-us-voter-turnout-1.11401.

impressive power. Cambridge Analytica took note of this power, sought to harness it, and influence voters in similar fashion, in service to the Trump campaign.

Ruptures in informational norms may not announce themselves so clearly after all. What if we don't know how, or care to detect said ruptures when they occur? What if we are being manipulated so slightly that we hardly notice them? Social media companies know what buttons to push, to make us confessional creatures. And we happily comply; we submit to the means that make us confess, wittingly or not. We are becoming central actors in this development, which starts to sound like rather profound social change – change that is not so gradual in the digital age. How can we be expected to sound the alarm over broken informational norms when we are at the heart of those transgressions – when we are made a driving force of the transgression itself? From the inside, captive to the change, seduced into churning it faster and faster, we hardly notice the transgressions.

If privacy is too context dependent and variable, it will be challenging to draw out useful policy recommendations. Perhaps we should focus instead on offering useful generalizations that will help courts decide privacy cases, and politicians craft pertinent and effective legislation. To this end – in line with these practical goals – we might also emphasize the social value of privacy.

The welfare of society and individuals is inextricably linked. When individual freedoms and rights are protected and promoted, within reasonable limits, society as a whole benefits. And individuals require a stable, nurturing society in order to achieve their personal goals and find fulfillment. Accordingly, we could evaluate attacks on privacy in terms of their impact on social functioning at large. If our privacy is routinely violated and our lives made an open book, this may undermine our ability and willingness to act as citizens and take part in society. We may feel vulnerable, and reluctant to enter into relationships with our peers, or with powerful entities, like corporations or the government. We may wish to retreat within our shells. But society cannot function so long as its members do not feel secure and confident to venture forth, and forge productive and nurturing bonds with one another, and larger institutions.

Democratic society is uniquely vulnerable to the "tyranny of the majority," as John Stuart Mill put it, which would steamroll minority interests and rights, and expunge the decision making of individual citizens. Group psychology indicates that collectives can exert pressure on individuals to conform, and even incite them to dispense with their conscience. In general, "the community can be suffocating to individuals" in that "social judgment . . . can stunt self-development."[27] In that case, privacy is necessary for individuals to fend off the pressure of society at large. Privacy provides that crucial space where we can be self-determining individuals, in tune with our unique wants, values, and designs – where we feel safe and emboldened to contemplate and cultivate them. Democratic society can only function as advertised when the majority is held in check in important ways, and individuals feel free to diverge from the official narrative and preponderant views. Citizens must be allowed to live as they see fit, and privacy ensures this. And democracy has an important lesson for societies more broadly: societies that function well are more democratic – they facilitate citizens choosing and pursuing their own paths, and thrive on the happy and willing contributions of diverse members.

Beyond this, it may be impossible to arrive at a concrete and specific definition of privacy – and pointless to keep trying. Perhaps we would be better off following Daniel Solove, who prefers to speak of privacy problems that "share family resemblances with each other" – and labels "the whole cluster privacy."[28] In this vein, Solove lays out a "taxonomy of privacy problems," which includes surveillance, identity theft, breaches of confidentiality, appropriation, and blackmail.[29] These are cases in which threats to privacy have come to light, chiefly in the legal sphere, where courts struggle to adjudicate. To advise lawyers and lawmakers alike in navigating this minefield, this general counsel applies: privacy should be protected, or not, when the needs and interests of democratic society are met, and in such a way that democratic citizens may thrive within that superstructure, and thanks to its generative, nurturing function.

Perusing this taxonomy of varying but related privacy problems, a few themes recur, notably, trust and vulnerability. Democratic society functions best when people feel they have something to gain personally from relationships – they cannot fear that they will be harmed or taken advantage of. In that respect, current privacy concerns walk a fine line: on one hand, privacy has been sacrificed in the name of amazing personal conveniences. By knowing my entire purchase history and consumer preferences, Amazon can anticipate what I might like to buy next; it satisfies my self-interest, helps me achieve my personal goals, and live as I wish. On the other hand, if I sense that Amazon's efforts are too intrusive – "creepy" – I may feel impotent and vulnerable in turn, and reluctant to engage with it, or similar companies. In this arrangement, we are presumed to be rational actors, looking on and deciding whether

---

[27]  Daniel Solove, *Understanding Privacy* (Cambridge, MA: Harvard University Press, 2008), 94.
[28]  Solove, 172.
[29]  Solove, 101.

or not certain interactions and relationships will benefit us personally. Society depends on us determining that said relations can be beneficial; it depends on us feeling safe. Legislators and courts are tasked with making society seem sufficiently hospitable to our wants and needs, deftly managing the interests of privacy, convenience, and security.

This argument for the social value of privacy still manages to prioritize the individual. Society relies on its individual members feeling that they have something to gain from it, and from their contributions, they build society into a humming machine – which aids and assists component members all the more. When individuals are mistrustful or feeling vulnerable, this makes for a negative feedback loop: they contribute less to society, and build weaker, fewer bonds – and society offers them less in turn. Privacy is a key ingredient allowing individuals to feel safe reaching out to others, and contributing to a democratic government devoted to serving the people.

I will soon take to task the individualism that clings to privacy, and perhaps defines it. For now, I will only ask: is this account powerful enough to prompt cultural change, and motivate people to respect privacy again – even somewhat? I find this argument sensible, and I appreciate its pragmatic tenor: privacy is important to society, which cannot function – for the benefit of each of us – without it. We require the space privacy provides, in order to remain comfortable and productive members of society. I would only point out that, thus far, we do not seem terribly cowed by all the exposure – it has not prompted us to retreat, feel intimidated, or withdraw socially. We seem too happy to engage with spying retailers; we seem content with our lack of space, and the conveniences we receive in turn. That might change, of course, with any given controversy, or string of events that suddenly makes people less apt to engage in the digital economy. But I am not sure what that might be. When it was revealed that the US government was collecting all our digital trails, from every transaction and communication, that did not prompt a mass conversion. And Facebook usage actually increased after the Cambridge Analytica scandal.[30] Apparently, the temptations of the digital economy are too powerful, and the speed with which it envelopes us hard to resist, or process. How are rational arguments in defense of privacy supposed to register with us, while we are caught up in the digital whirlwind, privy to its many wonders – on which we come to rely, on a daily basis. How are such arguments supposed to inspire

[30] Jake Kanter, "The backlash that never happened: New data shows people actually increased their Facebook usage after the Cambridge Analytica scandal," *Business Insider*, May 20, 2018, www .businessinsider.com/people-increased-facebook-usage-after-cambridge-analytica-scandal-2018-5.

a call to arms? Especially if, as I will soon show, privacy is threatened in ways that far exceed our comprehension – and imagination.

Some might say, at the very least, the arguments surveyed above may motivate and inspire our legislators and lawyers, who will lead the way in defending privacy. I am not optimistic about how successful their efforts will be without buy-in from the public at large. We are witnessing a broad popular retreat from privacy, and it is hard to see how regulations which seek to empower individuals to protect their privacy – though they are captive to confessional culture – can stymie or reverse the trend.

# 3

## Big Plans for Big Data

For the most part, our spies contend that we know we are spied upon, but accept the surveillance because of the many concrete benefits we receive in return. Marketers want us to know, for example, the more we divulge, the better they can serve us. Indeed, they can help us realize desires and aspirations before they occur to us – desires we never even knew we had. In that sense, they promise to empower us, help us get what we want, and improve our personal lives. In turn, this implies that savvy shoppers expose personal details, even if they seem arcane and unremarkable. Apparently, that is not for us to judge.

Marketers are banking on the fact that consumers will grow steadily more accustomed to the constant spying so long as they are preoccupied with the benefits, and ultimately forget the spying altogether. As one retail analyst summed it up, "shoppers (especially younger shoppers) seem to have developed an almost infinite capacity for tolerating [surveillance]. Make the incentive strong enough – and use the data in subtle enough ways so that you're not forcing the customer to know how far you've gone – and privacy will be a trivial concern."[1] What kind of sensitive surveillance is at issue? Consider the case of the mega-retailer Target, which, in 2012, was reported to be carrying out a remarkable data analysis initiative. While this incident may seem dated in an age where technology and surveillance methods evolve at light speed, it remains highly instructive, and helpful for understanding the bold ambitions of retail spies. Simply put, this case illuminates the ways corporations aim to monitor us, the kinds of data they want to collect, and their elaborate plans for said information. Taken together, it offers a troubling image of corporate ambitions that emerges throughout the surveillance economy.

---

[1]  Joseph Turow, *The Aisles Have Eyes* (New Haven, CT: Yale University Press, 2017), 237.

Thanks to its predictive analytics department, Target came up with a way to determine when female customers were in the second trimester of pregnancy, and barrage them with pertinent coupons. Immediately, several questions spring to mind: Why pregnant women? Why their second trimester? And of course, how did Target achieve this level of detailed knowledge? As to the first question, the mega-retailer would like to convince "customers that the only store they need is Target"; this is hard to pull off since "most shoppers don't buy everything they need at one store" – unless their "buying habits are in flux."[2] One such period in people's lives, researchers determined, is the arrival of a newborn. If couples can be compelled to visit Target to purchase all manner of baby-related merchandise, they will, out of sheer new parent exhaustion perhaps, start to grab other necessities when they are in the store – and their shopping habits, that is, devotion to Target, will be established for years to come. Target wanted to know when female customers were in the second trimester of pregnancy, meanwhile, so that they could beat out the competition, which showers new couples with coupons and promotions as soon as the baby arrives. The second trimester, furthermore, is when expecting couples tend to stock up on baby-related materials, and "build their nest."

Which leads to the next question: how did Target figure out *when* women were in the second trimester? People will likely say relevant tip-offs include purchases of pregnancy tests, diapers, pacifiers, or cribs. But that's all too obvious. Besides, many of the obvious pregnancy-related products will be purchased late in the game, but Target wants to know early on – as soon as possible. Luckily, the company's researchers discovered a way to do this: they identified "25 products that, when analyzed together, allowed them to assign each shopper a 'pregnancy prediction' score," and even "estimate her due date to within a small window, so that Target could send coupons timed to very specific stages of her pregnancy."[3] Researchers noted, for example, that expectant mothers tend to buy vitamin supplements early in their pregnancy, "larger quantities of unscented lotion around the beginnings of their second trimester," and "lots of scent-free soap and extra-big bags of cotton balls, in addition to sanitizers and washcloths" closer to their delivery date.[4]

Apparently, Target got very good at detecting pregnant customers – better than close family members, in at least one prominent case. A man stormed into a Target store complaining about pregnancy-related coupons and

[2]  Charles Duhigg, "How companies learn your secrets," *New York Times*, February 16, 2012, www.nytimes.com/2012/02/19/magazine/shopping-habits.html?mtrref=www.google.com.
[3]  Duhigg, "How companies learn your secrets."
[4]  Duhigg, "How companies learn your secrets."

promotions sent to his teenage daughter. "Are you trying to encourage her to get pregnant?" he fumed.[5] The store manager apologized profusely – but soon received a contrite phone call from the man, who found out his daughter was indeed pregnant. Target simply knew before he did.

The company decided to slow things down for fear of broader customer backlash, and conceal its outreach to pregnant customers. In its mailed flyers, for example, Target would mix ads for pregnancy-related products with ads for various, random products. One executive explained, "we found that as long as a pregnant woman thinks she hasn't been spied on, she'll use the coupons . . . As long as we don't spook her, it works."[6]

In general, retailers aim to make their data collection, prediction, and promotion efforts "frictionless" and "seamless," which are "current industry buzzwords for a process that doesn't provoke people to stop and ask questions about the technology influencing them."[7] When it comes to "frictionless" data collection, there is perhaps no better example than Amazon's virtual assistant "Alexa." Alone in your kitchen, chopping away – just you and Alexa – you will be more apt to muse aloud, and ask any number of questions about desired products. Or at least, you will certainly be less shy, guarded, or constrained than in a shop, posing questions to a merchant. Conversing with Alexa, "words can occur on the fly with . . . less inhibition, fretting, and comparing; less concern about the limits of one's bank account or where a product or service is sourced; less doubt and hesitation; less memory and remorse."[8] Interacting with Alexa is so seamless, in fact, that children have been inspired to order toys on the spot. In one case, a girl chatting with Alexa asked, "Can you play dollhouse with me and get me a dollhouse?" After she confirmed the order, the girl told Alexa "I love you so much!"[9]

As for "frictionless" promotions, consider this future scenario: soon, when you enter a store, you may find that retail items bear no price tag; instead, the store will recognize you by communicating with your cell phone – where the prices of items you inspect will appear. Retailers will be able to tap into your demographic data and purchase history (and who knows what else), and deliver personalized prices. Retail discrimination will likely result: stores will offer the best prices to customers deemed to have "high lifetime value,"

5   Duhigg, "How companies learn your secrets."
6   Duhigg, "How companies learn your secrets."
7   Turow, 177.
8   Shoshana Zuboff, *The Age of Surveillance Capitalism* (New York: Public Affairs, 2019), 261.
9   Jennifer Earl, "6 year-old orders $160 dollhouse, 4 pounds of cookies with Amazon's Echo Dot," *CBSNews*, January 5, 2017, https://www.cbsnews.com/news/6-year-old-brooke-neitzel-orders-dollhouse-cookies-with-amazon-echo-dot-alexa/.

customers who will be loyal and "profitable shoppers"; meanwhile, "retailers [will] downgrade the benefits of their loyalty program for customers judged to be of less value to the store based on the amounts they spend."[10] In short, wealthy customers will be rewarded – and courted – by retailers; the poor will not. This evokes a strikingly undemocratic future – will people be "comfortable with a society that reverts to the discriminatory elements of the peddler era in which selling was based on profiling each customer?"[11] I suspect they will, if the discriminatory marketing is sufficiently seamless, and discrete. Who won't want to take the better deal, provided they don't have to awkwardly confront poorer customers receiving higher prices? In that case, it will be handy when cash registers are removed from stores, too; you can simply click on your phone, purchase the item in question – at a price no one around you will see – and take it home.

With the kind of retail surveillance discussed above, companies know they may be going beyond the pale in some instances – pushing the envelope, if you will, outpacing consumers in the kinds of technology that are broadly acceptable. Which is why they try to conceal their elaborate designs. How would customers view Target if they knew how intimately the company monitors them, and seeks to compose a detailed account of their personal lives? In the aforementioned case, customer memory, and revulsion, was short-lived – if the surveillance program was widely known at all (though it was documented in the *New York Times* magazine). Target certainly withstood any public relations backlash. But tellingly, the journalist who detailed their pregnancy surveillance program was stonewalled by the company when he asked for comment. No one would speak to him when he flew to company headquarters to request an interview. Why did Target react this way – though it did nothing illegal? Clearly, the company felt it was doing something wrong, or something that would be perceived as wrong – but what? What exactly is disturbing or objectionable in Target's efforts, and others like them?

On one hand, the problem is the nature of the information Target sought out: it wanted a precise piece of intimate information. But as with the Cambridge Analytica "scandal" visited in the previous chapter, Target did not break any law in gaining this knowledge: it merely analyzed the data we had already given the company, data embedded in our purchase history. Perhaps more disturbing are the company's larger aspirations: Target wanted to transform customers from sometime visitors into devotees who would shop

<hr/>

[10]   Turow, 10–11.
[11]   Turow, 248.

nowhere else. This seems rather insidious – and corporate ambitions intolerably greedy.

Target's surveillance program suggests that it aims to utterly dominate the competition, and the market, and will not shrink from trying to manipulate us in that effort. To a lesser degree perhaps, this is also what is objectionable in the case of retailers delivering personalized prices on our cell phones. But again, the offense is hard to pinpoint. In itself, such marketing is innocuous – why wouldn't retailers want to know our demographic data, in order to market to us more effectively? Why wouldn't they want to deliver the best incentives and coupons to secure our business? It starts to seem less ordinary or innocuous, however, when we gain a better idea of the data that is sought. If they only want to know if we have college degrees, where we live, how much we earn, or other general data points, this is not terribly disturbing, or surprising. But when they want to know if we are pregnant – in the second trimester, no less – that's a different story. Why? Because, in those cases, companies are up to something that is far beyond our imagination and comprehension – and control. Indeed, thanks to increasingly sophisticated data analytics, corporations seem intent on controlling us.

Though retailers highlight the notion of a tradeoff to justify collecting our personal data, many people say they are not comfortable with the exchange, and do not find it particularly fair. But, researchers have found, this changes when people are faced with a "real-life tradeoff." Then, the discomfort dissipates. Why? Some suspect it's just because people are increasingly "resigned to giving up their data . . . Rather than feeling able to make choices, Americans believe it is futile to manage what companies can learn about them."[12] Marketers like to say that surveillance and data collection benefit and empower consumers. It enables marketers to offer us all manner of personalized promotions and discounts, showing us exactly what we want, exactly what will make our lives better. But consumers attest that they feel powerless in this exchange instead. They feel they are at a disadvantage because they "often don't have the basic knowledge to make informed cost-benefit choices about ways marketers use their information."[13] They don't know what information is sought about them, how, and why. And there is no autonomous decision making without said knowledge – they will not, cannot say they are in control of the information exchange. Under such circumstances, people "have

---

[12]  Nora Draper, Michael Hennessy, and Joseph Turow, "The Tradeoff Fallacy," A Report from the Annenberg School for Communication, University of Pennsylvania, www.asc.upenn.edu /sites/default/files/TradeoffFallacy_1.pdf.

[13]  Draper et al., "The Tradeoff Fallacy."

decided they ... cannot learn things, change government or business policy, or do anything else that will allow them to manage their personal information the way they want. Moreover, they feel that they would face significant social and economic penalties if they were to opt out of all the services of a modern economy that rely on an exchange of content for data."[14] In fact, when people learn *more* about the nature of the information exchange – when they gain deeper insight into all that is sought about them, and to what end, this does not make them feel more empowered. Researchers find that such people are more likely to be resigned.[15]

Consumer autonomy is also premised on the notion of privacy policies that consumers sign off on before doing business with companies online. But anyone who has glanced at such policies will dispute this; they are hopelessly opaque and complex, and individual consumers can do little with them. That's because such privacy policies are "legal tender not designed to be understood by ordinary people" – who typically don't even read them – but if people bothered to read every privacy policy they encountered, "they would spend 25 days a year engaged in this activity."[16] In any case, when you "refuse to opt in" to data sharing, many products offer "limited product functionality and data security."[17]

There is an illusion of autonomy at the heart of "privacy self-management," a misleading belief that "privacy can only be treated in terms of individual economic choices to disclose information; [occluding] the fact that these choices are demonstrably impossible to make in the manner imagined" – or proposed by corporations.[18] Just as panoptic surveillance sustains the illusion of self-determination on the part of the watched, so consent sustains the notion that we have some control and choice over data collection. This illusion of autonomy permits consumers to sink deeper into asymmetrical power relationships with their corporate spies. The data mining that now delivers our personal information makes "consent meaningless because the uses to which data will be put are not knowable to the user."[19]

Who knows, for example, that companies are interested in knowing if you are in the second trimester of pregnancy? Who will even imagine that

[14] Draper et al., "The Tradeoff Fallacy."
[15] Draper et al., "The Tradeoff Fallacy."
[16] Draper et al., "The Tradeoff Fallacy."
[17] Zuboff, 236.
[18] Gordon Hull, "Successful failure: What Foucault can teach us about privacy self-management in a world of Facebook and Big Data," *Ethics and Information Technology* 17/2 (2015), 90.
[19] Hull, 91.

companies are looking for such a thing? Who knows that companies want to know if you are obese – or if you buy "felt pads to keep [your] furniture from scuffing the floor" – because they have determined that these are indicators of credit risk?[20] Who knows that they have concluded the same about people who fill out loan applications in all capital letters?[21] And about people who invoke "God," and use words like "promise," "will pay," and "hospital" in said applications?[22] The industry of data analytics harbors immense ambitions, and aims to know us intimately – better than we know ourselves – and predict our behavior in detailed fashion. Apparently, it is an esoteric science, combing through our purchases, habits, and more, to discover what otherwise mundane or unremarkable facts reveal about us. Sometimes this science is faulty, and it has its critics and doubters – but not many in the corporate world, it seems. Big Data, as the industry of data collection and analytics is called, has proven sufficiently insightful and predictive to convince companies of its worth – or potential. For, even if corporations don't know what to make of every piece of information, "the basic promise of data [is]: save everything you can, and someday you'll figure out some use for it all."[23] The twenty-first-century consumer is the target of a massive offensive unleashed by corporations, locked in a vicious battle to expand market share – corporations that go to remarkable, unimaginable, almost demented lengths in this effort. If you think about it, it is rather fearsome for the individual consumer at the center of it all.

Governments are also paying close attention to the science, and promise, of data analytics. The Chinese government is rolling out an extensive program that deploys this science, dubbed the Social Credit system. China says this program will fix lingering and pervasive problems that simply cannot endure in a twenty-first-century economy – the biggest in the world. But there are also many non-economic reasons the Chinese government has turned to Big Data, and this is where the Social Credit system starts to sound ominous. Indeed, it looks to be a highly ambitious effort to exert control over a massive population, which, as it becomes wealthier and more cosmopolitan, will also be more restless, and demanding of civil rights and individual freedoms. China's government is anxious to slow this transition, or manage it (or maybe stop it in its tracks), and has decided that mass surveillance is a good bet.

[20] Hull, 91.
[21] Deborah Gage, "Big Data uncovers some weird correlations," *Wall Street Journal*, March 23, 2014, www.wsj.com/articles/big-data-helps-companies-find-some-surprising-correlations–1395168255.
[22] Seth Stephens-Davidowitz, *Everybody Lies* (New York: Dey St., 2017), 258.
[23] Bruce Schneier, *Data and Goliath* (New York: W. W. Norton & Co., 2015), 40.

As mentioned, China has sound economic reasons for turning to Big Data. Millions of its citizens lack official credit scores, and cannot get loans as a result. This also makes it difficult to hold citizens accountable when they enter into contracts – 50 percent of which are not kept.[24] The Chinese government hopes that by assigning Social Credit scores, calculated from a host of non-financial data points, these can be stand-ins for traditional credit scores, and also help enforce financial accountability. Millions of its citizens can then be pulled into the modern economy, and the environment for investment – foreign and domestic – made more appetizing and secure. The government also hopes this system will lead to "more effective oversight and accountability" of an economy marred by high levels of "micro-corruption," where the "sale of counterfeit and substandard products is a massive problem" and "63 percent of all fake goods, from watches to handbags to baby food, originate from China."[25]

The program becomes worrisome when you consider the kinds of information the government pays attention to in calculating Social Credit scores, and what else it plans on doing with these scores. The Chinese government has turned to the private sector to develop the system. Partner corporations include massive financial service and telecommunications firms who dominate several important sectors of the economy, including ride-hailing, online purchases and loans, and social media. They have decided upon five factors that go into calculating your Social Credit score, among which are some basic data points – when available – like credit history, proof that you are honoring contractual obligations, and personal information, such as your address and phone number. The fourth factor, however, is "behavior and preference." Here, the government will try to determine your character – your trustworthiness, to be precise – from your purchases and digital transactions. The Technology Director for Sesame Credit, one of the companies charged with developing the Social Credit system, put it thus: "Someone who plays video games for ten hours a day, for example, would be considered an idle person . . . Someone who frequently buys diapers would be considered as probably a parent, who on balance is more likely to have a sense of responsibility."[26] The fifth factor will be interpersonal relationships: are you associated with people who are often "idle"? Are you friends with anyone on social media who is delinquent on loan payments, or who breaks contracts? If so, this will reflect

[24] Rachel Botsman, "Big Data meets Big Brother as China moves to rate its citizens," *Wired*, October 21, 2017, www.wired.co.uk/article/chinese-government-social-credit-score-privacy-invasion.

[25] Botsman, "Big Data meets Big Brother."

[26] Botsman, "Big Data meets Big Brother."

poorly on you – thus, you may feel obliged to disconnect from them, or urge them to clean up their act.

With this, we start to see the kinds of social prodding – or social engineering – that the Chinese government hopes to implement. If you are deemed untrustworthy, and your personal behavior is hurting your friends, you might find your social circle shrinking. You will also miss out on a host of remarkable incentives for people with high Social Credit scores. Trustworthy people may be able to borrow greater sums of money and more easily, "rent a car without leaving a deposit," take advantage of "faster check-in at hotels," or even enjoy a more prominently featured dating profile online.[27] These incentives suggest why there has been no prominent objection to the program thus far – indeed, millions of Chinese citizens have already signed on for trial runs.

Foucault might raise an eyebrow here. China's Social Credit system looks to be an impressive way to use surveillance to compel conformity, where citizens will be their own principal drivers in the rush to behave – and accrue benefits. In a way, it "reflects a cunning paradigm shift," one commentator explained. "[Instead] of trying to enforce stability or conformity with a big stick and a good dose of top-down fear, the government is attempting to make obedience feel like gaming."[28] Gaming is not exactly the method Foucault depicted; this is a novel innovation. But it may well have the same effect: citizens will believe themselves free and self-determining in the race to conform. They will compete with one another to amass better scores and appear more trustworthy in the government's eyes. China is also banking on the fact that everyone will happily submit to surveillance on the promise of convenience. Faster hotel check-ins and rental car deliveries are at stake. Improved convenience is also sold as an important benefit of China's expansive deployment of facial recognition technology, aimed at supplementing the Social Credit system – and more.

In another ambitious program, entitled "Sharp Eyes," the Chinese government aims to connect security cameras in public spaces, like shopping malls, roads and train stations – even public toilets – with "private cameras on compounds and buildings, and integrate them into one nationwide surveillance and data-sharing platform."[29] Armed with facial recognition technology, the police can then monitor or follow suspects over this vast network.

[27] Botsman, "Big Data meets Big Brother."
[28] Botsman, "Big Data meets Big Brother."
[29] Simon Denyer, "Beijing bets on facial recognition in a big drive for total surveillance, *Washington Post*, January 7, 2018, www.washingtonpost.com/news/world/wp/2018/01/07/feature/in-china-facial-recognition-is-sharp-end-of-a-drive-for-total-surveillance/?utm_term=.adccf03dea09.

Alternately, the technology will be used to assist ordinary people in a host of daily tasks. When facial recognition cameras were recently installed in a high school in eastern China, "students got in and out of campus, picked up lunch, borrowed books and even bought drinks from a vending machine just by peering into the cameras. No more worrying about forgetting to carry your ID card."[30] Conceivably, the technology will soon enable people to purchase groceries simply by showing their face at the register; they could do the same when checking in to a hotel, or boarding a train. This is no small matter for a nation that seeks to deal with massive congestion. Indeed, Beijing's subway system plans to implement the technology to help "riders gain faster entry" to trains, and speed things along.[31] There are worries about the system's accuracy, and whether it may be liable to hacking, but this has not stopped the Chinese government from pushing ahead. Naturally, there are darker possibilities for the technology – as those high school students in eastern China ultimately learned. They soon found the facial recognition cameras installed in their classrooms, aimed at tracking their facial expressions, behavior patterns, and emotional states. The information was used to "create a running 'score' on each student and class. If a score reached a predetermined point, the system triggered an alert. Teachers were expected to take action: to talk to a student perceived to be disengaged ... or overly moody."[32] There were also plans to use the information to help teachers better understand the appeal and effectiveness of their lessons. It is not hard to foresee this technology being used in a coercive manner. Students would have to "keep up appearances" nearly all the time – an unnerving prospect. And as an educator myself, the notion that my students' emotional states will be measured during class, to assess my effectiveness, or student focus, is equally daunting and upsetting. The classroom environment, as any teacher will attest, varies according to a host of minor factors, internal and external to the classroom; much is beyond the control of the instructor. Parents of children at the Chinese high school issued enough complaints that the system was put on hold – not abandoned altogether, mind you.

The notion that authorities could, and perhaps would, monitor our emotional states is troubling. At first, it may be used in security lines at airports. Does anyone boarding the plane look especially nervous, worried, or stressed? Does he have evil plans for his flight, perhaps? In totalitarian regimes – and

---

[30]   Don Lee, "At this Chinese school, Big Brother was watching students – and charting every smile or frown," *LA Times*, June 30, 2018, http://www.latimes.com/world/la-fg-china-face-surveillance-2018-story.html.

[31]   Lee, "Big Brother was watching students."

[32]   Lee, "Big Brother was watching students."

what could be a scene out of 1984 – the government might inspect the faces of citizens amassed at a political rally: is everyone sincerely expressing devotion to the regime? Is anyone less than enthusiastic? Is anyone deceitful?

In the short run, the Chinese government will use "Sharp Eyes" to catch criminal suspects in a sea of faces – perhaps with the assistance of facial recognition glasses sported by police officers; it will also capture the faces of jaywalkers and broadcast them on large screens at the site of their infraction, in an effort to shame them.[33] The latter suggests similar aspirations to the Social Credit system: facial recognition will pressure people to behave better. In fact, "Sharp Eyes" may not even have to be fully operable to produce this effect. One criminal suspect confessed to police when they merely showed him their facial recognition glasses – which had not in fact spotted him. "Because he was afraid of being found out by the advanced technology," the police chief explained, "he confessed. We didn't even use any interrogation techniques. He simply gave it all up."[34] This demonstrates again how surveillance may be a highly efficient exercise of power – the authorities hardly have to do much of anything. In fact, the less the better.

Invoking the aspirations of Big Data, one critic said that China's expansive surveillance effort is "potentially a new way for the government to manage the economy and society. The goal is algorithmic government."[35] And yet, at this early stage in its development, it is reasonable to wonder how much video surveillance – and public shaming – people may tolerate? Will they accept seeing cameras everywhere they look? Will they put up with having their every transaction and chore recorded? Will they tolerate seeing their names listed in public places, announcing that they "can't pay their debts"?[36] While surveillance is light, as Foucault put it, some of China's potential initiatives start to sound heavy indeed. Short of outright rebellion, is it possible that the Chinese population might not behave in ways the government anticipates? That is – shamelessly, irresponsibly, recklessly? Might they be immune to all the social prompting after a while? For now, it seems, the Chinese population is submitting to all the surveillance – happily, in some cases, where welcome conveniences are on offer. They can take advantage of keyless entry into apartment buildings, for example, enabled by the facial recognition

---

[33] Paul Mozur, "Inside China's dystopian dreams: A.I., shame and lots of cameras," *New York Times*, July 8, 2018, https://www.nytimes.com/2018/07/08/business/china-surveillance-technology.html.

[34] Mozur, "Inside China's dystopian dreams."

[35] Mozur, "Inside China's dystopian dreams."

[36] Mozur, "Inside China's dystopian dreams."

technology; in the meantime, the government adds more and more faces to its database.[37]

As we might expect, the Chinese government is keen on using the video surveillance network, augmented by facial recognition technology, to identify and monitor political dissidents, especially in its western provinces, where there are concerns over separatist ambitions among the Muslim Uighur population.[38] Thanks to all the new kinds of data offered by this technology, will the government also expand its notion of political dissidence – or suspicion thereof? Perhaps it is discovered that you happen to frequent a coffee shop also favored by anti-government activists – and when you look at them while sipping your beverage, your facial expression is suspiciously friendly towards them? What's more, ordinary citizens untrained in detecting real political dissidence may rat on you. For, the Chinese government plans on enlisting their help in the security measures afforded by "Sharp Eyes." Citizens will be able to access security camera footage on home devices, and then relay suspicious behavior to the authorities. This quickly starts to smack of the total domination sought by totalitarian regimes. Perhaps it is no mistake then that the program's name is derived from Mao Zedong's favored slogan "the masses have sharp eyes," whereby he urged the citizens to spy on one another.[39]

We are justified in worrying about the social and political applications of China's vast surveillance efforts. Its government has made little pretense of caring about individual liberties and civil rights, and has indulged in overt oppression over the past half century. This was much worse under Mao Zedong of course, and his disastrous Cultural Revolution, but the modern Chinese government forcefully disbanded political protestors at Tiananmen Square in 1989 – and repressed coverage of the incident ever since – and routinely locks up journalists and political protestors. It may be easy to forget all this in light of China's booming, gleaming economy, which lures Silicon Valley companies rooted in the American culture of liberty. We may be inclined to think that the United States would never submit to the temptations of this technology; we will never see designs on total control, apparent in China's vast experiment.

And yet, it turns out, the United States has a "higher per capita penetration rate" of surveillance cameras.[40] Which means there is already an immense

---

[37]  Mozur, "Inside China's dystopian dreams."
[38]  Lee, "Big Brother was watching students."
[39]  Denyer, "Beijing bets on facial recognition."
[40]  Denyer, "Beijing bets on facial recognition."

video surveillance network in place, which could be employed in the Chinese manner if our government had an inkling to do so, or felt so empowered. And corporations and law enforcement are already using facial recognition technology in a variety of ways. Police have used facial recognition technology to expedite identification of criminal suspects, and airports have used it for similar ends, scanning the faces of people boarding international flights – and soon, domestic flights.[41] The US military is using the technology in a "drone-footage project involving Google, dubbed Project Maven, aimed to speed the job of looking for 'patterns of life, things that are suspicious, indications of potential attacks.'"[42] Concerned that the technology could be used for controversial and morally troubling ends, Google employees protested enough that the company pulled out of its partnership with the military. One Boston-based start-up developing the technology has rejected police and military applications of its product, citing similar concerns, and instead "partnered with automakers trying to help tired looking drivers stay awake, and with consumer brands that want to know whether people respond to a product with joy or disgust."[43] It is admirable perhaps that the company spurned government projects out of moral concern; however, the military and police will be keen to see how the technology evolves and develops in the private sector. They will surely learn a lot from marketers studying our faces and putting inferences to work.

It turns out American corporations are operating in ways reminiscent of the Chinese government, composing stand-ins for consumer credit scores, for example, when people lack official documents and formal information. So-called "E-scores" – a "sloppy substitute" for credit scores, by one account – are composed when companies "draw inferences about our wealth" from various informal data points, including our web browsing behavior, our purchasing habits, and our home location.[44] These are not the most accurate or fair indicators of creditworthiness, of course. They will likely produce outcomes that favor the rich, and punish the poor. E-scores largely rely on proxies – that is, are you buying the same things and living in the same neighborhood as other known entities? Entities that are creditworthy – or not? This opens the door for racism and class prejudice, though we have worked for decades to make the marketplace indifferent to such markers. Officially sanctioned credit scores – FICO scores – were

---

[41] "How much artificial intelligence surveillance is too much?" *Voice of America*, July 3, 2018, www .voanews.com/a/how-much-artificial-intelligence-surveillance-is-too-much-/4465586.html.
[42] "How much artificial intelligence surveillance is too much?"
[43] "How much artificial intelligence surveillance is too much?"
[44] Cathy O'Neil, *Weapons of Math Destruction* (New York: Broadway Books, 2016), 144.

meant to "ditch the proxies" and focus instead on the "individual in question –
and not on other people with similar attributes. E-scores, by contrast, march us
back in time. They analyze the individual through a veritable blizzard of
proxies."[45] And there is reason to worry that these "sloppy substitutes" can be
used for other dubious ends – to draw inferences on your character, for example.
Companies already look to credit reports to determine if you are hirable or worthy
of a promotion.[46] They will happily learn even more about you – and draw
conclusions on your character – from your E-score.

   Contemplating China's ambitious data collection analytics program, one
commentator opined that we in the United States "already live in a world of
predictive algorithms that determine if we are a threat, a risk, a good citizen and
even if we are trustworthy. We're getting closer to the Chinese system – the
expansion of credit scoring into life scoring – even if we don't know we are."[47]
When it comes to so-called "life scoring," consider all the data that effort has to
draw on – data that we consumers are contributing freely. We rate Uber drivers,
for example. This helps determine if they get more business in the future. Will
this publicly accessible rating be sucked up into one's E-Score? Why not?
Companies may determine that it gives insight into a person's work ethic and
creditworthiness; driving for Uber, after all, is a second job for many people –
suggesting that they are willing to work hard. We rate restaurants on Yelp.
Lenders could check this information to help determine if a given restaurant
is worthy of investment. Alternately, lenders might want to examine your own
Yelp posts – do you leave many? Does this mean you have time to kill? That you
don't work hard at your own job? That you are a profligate spender? If you are
prone to leaving snarky, critical or even rude reviews, perhaps this will indicate
something else unsavory about your character – you are temperamental, highly
judgmental, picky, or hard to please – and prompt a low E-score in turn. Similar
conclusions could be drawn from your Facebook posts, perhaps: are you
a diligent worker, or too busy sharing articles, pictures, and cat videos? If it
sounds outlandish that corporations might be interested in such information,
consider that the online lender Affirm, whose founder "believes that social data
can give more people access to credit," already studies "web browsing behavior,
activity on Facebook and Twitter, frequency of mobile phone calls and text
messages."[48] What is the company looking for? Apparently, it has its eye on your

---

[45]   O'Neil, 146.
[46]   O'Neil, 148.
[47]   Botsman, "Big Data meets Big Brother."
[48]   Andreas Weigend, "Our personal data is never going to be private again. We can work with
       that," *Quartz*, January 28, 2017, https://qz.com/896929/our-personal-data-is-never-going-to-be-
       private-again-we-can-work-with-that/.

personal associations, among many things. The former chief scientist of Amazon is an evangelizer for the company. Seeking to allay concern and empower consumers – but in language that could have been borrowed from the Chinese government itself – he said that you could "see an analysis of the data sources and how they affect your credit score. Once you've reviewed the data, you can decide on whether to change your behavior or change your data ... [You] might decide to unfriend a person who is dragging down your social data credit score ... "[49] Note the paradoxical reasoning implicit here: this technology gives you autonomy ... to limit yourself and curtail your behavior. But this presupposes you know what your spies are looking out for – you know what they have determined to be red flags. As established, however, the science of data analytics is arcane. It is unlikely that you will be so autonomous as this online lender suggests.

In the digital economy, it becomes clear, consumer or social information mixes easily with official data, such that they are neatly exchangeable, or nearly identical, at least in the eyes of some. The Chinese government is busy amassing and analyzing a plethora of data points on each of its citizens, in order to draw inferences – perhaps unfairly – about character. Corporate America is practically doing the same, as is our military and law enforcement. But Americans, and Westerners in general, should protest this new culture of character judgment. It goes against central democratic values, where individuals are innocent until proven guilty, equal before law enforcement and marketers alike, and they may exercise a degree of control over their fate. This is less often the case in the age of Big Data, when corporations, and governments, too, look to judge us without our input – or knowledge – and undermine our freedom in the marketplace, and society at large. Data analytics is advancing at such a fevered pace, and industry efforts are so elaborate and opaque, it's daunting to consider how we might stem the tide. We are quickly "entering an age where an individual's actions will be judged by standards they can't control and where that judgment can't be erased."[50]

Sensing the dangers at hand, many call for regulations on the collection and dispersal of consumer and citizen data. In 2018, the European Union enacted its General Data Protection Regulation (GDPR), which was seen to be a far-reaching effort at the time. Or at least, it was certainly far reaching compared to anything in the United States, where tech giants are relatively free from government intervention and, thanks to intense lobbying, dictate whether there will be data protection at all. Nevertheless, since the GDPR impacted

[49]   Weigend, "Our personal data is never going to be private again."
[50]   Botsman, "Big Data meets Big Brother."

the behavior of numerous transnational corporations, even if they were not based in Europe, the law had a nearly global reach, and influenced how many American companies treat our data – or at least, disclose how they treat it.

Among the regulations, which many would like to see implemented in the United States or worldwide, are the following: companies must provide "documentation of why people's information is being collected and processed, descriptions of the information that's held, how long it's being kept for and descriptions of the technical security measures in place"; they must also secure consumer consent before data is collected, which entails, at the outset of each consumer experience, stating how and to what end the collected data may be used.[51] This latter measure stipulates that consumers must now opt-in to a company's website, and approve how it uses consumer data. Previously, consumers had to opt-out if they did not want a company to collect and share their data; this required researching the company website to find out the relevant privacy policy, and then discover the terms and consequences of opting-out. This made sharing data all too easy. People could do business with companies online, and never think of the consequences of data sharing – indeed, it was never mentioned at all. GDPR aims to bring data collection foremost to our minds; the European Union wants this to be the first thing we reckon with when interacting with a company digitally.

In a way, GDPR aims to effect a cultural change when it comes to data sharing. It wants people to pause and consider the possible consequences before they share personal information with corporations. People are no longer to be automatically sucked into the data analytics system. GDPR "mandates that firms obtain explicit consent from consumers for every possible use of their information, and allow them to delete and request copies of all data companies have on them."[52] The new law also forces companies to repackage privacy policies, to make them more easily understandable and manageable for the average reader. Companies must, for example, retreat from legalese as far as possible. Technology giants have complied with the law by coming up with "new tools for people to download and delete their data."[53]

---

[51]  Matt Burgess, "What is GDPR? The summary guide to GDPR compliance in the UK," *Wired*, June 4, 2018, www.wired.co.uk/article/what-is-gdpr-uk-eu-legislation-compliance-summary-fines–2018.

[52]  Elizabeth Dwoskin, "New privacy rules could spell the end of legalese – or create a lot more fine print," *Washington Post*, May 24, 2018, www.washingtonpost.com/news/the-switch/wp/2018/05/24/new-privacy-rules-could-spell-the-end-of-legalese-or-create-a-lot-more-fine-print/?utm_term=.09c9b7982269.

[53]  Dwoskin, "New privacy rules could spell the end of legalese."

But there are concerns about how effective the new data protections might be. In general, the law seeks to empower individuals – but will individuals really be so empowered or motivated to do much? Will they actively, vigilantly look to see what companies know about them? Will they seek to delete all the embarrassing or compromising details that have amassed over a vast network over many years? Will individuals read the privacy policies closely – even if they are more readable – to understand and approve what companies are doing with their personal information? Critics note that "the requirement of companies to disclose more about their data practices than ever before could result in more-lengthy explanations."[54] Will people eager to make use of digital conveniences really plow through those statements, and digest them one by one – keeping tabs on which websites collect what information, etc? As of this writing, it is too soon to render judgment on GDPR. It may well happen that individual consumers pay closer attention to privacy policies – and companies will be forced to treat consumer data with greater care. But I am not optimistic. This is a lot to ask or expect of individual consumers locked in a fast-moving and all-encompassing surveillance economy – where the price of doing business with anyone or any firm is sharing data. And the terms of exchange repeatedly insist that you give more data to receive more benefits in turn. What's more, GDPR seeks to empower individuals to deal with some of the biggest, richest corporations on earth – whose inner machinations are quite inscrutable – and set consumers on equal footing with these behemoths. That seems hardly plausible. Any single individual tasked with protecting his privacy in the surveillance economy is at a profound disadvantage. The asymmetries of power and knowledge between consumers and corporations are stark.

We, ordinary citizens and consumers, have little idea of the information sought about us, why it is sought, to what end or consequence. This is far beyond our imagination and comprehension. To put it otherwise, we have no idea what we reveal about ourselves, what our spies learn, from even basic snippets of our behavior. For example, one group of researchers said that, through automated analysis of Facebook "likes," it was able to predict people's race with 95 percent accuracy, and gender with 93 percent accuracy – and if they were Christian or Muslim, Democrat or Republican.[55] And Facebook has figured out how to determine from user information if a person is falling in

54   Dwoskin, "New privacy rules could spell the end of legalese."
55   Michal Kosinski, David Stillwell and Thore Graepel, "Private Traits and Attributes are Predictable from Digital Records of Human Behavior," *Proceedings of the National Academy of Sciences of the United States of America*, April 9, 2013, www.pnas.org/content/110/15/5802.

love. The social media giant analyzed data from users who had changed their relationship status, and looked for salient and predictive tip-offs. For example:

> The data says that in the 100 days before people change their status they make increasing numbers of posts on each other's walls. Couples about to be "official" will post . . . 1.67 times per day in the 12 days before they publicly change their profile to "in a relationship." The number of posts then falls to 1.53 posts per day in the next 85 days . . . [While] the number of interactions drops as the relationship starts, there's also an uptick in the level of positivity. This includes the use of words like love, nice, happy, and to get the overall trend, Facebook subtracted negative words like hate, hurt and bad.[56]

What does it say about us that we betray such intimate feelings in simple, otherwise unremarkable behavior patterns? More importantly: what does it say about Facebook that it is taking note of such trends – sifting through our words, measuring our every communication, drawing conclusions about our personal lives? Why would Facebook want to know if users are falling in love? What could it do with that information?

Obviously, the answer is a lot. And clearly, the fact that Facebook is researching this at all indicates that the company deems it marketable. It could, for example, sell advertising space on your Facebook page to florists or jewelers if it determines you are falling in love. Alternately, if could invite Ben and Jerry's or alcohol purveyors when it knows you are in the midst of a break-up. And it is "only a short jump from identifying vulnerabilities to figuring out how to create them."[57] Isn't that precisely what marketers always long for? Facebook's knowledge here – about our love lives – reveals why companies don't wish to divulge the nature, extent, and aim of their data analysis: because of the potential power it lends them – over us. It is also a distinctly unflattering view of these companies who want such power over us. Perhaps this is why Facebook, alone among the Silicon Valley elite, sought to elude the new EU data protection laws – and continue to conceal what it plans for our data – by moving "70 percent of its users to be registered in the US, instead of Ireland," as had previously been the case.[58]

How can corporations, and any of our would-be spies, resist compiling and analyzing data, when they have determined that revelatory indicators are so

---

[56] Ian Morris, "Facebook knows when you fall in love, and that's pretty creepy," *Forbes*, December 31, 2016, www.forbes.com/sites/ianmorris/2016/12/31/facebook-knows-when-you-fall-in-love-and-thats-pretty-creepy/#355c482e6f52.

[57] Zeynep Tufekci, "Is the Internet good or bad? Yes," *Medium*, February 12, 2014, https://medium.com/matter/is-the-internet-good-or-bad-yes-76d9913c6011.

[58] Burgess, "What is GDPR?"

widely and easily available? One study looked at people's network of friends and "accurately predicted whether someone was in a relationship 60% of the time" – also when the relationship was about to end – leading researchers to conclude that "crucial aspects of our everyday lives may be encoded in the network structure among our friends, if we know how to look."[59] Our spies don't need access to the content of our communications at all. They have learned that the form of our communications is as illuminating, or more so. Researchers believe it tells them personality type, and can inform subsequent commercial pitches. "The price you are offered does not derive from what you write about but how you write it," one scholar explains. "It is not what is in your sentences but in their length and complexity, not what you list but that you list, not the picture but the choice of filter and the degree of saturation, not what you disclose but how you share or fail to, not where you make plans to see your friends but how you do so ... "[60]

After Snowden's revelations, the US government sought to downplay its spying operations, saying the NSA was only collecting our "metadata" – the data of our data: it was not reading our emails or studying what we purchased at the hardware store, but only taking note of the time, destination, and duration of our communications, where we were shopping, and making digital transactions. If the NSA detected troubling patterns in our metadata, only then did it ask a judge if it could inspect the data itself. Thus, the argument goes, this was not so invasive after all. And yet, analyzing metadata has the potential to provide a surprisingly "revealing picture of people": depending on where I travel in a day – and the digital clues I leave at each destination – the metadata could indicate "whether I'm negotiating to leave my employer and take a new job or a secret business deal, whether I'm having an extramarital affair, whether I'm seeing a psychiatrist."[61]

Some might be assuaged by the fact that there is an ocean of data out there, and you can remain somewhat obscured amidst it all. But that is not the case. It is not hard for our spies to determine our precise identity through it all. Beyond a certain point – "if you eliminate the top 100 movies everyone watches," for example, "our movie-watching habits are all pretty individual."[62] The same goes for our book preferences and our shopping

---

[59] Leo Mirani, "What your Facebook friends list reveals about your love life," *Quartz*, October 28, 2013, https://qz.com/140357/what-your-facebook-friends-list-reveals-about-your-love-life/.

[60] Zuboff, 275.

[61] Barton Gellman, interviewed by Robert Siegel, "NSA harvests contact lists from email, Facebook," *All Things Considered*, NPR, October 15, 2013, www.npr.org/sections/thetwo-way/2013/10/15/234776676/report-nsa-harvests-contact-lists-from-email-facebook.

[62] Schneier, 52.

proclivities. Taken together, all of these patterns point to a unique person, with distinctive habits and proclivities. Not to mention that we betray our identity through the location data on our cell phones. But "you don't even need all that data; 95 percent of Americans can be identified by *name* from just four time/ data/location points."[63]

Some activists have suggested we employ methods of obfuscation, that is the "deliberate addition of ambiguous, confusing or misleading information to interfere with surveillance and data collection."[64] Methods can include something as simple as the use of various pseudonyms online, or something more sophisticated, like browser plug-ins that initiate a host of web searches on random topics, just to throw off our spies. The aim of the latter is information overload – behind which we can hide. Sooner or later, however, our spies reconfigure the tools of data analysis, and learn to cut through the information overload perpetrated by individual users – who must then discover new methods of obfuscation. Would-be obfuscators work on "emerging methods for foiling face recognition systems, like strange makeup or eyeglasses," but these only work until the technology catches up.[65] Obfuscation is a full-time job, in other words. At best, it is a stalling tactic – a starting point for the digital resistance – but not a long-term solution to the onslaught of Big Data.[66] In any case, the surveillance economy will not be upended by individual activists dodging and ducking the system for so long.

Perhaps we can't help but be known intimately by our corporate and government spies. Perhaps it is just too easy for us to betray personal information – sooner or later. In that case, the best response might be to watch the watchers.[67] We might keep an eye on what they collect and know, and then do with it. Data brokers already offer consumers such insight, if they want it; and this is something that GDPR seeks to mandate for companies we do business with digitally. However, the reports that data brokers offer are "highly curated," it turns out, and "include the facts but not always the conclusions data brokers' algorithms have drawn from them."[68] In that case, how can we know which data are salient, and which are not? And if we are privy to the conclusions, how can we know how they are arrived at? And can we ever be

[63] Schneier, 53 (his emphasis).
[64] Helen Nissenbaum and Finn Bruton, *Obfuscation: A User's Guide for Privacy and Protest* (Cambridge, MA: MIT Press, 2015), 1.
[65] D. J. Pangburn, "How to disappear in a fog of data (and why)," *Vice*, November 16, 2016, www.vice.com/en_us/article/yp3ex7/obfuscate-yourself-nissenbaum-brunton.
[66] Pangburn, "How to disappear in a fog of data."
[67] Botsman, "Big Data meets Big Brother."
[68] O'Neil, 152.

sure we are shown all the conclusions companies have drawn about us? Or how they might analyze said data in the future? Or which data will be salient in the future? "The sheer volume of data inputs and methods of analysis moves beyond human comprehension," one scholar contends; individuals cannot hope to contest surveillance algorithms without the help of "new counter-vailing authority and power," like a government agency tasked with regulating the use of said algorithms and equipped with "machine resources and exper-tise to reach into the core disciplines of machine intelligence."[69]

When it comes to data protection, the power differential between indivi-duals and our spies is vast. We don't really know what these parties know about us – we can't see how they analyze basic data points, and draw inferences about our identity. And we have little comprehension of their plans for our data – now or in the future. Regulatory efforts like GDPR, which seek to give individuals the opportunity to manage their data, seem less potent when you consider how we are so very immersed in the surveillance economy, soon to sink deeper.

[69]  Zuboff, 484.

# 4

## The Surveillance Economy

In the face of rapid technological changes transforming our lives in profound ways, the forecast for privacy looks dark. Its demise is hastened by "an unstoppable arms race in communication tools and data mining capabilities, which in turn are both due to the continued progression of Moore's Law. The cost of keeping secrets increases inversely to decreases in the cost of computing."[1] Roughly, Moore's Law holds that computing power will grow exponentially; digital devices will become faster and more powerful in rapid succession. Where technological changes may have once developed gradually, that is precisely *not* the case in the digital age, where breakneck speed of change is the rule. And digital technology will become cheaper, more accessible, and broadly distributed in the process. Taken together, this means that the cost and hassle of protecting privacy grows exponentially, too. In the digital net that envelops our everyday lives, it will become increasingly more difficult and rare to perform any task without revealing ourselves, and opening our lives to spying eyes. And our spies are not content to watch us from without; they will install sentinels in our very bodies, and monitor us from within.

Surveillance is poised to dominate our driving. Insurance companies are installing in the cars of willing customers devices that monitor how much they drive, if they brake too hard or travel too fast, even what hours of the day they are on the road. The industry determined that these factors are far more predictive of driving behavior, specifically, if drivers are more or less likely to be in an accident. Insurance companies are also happy to monitor behavior in this way because they know it influences how customers drive, and makes them more cautious. Customers meanwhile agree to be monitored at the promise of lower

[1] Nova Spivack, "The post-privacy world," *Wired*, July 26, 2013, www.wired.com/insights/2013/07/the-post-privacy-world/.

premiums. Insurance companies may make such monitoring a requirement in the near future; without it, you will get no car insurance at all. And soon, insurance companies will monitor drivers without physical devices in their cars, but simply track their driving behavior through mobile-phone apps.

One such app has been developed by FICO, the company that gives people credit scores, and eDriving, which provides driver training. The eDriver Mentor Smartphone app will calculate your driving score, which you may then use to shop for car insurance and get the best rates. The app will tell people "how they could improve their skills. The app tracks drivers' acceleration, braking, cornering, speeding and how they engage with their training on the app."[2] The CEO of eDriving explained that "we are taking a Weight Watchers or FitBit approach" to influence people's driving behavior. "It's a little bit of gamification and a little bit of shamification."[3] FitBit monitors people's physical activity, providing a sly encouragement to exercise more – or, as the executive notes, it shames you for bad behavior (i.e. when you are lazy). People will sign up for such monitoring at the prospect of self-improvement or saving money, and also because it is fun. At least, that's the proposal. But gamification is a recurring element of increased monitoring – as we saw in the case of China's ambitious surveillance system, too. Or rather, I should say that gamification is a recurring *enticement*. In this case, it's as if I inserted myself in a video game where I am the main contestant . . . to prove that I am a safe and compliant driver. This may not sound like the most exciting game, but I wager people will play it if they can save money, and earn other perks that insurance companies will dream up. And as we will see, corporate America is busy turning much of our lives into video games, where we happily compete in exchange for being watched.

Ford motor company now installs in its cars the tools for monitoring. It equips new vehicles with a system called SYNC-3, "a fully integrated, voice-activated communications, entertainment and information system . . . a revolutionary way to interact with your vehicle."[4] This computer, which helps drivers navigate roads and the car's entertainment system alike, and relays important information about the engine and the trip at hand, now also monitors driver behavior, composing a score that can be presented to insurance companies. One advantage of this innovation is that it can help provide

2   Tom Anderson, "More auto insurers want to track your driving behavior in exchange for lower rates," CNBC, October 23, 2016, www.cnbc.com/2016/10/23/more-auto-insurers-want-to-track-your-driving-behavior-in-exchange-for-lower-rates.html.
3   Anderson, "Auto insurers want to track your driving behavior."
4   Ford Motor Company, "SYNC 3 and SYNC Hands-Free, Smart Entertainment & Vehicle Information Systems," www.ford.com/technology/sync/ (accessed November 20, 2017).

a more accurate and personalized driving score. For one thing, the computer can identify different drivers, connecting to their different cell phones; thus, a teenage driver won't ruin his parent's driving score.[5] Furthermore, the system may constantly determine your driving score and calculate it with greater precision, changing over time. For example, it can gauge how drivers perform in "highly accident-prone intersections," allowing them to prove they are good drivers, and improve their driving score – on a daily basis.[6] One Ford executive suggests how empowering this will be: "the more data [drivers] get, the more they'll be able to fine tune their algorithms over time."[7]

FICO touts this monitoring as a kind of mentorship. It will train you, improve your driving skills, and save you money. Ford now offers the ability to constantly hone your skills and prove your progress. But it is easy to imagine how this driving score could also be punitive. Presumably it will, like your credit score, follow you around, and, in some cases, be a black mark on your record. Or life. Most car insurance companies already look at your credit score to set your premiums, which is why, I suppose, it makes sense that FICO is involved in determining driving scores. Why would car insurance companies be interested in your credit score? If you are a responsible individual, you are more likely to be a good, careful driver. Perhaps banks – or other businesses and government agencies – will be interested in your driving score, in turn?

In fact, "the use of sensory technologies that permit behavioral underwriting by insurers is likely to be expanded beyond auto insurance into homeowners, life and health coverages, and perhaps even . . . workers' compensation. Your whole life could become an exercise in keeping your premiums down – safer and cheaper – but a lot less exciting."[8] A company might not want to give you homeowner's insurance, for example, if it determines you smoke and are a fire hazard – or if it decides that smoking is an indicator of reckless behavior more broadly. As fewer Americans smoke, companies may look for other indicators of fire hazard, or general risk, no matter how seemingly remote. Like if you cook a lot and are thus more liable to set a pot on fire. Or if you use your appliances too often – or have too many – and run the risk of an electrical short. How, you might ask, will companies know? If tech companies have their

---

[5]  Hope Reese, "CES 2017: Ford's DriverScore app tracks driving data to reward good drivers with low insurance rates," *Techrepublic*, January 4, 2017, www.techrepublic.com/article/ces-2017-fords-driverscore-app-tracks-driving-data-to-reward-good-drivers-with-low-insurance-rates/.

[6]  Reese, "Ford's DriverScore app."

[7]  Reese, "Ford's DriverScore app."

[8]  Leo Mirani, "Car insurance companies want to track your every move – and you're going to let them," *Quartz*, July 9, 2014, https://qz.com/230055/car-insurance-companies-want-to-track-your-every-move-and-youre-going-to-let-them/.

way, we will soon inhabit "smart homes" filled with internet-connected appliances – even furniture – that make notes of our habits and energy use. To offer tips, and serve us better of course.

One couple who subjected themselves to a "smart home" experiment, installing internet-connected lights, coffee maker, baby monitor, kid's toys, and toothbrush, among other things, found that their new "smart bed" could monitor "our breathing rate, heart rate, how often we toss and turn, and then it will give us a sleep report each morning."[9] Their internet-connected vacuum, meanwhile, was touted for collecting a "rich map of the home," which could be shared with "Apple, Amazon, or Alphabet, the three companies that hope to dominate the smart home market."[10] The point – or rather, the dream – is that your appliances will talk to one another, and relay key information about you beyond the home – information that can be monetized. This will be facilitated by a burgeoning list of "smart" products, "from smart vodka bottles to internet enabled rectal thermometers" – also "smart lightbulbs, smart coffee mugs … smart juicers, and smart utensils said to improve your digestion."[11] Together, these smart devices might help compose a more detailed and thorough picture of your life and behavior, for the benefit of your own knowledge, but also that of your spies. Back to insurance: perhaps a company that offers life insurance is wary of your sleep habits, dental hygiene, or coffee addiction, and it deems you a bad investment. Or a company determines you are a bad bet for home insurance because you don't vacuum enough – or the smart vacuum's map of your home indicates plenty of clutter, which might be a fire hazard.

Who knows what kinds of things insurance companies might like to learn about you, when determining your policies? Who knows what lifestyle changes they might suggest – or require – so you can secure the best price, or get their product at all? The growing digitalization of our cars and homes provides insurers with immense power to monitor us and nudge us to tweak our habits. We may look to curb our behavior and make it progressively safer, and more predictable – more conforming, less likely to raise red flags. Which sounds like we will be less free, in a way – less free to take risks and learn from them, less likely to derive thrills from risky behavior, or indulge quirky habits. Or maybe not. Maybe we will just have to figure out different ways to remain distinct, and cling to unique behavior traits amidst the economic pressures of

9   Kashmir Hill, "The house that spied on me," *Gizmodo*, February 7, 2018, https://gizmodo.com
    /the-house-that-spied-on-me–1822429852.
10  Hill, "The house that spied on me."
11  Shoshana Zuboff, *The Age of Surveillance Capitalism* (New York: Public Affairs, 2019), 238–9.

the insurance industry. For, this pressure will not retreat any time soon. If anything, it promises to get worse. In that case, we may have to consider other, perhaps more significant, ways to remain free and independent through it all.

And we have not yet broached the topic of driverless cars, which remove the single greatest factor behind car accidents – the human driver – and replace him with an all-knowing computer. Thanks to their life-saving capabilities, there will be considerable pressure to adopt driverless cars, though many are wary of the technology at the moment. Financial incentives will also be strong. Driverless cars may provide considerable savings for consumers, for one thing due to averted accidents, but also because they will automatically avoid traffic jams and obey the speed limit, both of which spell fuel savings, and help the environment. They also promise to offer amazing conveniences, which, as usual, involve exposing our personal lives in expansive ways. These vehicles will know and record the details of any trip we take – or desire. Marketers are eager to descend upon driverless cars and transform advertising into so much more.

In the not too distant future, your car's computer may remind you to pick up your dry cleaning when you are near the business in question, or if you drive by a certain restaurant, your car may recommend it – knowing your tastes. Or when you pass the grocery store, it might tell you what special items are on sale – and not any old items, but brands and products you favor. Here's how this will work:

> [The car] knows your preferences because the vehicle has combed through your emails, identified key words, and assessed related messages for emotional tone. Similarly, the car knew which sale items to show you from the grocery store because it reviewed your past shopping activity. Plus there was that one time you told a friend who was sitting in the car with you how much you liked a particular beer you'd tried the night before. The car heard your conversation, picked up on brand keywords, and knew to suggest the same beer for your shopping list when it went on sale.[12]

You might say this sounds too fantastical. Even if this technology becomes a reality, will people tolerate cars listening in on their conversations? Will we put up with this level of "convenience"? How many will accept, or welcome, the services listed here – in exchange for your car spying on you? I suspect that many will be enamored by it all at first, and gladly trade privacy – at least as a kind of stunt, if you will, to see what the car can do,

---

[12]   Adrienne LaFrance, "Self-driving cars have a privacy problem," *The Atlantic*, March 21, 2016, www.theatlantic.com/technology/archive/2016/03/self-driving-cars-and-the-looming-privacy-apocalypse/474600/.

what it can get right. Suddenly, your car is a multifaceted resource, too; like your cellphone, it will provide information, and perhaps reviews of businesses and sites in your vicinity. The only difference is that, now, the car will bring you directly to them. Will these conveniences become second nature? Will they become habit – meaning that we will hardly think of the privacy lost in the exchange? Perhaps. There is little evidence to suggest we will resist the siren call of digital technology and enhanced convenience. We are already steadily immersed in the new world of digitized cars. Consider that in 2017, "more new cars [were] added to cellular networks than new cellphones."[13]

The companies developing driverless cars do not seem to put much stock in our privacy – though they solemnly say otherwise. The companies do not limit their designers in this regard, but instead empower them in the opposite direction, urging them to think of countless and newfound ways to monitor and track us so as to offer ever more wondrous services. If certain methods of surveillance annoy customers – or if the services rendered are annoying, or do not seem worth the bother – companies can always discontinue them. But it's better to know all the possibilities and powers up front. As one privacy advocate put it, "Sometimes it's just that the people who are designing the gizmo don't even think in terms of privacy . . . They just think: More data is always better. In their minds it's just 'We may not know what we're going to do with that data.'"[14]

I suppose we should be hardly surprised that businesses are also interested in monitoring employees in addition to customers. This trend has developed rather seamlessly from companies' desire to lower employee healthcare costs. Many have been doling out wearable fitness trackers to employees, which monitor physical activity, and hopefully encourage good eating, sleeping, and exercise habits. In so doing, companies negotiate "lower rates on collective insurance policies. Underwriters are more trusting of these devices than the self-reporting of employees."[15] This puts fitness trackers dispensed by employers in a rather insidious light. The devices are touted as means for workers to better monitor their physical activity, and with that knowledge, improve it – again, as if they were in a game or contest, challenging themselves to walk more, and compete with co-workers, family, or friends. In point of fact,

[13] Jonathan Gitlin, "Car companies are preparing to sell driver data to the highest bidder," *Ars Technica*, February 22, 2018, https://arstechnica.com/cars/2018/02/no-one-has-a-clue-whats-happening-with-their-connected-cars-data/.

[14] LaFrance, "Self-driving cars have a privacy problem."

[15] Olivia Solon, "Wearable technology creeps into the workplace," *Bloomberg*, August 1, 2015, www.bloomberg.com/news/articles/2015-08-07/wearable-technology-creeps-into-the-workplace.

insurance underwriters know that such encouragement and self-monitoring only goes so far. The real point is to spy on workers – because they cannot be counted on to volunteer sensitive information that employers want to know. And there is a coercive element, too. It is not enough to ask employees to become healthier, and allow them to volunteer health data. No, companies will give them foolproof devices that calculate how they exercise, and then collect that data. And perhaps, if employees do not change their behavior and become healthier, the data can be used against them.

Businesses are also happy to use surveillance to know how productive their employees are, and, more importantly, squeeze more work out of them. They can use sensors to track how long workers sit at their desks, and even take "screen grabs" of their computers, to make sure they stay on task.[16] Sensors can also "track [employee] movements and speech patterns," enabling executives to "look for trends and make adjustments aimed at boosting performance – perhaps by redesigning office spaces to encourage communication and collaboration."[17] This may be spun in a positive light: benevolent bosses will be able to tell when employees – by their speech patterns, for example – are bored or uninspired in the company of certain peers, and, by mixing and matching employee combinations, light the fire of innovation and creativity. Alternately, of course, bosses could know if you are slacking off; they might see what non-work-related websites you visit throughout the day, how often you take breaks, or just zone off, and punish accordingly. This corporate effort is dubbed "the quantified self at work," or the "quantified workplace."[18] And it starts to make the workplace sound increasingly uncomfortable, or downright oppressive.

Some companies, for example, are looking to microchip workers. Recently, a Swedish firm dabbled in this effort, inserting "near field communication chips" (NFC chips) in volunteers. The inserted microchip allows an employee to "swipe into his office, set the alarm system, register loyalty points at nearby retailers and access his gym ... [eliminating] the need for key-fobs or electronic entry cards" – and cash or credit cards, too, apparently.[19] This may sound extreme, and troubling: corporations will now lay claim to their work-ers' bodies from the inside. An executive from the company sought to

---

[16] Jane Wild, "Wearables in the workplace and the dangers of staff surveillance," *Financial Times*, February 28, 2017, www.ft.com/content/o89codoo-d739-11e6-944b-e7eb37a6aa8e.
[17] Wylie Wong, "Want to improve employee productivity? Wearables could be the answer," *Biztech*, February 10, 2017, https://biztechmagazine.com/article/2017/02/want-improve-employee-productivity-wearables-could-be-answer.
[18] Wong, "Want to improve employee productivity?"
[19] Solon, "Wearable technology creeps into the workplace."

downplay concerns, reminding us that we have been implanting things in our bodies for some time now – like pacemakers. "That's a way, way more serious thing than having a small chip that can actually communicate with devices," he insisted.[20] What if this chip is read by other devices such that it reveals intimate details about yourself? That looks like a future possibility, too. One microbiologist said that NFC chips could communicate health data, in addition to data about your specific whereabouts and movements.[21]

As we saw in the case of retail surveillance, it is difficult to imagine or predict what kind of data employers might like to know about their staff, and how they plan on using that information. Perhaps, as Target learned with pregnant customers, employers will discover that unexpected, random, or arcane features are especially revealing about worker productivity. Perhaps employers will discover unexpected buttons to press, to make their charges more efficient. Companies already display interest in data pertaining to non-work-related behavior, which indicates how productive you are, or will be. This includes your sleep patterns, which can be revealed by wearable technology.[22] An executive might look to see how well employees have slept on a given night, and then decide who is most rested and best able to deliver a crucial sales pitch. It is easy to imagine how this information could be used against employees – unfairly. Poor or fitful sleepers might face discrimination from employers looking for excuses to cull the staff. Employees could collect and show off their sleep data, among other things, as part of their "biometric curriculum vitae."[23] They could wield this CV when applying for new jobs, or lobbying for promotions, and demonstrate how they perform under stress, and remain productive and in good health. If anyone is worried about worker oppression, we might remind them that executives could also be compelled to compile a biometric CV. Presumably, shareholders would love to see how executives hold up under stress, or know about their poor health, bad sleeping habits, or wild lifestyle choices, which might impact stock performance.

One defender of workplace surveillance said, "it's in nobody's interest to have overworked, stressed and anxious employees who often aren't even aware of their own condition. Making things visible is a good thing if there is

---

[20]   "A Swedish start-up has started implanting microchips into its employees," *CNBC*, April 3, 2017, hwww.cnbc.com/2017/04/03/start-up-epicenter-implants-employees-with-microchips.html.
[21]   "A Swedish start-up has started implanting microchips into its employees."
[22]   Patience Haggin, "How should companies handle data from employees' wearable devices?" *Wall Street Journal*, May 22, 2016, www.wsj.com/articles/how-should-companies-handle-data-from-employees-wearable-devices–1463968803.
[23]   Haggin, "How should companies handle data from employees' wearable devices?"

a culture of trust and accountability."[24] But what if all this constant and pervasive surveillance undermines a culture of trust? What if the surveillance sends a message of profound suspicion – a message to employees that they are not trusted to do the right thing, but sometimes behave in ways that undermine their performance in the workplace, and prove a corporate liability in their personal lives? This mistrust may sour the relationship between employer and employee, and transform workplace monitoring from assistance to coercion.

But there is no turning back. Due to a variety of factors, workplace surveillance is here to stay, and is bound to become more expansive and intrusive. As one technology researcher puts it,

> Sport science has evolved remarkably in the last 10 years and we can expect the same from management science. Is it reasonable for a team to expect a football player to wear a sensor in his shirt to monitor granular movement and injury susceptibility – things that video, psychologists and pitchside observers just don't pick up? Nowadays you can't compete at top-level sport without this kind of wearable insight and analytics. In the near future, we'll see the same kind of thing in all fields of endeavor. In most fields, it may be a similar question, not so much of whether you should be able to require wearables as whether you can compete without them.[25]

This is an odd, if illuminating, analogy. It is strange, and even a bit outrageous, to suggest that employees be treated like professional athletes. The latter can and will submit to extreme monitoring because they are expensive investments, and clubs have a right to know that their investments are in good shape. When a top athlete signs on with a club for an exorbitant amount, the club has good justification to investigate his physical condition, and insist that he curtail his behavior lest he injure himself. But average employees in an average firm? Are they to be held to the same standards of rigor and performance? Do we really need to make sure that they, too, are performing at top levels like professional athletes? Must we ensure that every employee contributes to the team in top form? Slackers beware? Apparently, companies think this way, likely because competition is so fierce, or is perceived to be, and they will do whatever they can to expand or dominate market share. This includes hiring employees who, like athletes, are "most fit" – or companies will help them get into great shape – or pressure them to operate at the top level, through non-stop monitoring and measuring.

[24] Haggin, "How should companies handle data from employees' wearable devices?"
[25] Haggin, "How should companies handle data from employees' wearable devices?"

As this researcher indicates, sport science is at the forefront of wearable technology, developing "smart clothing" that may have broad applications in society. Some researchers, for example, are developing leggings that "measure muscle fatigue in runners" and could help athletes determine appropriate exercise regimens, and avoid injury.[26] Others are working on a "smart sports bra" that monitors body temperature, and opens vents if you are too hot.[27] Conceivably, these features will likely have appeal beyond the realm of sports. The relevant technology is in early developmental phases, and is still too cumbersome and expensive. But again, "wearables have Moore's law on their side," which means they will get sleeker, lighter, cheaper – and pervasive.[28]

That researchers are excited about the application of wearable technology in sports performance points to another vast frontier: healthcare. With this, we turn to what is perhaps the most certain and forceful pressure for intimate and ongoing surveillance – willingly entered into by us all.

"Until recently, continuous monitoring of physiological parameters was possible only in the hospital setting," a group of medical researchers wrote in 2012. "But today, with developments in the field of wearable technology, the possibility of accurate, continuous, real-time monitoring of physiological signals is a reality."[29] Continuous monitoring, I wager, is something that many people will welcome, in the interest of averting sudden health crises, or improving their well-being long term, and reducing health-related costs. These researchers detail how electrodes woven into the fabric of clothing, for example, will collect "electrocardiographic and electromyographic data" that can help diagnose and treat a host of "neurological, cardiovascular and pulmonary diseases such as seizures, hypertension, disrhythmias and asthma."[30] They offer an image of a particularly unflattering garment, covering one's entire torso, with all manner of electrodes and sensors embedded in it. If this is too unwieldy or unsightly, more elegant innovations await. Such as a ring sensor, which is "completely self-contained" – meaning it has no wires extending into or out of it – and whose applications range from the "diagnosis of

[26] Virgina Postrel, "Why nobody's wearing wearables," *Bloomberg View*, March 3, 2016, www .bloomberg.com/view/articles/2016-03-03/why-nobody-s-wearing-wearables.
[27] Postrel, "Why nobody's wearing wearables."
[28] Postrel, "Why nobody's wearing wearables."
[29] Paolo Bonato, Leighton Chan, Hyung Park, Shyamal Patel, and Mary Rodgers, "A review of wearable sensors and systems with application in rehabilitation," *Journal of Neuroengineering and Rehabilitation* 9/21 (2012), https://jneuroengrehab.biomedcentral.com/articles/10.1186 /1743-0003-9-21.
[30] Bonato et al., "Review of wearable sensors."

hypertension to the management of congestive heart failure."[31] Or
a miniature microphone that, when placed on your neck, can record
breathing irregularities.[32] No doubt this sensor can be made to look like
a necklace, or discreetly fitted into fashionable jewelry.

These innovations are anticipated thanks to specific medical challenges we
face now and in the future. As more people live longer, they will be liable to
more health crises, many of which are treatable but expensive when they pile
up or fester. And we are entering an era in the United States where the baby
boomers are growing old, and this population bulge will tax the healthcare
system.[33] What's more, thanks to Obamacare, we have extended health insurance to tens of millions of new patients, and must figure out a way to provide
their care affordably and effectively. Medical surveillance, many think, will be
key to this and a host of related questions: "How do we care for an increasing
number of individuals with complex medical conditions? How do we provide
quality care to those in areas with reduced access to providers? How do we
maximize the independence and participation of an increasing number of
individuals with disabilities?"[34]

Lowering healthcare costs has been a major policy concern in the United
States for many years – decades, really. When President Obama finally
enacted major reforms to the healthcare system in 2010, he had two principal
aims: provide insurance to tens of millions of Americans who had none; and
lower healthcare costs, which, it turns out, were a major force driving people to
declare personal bankruptcy – and threatening to bankrupt the federal government, already on the hook for healthcare costs of millions of people thanks to
Medicare, Medicaid, and the Veterans Health Administration. The only
problem was, due to pressure from the pharmaceutical industry and the
doctors' lobby, among others, President Obama's resulting reform bill did
not include significant measures to lower healthcare costs, effectively giving
lie to the bill's official name, the "Affordable Care Act." For cost savings,
healthcare reform basically had to rely on the dubious prospect of Americans
becoming healthier, and thus cheaper, patients. If more people had health
insurance, the thinking went, they would be more inclined to visit a doctor
and get their health in order. Of itself, this would be no small victory, since
much of the rise in healthcare spending is due to certain epidemics related to
our high-fat diet, and sedentary, workaholic, car-dependent lifestyle: diabetes,

[31]  Bonato et al., "Review of wearable sensors."
[32]  Bonato et al., "Review of wearable sensors."
[33]  Bonato et al., "Review of wearable sensors."
[34]  Bonato et al., "Review of wearable sensors."

hypertension, heart disease, and obesity. If Americans could become more active, and incentivized to live more healthily, and subjected to monitoring for expensive conditions that could be nipped in the bud, considerable savings would follow.

Among our national epidemics, diabetes is the most expensive, but "constant adjustments to diet and lifestyle can reverse" the disease.[35] Diabetes is never treated this way because people typically don't live in a way that allows for constant adjustments. They have to rely on their own attention in adjusting diet and activity, but doctors know this is far from ideal. Patients might not know exactly what to look for, and when, and they don't know precisely how to adjust their intake; they need to be prompted, and advised – constantly. What's more, people are often too busy to pay attention to minute but consequential health indicators, or they are just negligent. Accordingly, diabetics would do best with a "live-in doctor," and the company Virta Health has come up with the next best thing, outfitting patients with a fitness tracker that monitors salient health data, submits it for analysis by artificial intelligence software, and relays doctor recommendations. With ongoing streams of data, and constant communication with patients, doctors can tweak diets and medications continuously. The technology also enables doctors to treat many more patients at once. Virta's program has proven stunningly effective: 87 percent of patients who relied on insulin to control their diabetes either decreased their dose of the medication, or dispensed with it altogether.[36] That is a tantalizing discovery. The vast majority of diabetics could get their expensive and debilitating disease under control through continuous communication with doctors, who virtually watch their every movement and intake. When healthcare is no longer a luxury or consumer good, but a universal right – which has been the cultural transition wrought by Obamacare, whether Republicans like it or not – and we are charged with extending effective healthcare to everyone without breaking the bank, innovations such as Virta's will be in high demand. And they will become the norm.

Virta's innovation, and others like it, is doubly appealing because it offers the prospect of treating diseases along the way, or in their early stages, before they get too expensive and become even more painful. Diabetes may culminate in kidney failure, for example. The ensuing dialysis is a costly and onerous treatment, which requires significant effort from patients, and poses

---

[35] Kevin Maney, "How artificial intelligence will cure America's sick health care system," *Newsweek*, May 24, 2017, www.newsweek.com/2017/06/02/ai-cure-america-sick-health-care-system-614583.html.

[36] Maney, "How artificial intelligence will cure America's sick health care system."

challenges to the poor if they lack a car, and have difficulty traveling to a clinic. It is far better if we can catch diseases along the way – and this appears to be a central ambition of medical surveillance. IBM's supercomputer Watson can play an important role here. Watson promises to be the "best diagnostician on the planet," since it can process reams of patient data, thousands of research papers from over the years, as well as cutting-edge discoveries and medical dispatches from around the world – in record time.[37] In order to work its magic and deliver the most precise diagnoses, Watson only needs to know everything about you. Some hope that if we allow Watson to simply analyze our genetic data, and process that alongside all other information at its disposal, it can provide a preliminary diagnosis of incipient or impending afflictions. This would be no small feat – it would effectively "supplant that first visit to a doctor when you're sick – which, of course, is when you least want to travel to a doctor's office."[38] Healthcare becomes costly when people put off going to the doctor, and allow ailments to worsen. Watson can provide the first step in anticipating or recognizing said ailments, prompting necessary lifestyle changes or treatment – early on, when treatment is easier, cheaper and more effective. How can we resist?

In a report on the "quantified-self movement," the Center for Digital Democracy (CDD) describes how researchers are developing all manner of biosensors that will monitor not only our vital signs – from the inside – but also "brain activity, moods and emotion."[39] A major breakthrough that has driven the quantified-self movement, and expanded new frontiers of data collection, is the fact that storing the vast amounts of information produced in the digital age has gotten steadily easier and cheaper – as have the means of processing it and translating it. Thus, our many potential or eventual spies are inclined to extract ever more information, with greater hope or expectation that they will make sense of it – if not now, then someday. Researchers are developing a pill with biosensors that, when swallowed, will relay data about the state of your digestive tract; they are working on another pill that will communicate your blood alcohol level, and potentially turn off your car before you drive over the legal limit.[40] Google, for its part, is developing a "digital contact lens" that will measure "blood glucose levels" from your tears.[41]

---

[37]  Maney, "How artificial intelligence will cure America's sick health care system."
[38]  Maney, "How artificial intelligence will cure America's sick health care system."
[39]  Kathryn Montgomery, Jeff Chester, and Katharina Kopp, "Health wearable devices in the big data era: Ensuring privacy, security and consumer protection," *Center for Digital Democracy*, December 15, 2016, www.democraticmedia.org/sites/default/files/field/public/2016/aucdd_wearablesreport_final121516.pdf.
[40]  Montgomery et al., "Health wearable devices in the big data era."
[41]  Montgomery et al., "Health wearable devices in the big data era."

Nanotechnology promises amazing potential in the realm of diagnosis. Currently, researchers are working on nanosensors, one billionth of a meter in size, which could measure the "build-up of bacteria on implants," like hip replacements or pacemakers, and communicate whether an infection is brewing, and antibiotics are necessary.[42] Typically, by the time an infection in an implant reveals itself, the condition is very serious, perhaps life threatening, and requires serious or invasive treatment. In the case of pacemaker infections, especially in older people, patients are often too weak to undergo surgery. Lives would be saved, quality of life preserved, and costs managed if we could detect and treat these bacterial infections early on.

There are many medical conditions whose symptoms are evident only when it is too late for effective treatment – like pancreatic cancer, which is notoriously difficult to diagnose. When symptoms of pancreatic cancer emerge and the disease is noticeable, it is typically too late to do anything, and patients are already close to death. If researchers were able to develop nanotechnology that could alert us to the first signs of pancreatic cancer, that would be a welcome find. I would likely take advantage of this technology, having seen close family members and friends suffer this awful disease, which often strikes in the prime of life. When I think of my own children, and the importance of being around for them – and the lengths I would go to make sure of it – I know other parents feel the same. Dying when your children are young, this is every parent's nightmare. Many would sign up for constant, internal surveillance if it promised to alert them to the first signs of cancer, or any fatal disease or crippling condition, when it could be averted or caught early on.

Because people are especially attentive or anxious when it comes to their health, marketers find medical surveillance a natural target for their outreach. We may be subjected to specialized advertisements, for example, when we consult our wearable devices to gauge nutritional and fitness goals, and communicate with peers.[43] The company FitAd specializes in such ads for fitness-minded people, issued at what it calls special "Moments" when they deem it best to market in a native format: "Moments mark the start, completion or achievement of an important milestone within a fitness and health app or website. At these Moments, it is appropriate to match advertising to the Moment so that brands can acknowledge, recognize, reward or challenge users."[44] The native format of this kind of advertising refers, at least in part,

---

[42]  James McIntosh, "Nanosensors: The future of diagnostic medicine?" *Medical News Today*, January 14, 2016, www.medicalnewstoday.com/articles/299663.php.
[43]  Montgomery et al., "Health wearable devices in the big data era."
[44]  Montgomery et al., "Health wearable devices in the big data era."

to the way it is insinuated or interwoven into gamified surveillance: Gatorade will cheer you on, for example, and issue you special promotions if you reach fitness goals. But it is not hard to imagine that marketers might also take advantage of an individual's vulnerabilities in these Moments. If they determine that you are exercising to lose weight, marketers might send you "native ads" that prey on your insecurities.

Generally speaking, is it beyond the realm of imagination that marketers might determine you have cancer, and tout products of interest to you, in your state? Multi-vitamins, high-energy foods, spa treatments, wigs, or headscarves – insurance or investment products? Cancer patients are especially vulnerable – that is to say, their condition makes them highly vulnerable in certain respects, and perhaps easily taken advantage of or manipulated by marketers. Will marketers, together with behavioral scientists, discover that cancer patients are especially fertile customers and, if they survive, potentially faithful clients for years to come? As Target learned about pregnancy, cancer is also a life-changing event that radically restructures people's lives, habits, and priorities, potentially making them fair game for new retail loyalties.

Closing the circle on retail and medical innovation, your smartphone or smartwatch could soon access your medical records and fitness data, and then communicate with sensors in the grocery store "to provide real time shopping and health advice."[45] I suspect it might be hard to ignore this advice – or at least, harder to ignore than advice pertaining to style or taste preferences – especially if your medical records divulge a serious illness. People go to great lengths to preserve and promote their health, stay fit, and lose weight. Retailers know this. Which is why, for them, the lure of medical surveillance will be strong. And for us, who will be monitored and watched, the surveillance promises to be intense indeed, providing us with near constant reminders how to improve ourselves and our lives – will we stand the intensity? Will you, for example, put up with the "smart shoes and biometric shorts" under development, which will "remind you to straighten your posture, hydrate and run and walk with correct form"?[46] I am unsure. On one hand, I could see that people might be annoyed by perpetual correction. On the other hand, if it is provided in the right way – slightly, implicitly, not overtly – and people hardly notice that they are being corrected, but reap the rewards, then it might work marvelously.

Privacy is in great danger. A variety of economic, social, and cultural pressures are conspiring to do it in – with our willing support. I suspect

---

45  Montgomery et al., "Health wearable devices in the big data era."
46  Montgomery et al., "Health wearable devices in the big data era."

that medical pressures will be preeminent. Increasingly, ours is a society that expects universally accessible and affordable healthcare. In this respect, the United States is joining the ranks of other industrial democracies, and approaching socialized medicine, which satisfies human rights concerns, and, it turns out, is very economical. Any nation that looks to provide medical treatment for all its citizens must work hard to get costs under control – perhaps dramatically. Medical surveillance promises to be an attractive tool in this effort. In the United States, in fact, the imperative is greater: we suffer the highest healthcare costs in the developed world – it's not even close. If we would pull off similar reforms here, where everyone can access a basic degree of effective healthcare, we must work very hard to lower such costs. Granted, our problem is exacerbated by gross inefficiencies; but even if the latter are solved and ironed out, the pressure to deploy medical surveillance will still be strong. As mentioned, it could be all too useful in tackling the deleterious lifestyle trends responsible for common epidemics, and also rooting out isolated afflictions. When it comes to medical surveillance, there is no turning back: we will surrender, or submit. And the kind of surveillance medical innovation promises will be expansive indeed – it is of a special character, in comparison to other forms of surveillance discussed earlier. Medical surveillance will be most effective when the spying eyes are embedded deep within our bodies, monitoring and reporting our every breath, our every move, our every bite.

Some who read over the accounts and predictions in this chapter may find them objectionable. And I tend to agree – for now. I may well find them all too comfortable in a couple of years, and give them nary a thought. That said, the future of surveillance bears ominous trends, and ominous threats. Medical surveillance may make us especially vulnerable to outside manipulation – it will offer personal information and insight that our spies never dreamed of. But I fear there is no turning back. We are running headlong into this brave new world; the various forces or pressures compelling this evolution are hard to overcome or resist. Indeed, we, the watched, are helping drive this evolution. It is implausible to remind people of the virtues of privacy, and then convince them to – what exactly, leave the digital world? That is largely unacceptable. Or is the solution to become more guarded and wary in one's digital dealings? Evidence suggests that is an unlikely proposition. In any case, and as mentioned, our spies need only few data points to pinpoint our identity. Which is to say, our spies may not need sophisticated technology to watch us and know us – intimately. What's more, individual citizens and consumers seem especially ill equipped to muster much of a defense against the forces of surveillance – both those that are sophisticated, and those that are not. We don't even know what our watchers look for, in many cases.

We are facing a situation where surveillance is unavoidable, and the proper response will not be on the micro level, but the macro level. Which is to say, we ought not focus on individuals facing the dangers and seduction of surveillance; we ought not focus on advising them to rebuff, resist, or elude surveillance, or loosen their devotion to digital technology – by, among other things, reminding them of the forgotten virtues of privacy. Rather, we must work to empower people politically in the face of their many spies. We must make it so that the inevitable surveillance is less destructive or damaging politically. We must ensure that it won't diminish us or compromise us as democratic citizens – and human beings. That is the challenge.

# 5

## Privacy Past and Present

Before anyone despairs over the demise of privacy, it is helpful to consider the history of this institution, and how it developed into its modern incarnation. In one respect, privacy is a very young value, and humans have long lived – and communities flourished – without it. Privacy has always been embattled. That is nothing new – you might even say that is its native state. When people managed to achieve some degree or form of privacy in the past, it was in much lesser quantities, and far more selectively and rarely enjoyed than advocates and critics say we need and deserve. The amount of privacy we have come to expect or take for granted in contemporary suburban living, by contrast, is almost absurdly generous. It is hard to imagine or conceive of an architecture and landscape that prioritizes privacy better. But appearances are deceiving: on one hand, and as I have been arguing thus far, our lives have never been more transparent within our suburban bubbles. Do we care? Better yet: what does this indicate we value in or about privacy? Does it suggest we esteem privacy at all – or something else altogether?

At the same time, privacy is also much older than many scholars and even its own advocates admit. Or rather, I should say, privacy of some form is quite ancient, and its roots stretch back far indeed. Something akin to privacy, or evocative of it, is depicted and elevated in the teachings of the Stoics, and the Gospel. This offers two compelling suggestions: many argue that privacy is inherent and essential to democracy; but this may not be the case, since privacy of a kind is visible far earlier than the full emergence and maturation of democracy in the nineteenth and twentieth centuries. At the very least, we must reconsider and evaluate the relationship between privacy and democracy, and what each gains from or contributes to the other. What's more, the Stoics and early Christian writings, insofar as they eulogize something like privacy – but without our legal and physical architecture of privacy – suggest that we may not require that legal or physical architecture at all. Which is to say: the virtues of privacy can be achieved by other means – perhaps the autonomy and authenticity and free thinking that theorists say privacy delivers, and which make the institution essential, need not be gained by privacy at all.

In *Olmstead* v. *United States*, which concerned law enforcement's right to gather evidence from private phone calls via wiretapping, Louis Brandeis declared that the nation's founders "conferred, as against the Government, the right to be let alone – the most comprehensive of rights and the right most valued by civilized men."[1] Justice Douglas echoed Brandeis' assertion in a later court opinion, stating that marriage included and presumed a preexisting right to privacy, a right that is "older than the Bill of Rights, older than our political parties, older than our school system."[2]

A central debate surrounding privacy is whether it is a universal aspiration, and an enduring, consistent value or institution. Some, like Brandeis and Douglas apparently, deem privacy an eternal good. It is a goal that all civilized men yearn for intuitively or overtly, and there are certain experiences and arrangements in our lives that naturally demand it. Like marriage, Douglas would say. This is a common view today, that marriage requires privacy. But why? In one respect, it's because we also presume that marriage requires autonomy. We tend to think that a healthy, solid, nurturing marriage requires partners who are together of their own free will and decision, fully cognizant of what they enter into. And they need privacy to make up their minds – they must be protected from outside influences or pressures. The choice must be theirs alone. Spouses also require privacy in order to be intimate, to bare themselves to one another honestly and safely, and develop a lasting bond that may withstand the challenges of a long-term relationship. But these assumptions are all quite recent – that I will only marry whom I love, and that it must be a personal, lucid, independent decision. For the vast majority of our history, people did not marry for love – and marriage did not involve, much less require, privacy. Marriage was decided by one's family, or the community at large. It is amazing how quickly and thoroughly this has been forgotten, though it was predominant only a few generations ago. Until recently, the key deciding factor in choosing a spouse was if your family deemed him or her a good match, for social or economic reasons. Love might develop later, but it was not a deciding factor at the start – nor was it necessarily the product of privacy, which was in short supply. Very often, after all, your larger family lived on top of you, and in close quarters.

---

[1]  *Olmstead* v. *United States*, 277 US 438 (1928).
[2]  *Griswold* v. *Connecticut*, 381 US 479 (1965).

The latter is such an outrageous proposition to us today that we have a sitcom spoofing the forsaken private lives of a married couple – *Everybody Loves Raymond*. Ray's parents live next door, his brother nearby, and they are always barging in, weighing in, leaving the couple little peace. This is an absurd arrangement for most Americans; or rather, it is far from the ideal, or what we are taught to expect. This set up is of course hardly new, nor is it out of the ordinary for many societies today – even many families in the United States. In any case, the prevalent model for twenty-first-century American family life involves strict segregation: grandparents do not reside with you, but in a retirement home; children stay at home until they are 18, then move away to college – if they can't afford their post-collegiate abode, many parents help them do so (even in a very expensive city perhaps); cousins, aunts, and uncles, well, they generally stay away until the holidays. American families are highly mobile, furthermore: a quarter of all adults move every five years.[3] Independence is prized – the independence of families, left to themselves, enjoying their own company – and independence *within* families.

Perhaps Douglas would have been on surer footing had he said that love, not marriage, requires privacy. Marriage as an institution has not always, or often, needed privacy because, as mentioned, it did not involve love – it was more of a contractual relationship. But things are different for love, no? Lovers would seem to need privacy, or at least, they will always want it. And yet, love has existed, and even flourished, in societies with little privacy.[4] What does this mean for privacy? That lovers may desire it, but not in fact need much for their relationship to bloom – or thrive? On one hand, consider how the notion of "forbidden pleasure" – often supplied by lack of privacy and "alone time" – sparks infatuation and invigorates a romance. On the other hand, I am the first to admit how my wife and I cherish moments of privacy, and need them to sustain and nourish our partnership. With our four kids, my wife and I find alone time in a few brief arrangements and activities – like taking a walk, going out to dinner, watching TV. Perhaps the privacy that lovers require can be attained periodically or only briefly, and in a variety of ways that might otherwise seem mundane or insignificant – like when my wife and I bond during a late-night trip to the grocery store.

Privacy may be understood and achieved differently, by lovers past and present. It is easy for us to look at historical romances, or marriages, and

---

[3]  Adam Chandler, "Why do Americans move so much more than Europeans?", *The Atlantic*, October 21, 2016, www.theatlantic.com/business/archive/2016/10/us-geographic-mobility/5049 68/.

[4]  Richard Posner, "The Right of Privacy," *Georgia Law Review*, 12/3 (1978), 408.

wonder if they enjoyed any privacy at all. It certainly seems they enjoyed less than couples demand and take for granted today. But they may also have enjoyed a different – lesser? – form of privacy than we have come to know. As suggested above, lovers may find privacy in unexpected ways, in unexpected moments, and unexpected mediums. They may not require a bedroom suite with lock and key to discover privacy. They may be able to silently commune, if briefly, gazing into one another's eyes, exchanging a secret message only they know – in a language only they know. This is the product of love, after all: lovers know how to read one another immediately and implicitly, on the basis of subtle gestures, flinches, postures, movements – tremors, pursed lips, knitted brows, smirks, and the like. The overarching point is this: it is wrong to believe that privacy was always esteemed, much less understood and expected, in the same form and fashion. Rather, the privacy that advocates such as Justice Douglas extol is the result of a specific evolution, and humans have lived and thrived without it.

As mentioned in Chapter 1, the American notion of privacy owes much to English legal and cultural traditions. And in the English experience, "the private realm . . . which became a defining feature of liberal democracy, can only distantly be glimpsed in the conflicts between households and authorities" in the fourteenth century.[5] In particular, claims to privacy emerged in and from disputes over property, its protections, and the desire to enjoy it free from physical intrusion or wandering eyes. In medieval London, however, "privacy was a scarce and contested commodity. It was not a possession or a secure right, but . . . an aspiration."[6] The average home had few rooms – if any – and none that were devoted to a single purpose. Indeed, the pre-modern home was hardly a refuge in itself, and, since it commonly harbored a workplace as well, was largely an extension of the public realm. Over the next few centuries, homes came to include several rooms (or at least a few), rooms that offered some seclusion, and which were specialized – for sleeping, eating, bathing, or entertaining. At first, however, the seclusion realized in specialized rooms was the privilege of the rich. As with all things enjoyed by the rich, such an arrangement was coveted, and ultimately demanded by everyone else.

The ascendancy of privacy roughly follows greater social prosperity. When people had more money – or when society supplied funding – they could build the infrastructure that we deem essential to privacy. Ultimately, this will feature the single-family home, which, in the American model, stands alone

---

[5]  David Vincent, *Privacy: A Short History* (Cambridge, UK: Polity Press, 2016), 3.
[6]  Vincent, 5.

on an expansive lawn, fenced off from neighbors. In addition to growing prosperity, historians have identified other important drivers behind the rise of privacy. For one thing, the state increased its power to encompass tasks and services previously carried out by private agents, or local communities. In France, this process was accelerated under the reign of Louis XIV, who sought to replace clientelistic networks with an administrative state. By the end of the seventeenth century, "the public realm is now quite 'deprivatized' ... it became possible to create a closed private preserve, or at any rate, a private realm totally divorced from the public sphere and completely autonomous."[7] Though paradoxical, perhaps it should come as little surprise that the private realm is the fruit of strong central government, which takes over tasks that might otherwise or previously fall to private agents. This gives people more time and space to enjoy private pursuits and personal interests, to some extent at least. A strong government is also necessary to help protect and preserve people's private sphere.

According to our founding fathers, and echoed by many political theorists, the government is a principal threat to privacy. However, it certainly makes sense that weak – or absent – government makes privacy untenable; how can you hope to enjoy your private realm amidst anarchic chaos? A competent government, which assumes and addresses public services, is an essential help for anyone who hopes to carve out and enjoy a private space. In any case, if privacy requires strong government – and I am persuaded it does – then it follows that the private realm will always be threatened by the very thing that sustains it. And indeed, the early modern state sought to intrude on the individual space of citizens, or aimed to exert control even there, insofar as it "instituted a new way of being in society, characterized by strict control of the instincts, firmer mastery of the emotions, and a heightened sense of modesty."[8] Paradoxically, this "new way of being" that the state commanded likewise required privacy of a kind, in order to nurture and preserve personal virtue. The early modern moral code clearly draws on Ancient Stoicism, which saw a notable resurgence in this time period.

Stoic philosophy, as articulated by Seneca, Marcus Aurelius, and Cicero, praises the virtue of emotional resilience and equilibrium. The Stoics called it "constancy," where one is not overly excited or deflated by external events, the opinions of others, or personal interactions. When you properly understand the

---

[7] Philippe Ariès, "Introduction," in *A History of Private Life, Volume III*, trans. Arthur Goldhammer (Cambridge, MA: Harvard University Press, 1989), 10.

[8] Roger Chartier, "Figures of Modernity," in *A History of Private Life, Volume III*, trans. Arthur Goldhammer (Cambridge, MA: Harvard University Press, 1989), 16.

nature of things, including your own nature – and limitations – you will not
find anything surprising or tragic that fate sends your way; and you will be
morally steeled to perform your duties. This mindset demands a good deal of
introspection, and is practiced effectively, though not literally, alone. The Stoic
emperor Marcus Aurelius, for example, spoke warily of the corrupting influence of the masses, and sought to insulate himself from them – mentally.
Physically, he could not do so, of course, because he had a job to do. As
emperor, he had to mix with people of all kinds of moral states – some quite
sinister and corrupt indeed. He was especially dismayed when he had to
preside over the gladiatorial games, with their howling, bloodthirsty crowds.
And yet, Marcus aimed to make of his mind a "citadel," where he could
develop and entertain rational thoughts, alien and resistant to the impassioned
masses – rational thoughts that might transform his emotional state, and help
him greet the pressures of his job and the general absurdity of life with
equanimity.

Upon reflection, Stoicism likely played a crucial role in the evolution of
privacy. This school of philosophy gained many adherents in early modern
Europe, ravaged by the wars of religion following the Protestant Reformation,
for it claimed to help people find emotional refuge amidst chaos and turmoil.
And thanks to its resurgence, Stoicism influenced the most important philosophers of this time period – Spinoza, Leibniz, Descartes, Machiavelli,
Montaigne – thinkers who would be responsible for crafting the modern
subject, the free-thinking, self-ruling agent who would drive scientific inquiry
and democratic politics. And yet, Stoicism has always been misunderstood in
significant ways, by admirers and critics alike. For example, its social aspect is
often ignored or downplayed, and Stoicism is instead deemed a highly or even
exclusively individualistic form of morality, which recommends retreating
within oneself, and casting scorn on the outside world, or at least, the things
that men commonly value.

It is true that Stoicism focuses on the individual subject as the source of
moral reform – through psychotherapy, transforming irrational emotions (or
passions) into their rational counterparts – but such reform is not performed in
isolation, nor does it demand retreat. Indeed, as the Stoics conceive it, how
you interact with your surroundings is instrumental to how you transform your
mind and behavior. Duty is essential to achieving Stoic detachment.

Seneca offers perhaps the most persuasive account of duty in his essay "On
the Tranquillity of the Mind," where he advises one Serenus, who suffers from
restlessness and boredom, and looks for fulfillment in all kinds of activities – none
of which he performs adequately or completely, and is thus perennially

discouraged and dissatisfied. Seneca recommends that Serenus throw himself into his duties, both those of a citizen, and those of his professional post. Instead of pursuing, or discovering, what it is he wants to do, and what offers him fulfillment, Serenus ought to assume his obligations, as he recognizes them. How shall he know what those duties are? His place in society and history are an indication, Seneca maintains; also his nature – his specific character, talents, and limitations; and what society needs. In sum: your duties are the things you are best equipped or outfitted by nature to do, which present themselves to you, and which society requires of you at that particular time. Duties may vary according to your station, or if your nature is compromised, but the fact that you have duties never changes: "if Fortune … cuts off any opportunity for action … let him find some employment where he may be of service to the state. Service in the army is denied him: let him seek public office. He must live in private capacity: let him plead cases. He is condemned to observe silence: let him aid his fellow citizens by his unvoiced support."[9]

Seneca likens duty to playing a part or role that has been assigned you – not of your choosing. It is something you must take on and assume. This is meant to be therapeutic: it creates a needed distance between you and your job – any job (including parenting) – and the fruits of your labor. Too often, people fail at a job – or obligation – because they are too personally invested in it, and too anxious as a result. Or they are overly disgusted when they fail, or do not perceive the fruits of their labor, and throw up their hands in despair. The Stoics aim to make us reliably diligent, no matter what work faces us. Do your job, whatever job presents itself to you at the time, and do it thoroughly and consistently. Do not shrink from your obligation; always look to help, in whatever way you can. And though you merely play a role or part in some larger drama – not of your design – play it seriously. Seneca lauds the disposition of Canus who was falsely accused and condemned to death. At the time of his execution, Canus "was playing draughts when the centurion … gave the order for him as well to be summoned. When he was called he counted the pieces and said to his companion, 'Mind you don't pretend you won after I'm dead'; then with a nod to the centurion he added, 'You will testify that I was one piece ahead.' Do you suppose that Canus played a game at that board?"[10] Canus seems terribly serious, if a bit joyless – and in the next breath, Seneca says the person who laughs at the absurdity of the human condition is more valuable than he who laments it – but the point is clear: we may be

<hr />

[9] Seneca, "On the Tranquillity of the Mind," in *Dialogues and Essays*, trans. John Davie (New York: Oxford University Press, 2007), 120.
[10] Seneca, 134.

playing a game, but our respective roles are duties. Play them seriously; don't take them lightly. See them through.

Early modern thinkers seized upon the individualism inherent in Stoicism, and ignored the social aspect implicit in duty. Machiavelli was enamored by what Stoic virtue could do for soldiers, making them dispassionate, resilient, and resistant to pain or tragedy (a famous Stoic saying is "the wise man is happy even on the rack"); they could be fearsome individuals on the battlefield. Montaigne engages in Stoic contemplation and therapy alone in his tower, demonstrating how it can steel an individual for the pain, suffering, and loss that fate throws at him. And Justus Lipsius, one of the most popular moralists of the sixteenth century, admires how Stoicism can make a person safe and content, like a ship moored in a harbor during a storm. When you realize that Lipsius is talking about insulating the individual from the anxiety and fear of social strife – which he witnessed aplenty during the wars of religion – an unflattering and oft criticized image of Stoicism emerges: the individual turned inward, detached from social concerns. This is precisely *not* what the Stoics intended. But they walk a fine line, at least from our vantage point. For, they aimed to deliver "apatheia," which is a pejorative term today; we consider an apathetic person one who is absent feelings and emotion – cold and indifferent, in the worst sense of the word. For the Stoics, however, it simply meant to be "without passions" – irrational emotions like fear, anger, and desire, which wreak havoc on an individual, and on social relations. Instead, you ought to be filled with rational emotions – you ought to be happy or cautious or hopeful, and for the right reasons, with a right understanding of self and world. The Stoics invoke a kind of autonomy, and bemoan heteronomy: when reason is ascendant, I am no longer batted about by outside pressures and events, rising and falling at their mercy; rather, I am in control of how I feel and react – because I understand, and diligently perform my duties.

Stoicism is of special interest to us because, for one thing, it is apparent how the resurgent popularity of this philosophy, and the elements that modern philosophers focused on, helped shape the value of privacy as we have come to know it. According to its advocates, privacy is that space where I can be alone, uncorrupted and untouched by outside influences; and in my isolation, I may have or develop or discover the autonomy to shape my opinions and outlook, my emotional state and personality, and fate. Privacy invokes the Stoic vigilance against heteronomy, which involves no small degree of introspection. On the other hand – and this is why the Stoics are additionally compelling – they never imagined that anyone would need or achieve privacy, understood as isolation or protected seclusion, to be autonomous. I can only hope to be autonomous in and through my interactions with other people – who are desirous, fearful, angry – besotted by passions. The task, and challenge, is to become autonomous in their midst, and constant company.

Another important force elevating privacy in the early modern period was the revolution in religious practice wrought by the Protestant Reformation, and its Catholic response. In the early modern period, one historian notes, "the most frequent use of the word private is to be found in the personal writing of godly men and women."[11] A cursory glance at the major claims and concerns of the Reformation and Counter-Reformation indicate the growing importance of privacy in the life of the believer. But a deeper look at Christian texts reveals that privacy – of a kind – was a central concern and recurring theme from early on.

Luther emancipates the individual believer from priestly mediation: one can commune directly with God, alone, or of his own efforts. What's more, Luther affirms the primacy of faith over works. While Catholicism maintains that individuals must perform sacraments and acts of charity to avail themselves of God's grace, and purify themselves spiritually, the equation is reverse for Luther: "It is always necessary that the substance or person himself be good before there can be any good works, and that good works follow and proceed from the good person."[12] A person must have faith – first. And faith is achieved through profound, sincere reflection and prayer, and honest assessment of one's sins. God "teaches us inwardly through the living instructions of his Spirit."[13] Faith is an individual affair, and challenge. The community of believers is secondary; one's personal relationship with God is preeminent. Faith "unites the soul with Christ as a bride is united with her bridegroom," Luther tells us.[14] And it requires protection from outside corruption and temptation. Faith entails cultivating the "inner man," in peace and purity. It is a retreat into a realm of prayerful silence, where you face God alone – and alone under His gaze, you present yourself genuinely, as you are, and discern his teachings purely and directly.

The Catholic Counter-Reformation also emphasized individual self-reflection and prayer, as exemplified by Ignatius of Loyola's *Spiritual Exercises*. As the title suggests, Ignatius details a program of contemplation where a person, ideally withdrawn "from daily life for four weeks of meditation … looks in gratitude for God's gifts in [his] life, and then, at [his] own sinfulness"; using his imagination – and five senses – he will reflect

[11]  Vincent, 13.
[12]  Martin Luther, *On Christian Liberty*, trans. W. A. Lambert (Minneapolis: Fortress Press, 2003), 39.
[13]  Luther, 24.
[14]  Luther, 18.

on the life, teachings, and passion of Christ, seeking to empathize with his suffering.[15] There is a strongly personal element in Ignatius' *Exercises*: the individual must plumb the depths of his soul, admit the many facets of his sinfulness, and learn to recognize signs of God's grace in his life. As with Luther, Ignatian prayer invokes a retreat into an inner space, where you can present yourself authentically – to yourself and God.

Historian David Vincent thinks that Post-Reformation writings on prayer "represented the true beginning of privacy as a withdrawal from the society of others for the purpose of managing a personal archive of emotion and knowledge."[16] And yet, to the extent that "managing this archive" sought to purify your intentions before God and make you face Him honestly, where God's imprint and your sins are clear to see, this was not a new effort. In fact, this notion is rooted in some of the most arresting and challenging teachings of the New Testament – teachings that assert what was new and distinctive in Jesus' reforms.

In Matthew's account of the Sermon on the Mount, Jesus says it is not enough to simply refrain from murder and adultery; you "commit murder in your heart" when you are angry with another person, and you "commit adultery in your heart" when you lust after another.[17] Thus, you must pay careful attention to your personal intentions, and correct them. The Pharisees – whom Jesus calls hypocrites – focus on outward signs of faith, but real goodness reigns and flows from within. Naturally, Jesus does not dismiss or diminish acts of charity; he puts special emphasis on embracing and assisting the poor and social outcasts. But, he says, "take heed that you do not do your charitable deeds before men, to be seen by them."[18] You will purify your intentions if you act for no one else's attention and approval. The hypocrites, meanwhile, make a big show of their charity and devoutness, and Jesus deems them insincere. They aim at personal glory – to be respected in the eyes of men. But Jesus has a notable prescription for prayer: "When you pray, you shall not be like the hypocrites. For they love to pray standing in the synagogues and on the corners of the street that they may be seen by men … But you, when you pray, go into your room, and when you have shut your door, pray to your Father who is in the secret place; and your Father who sees in secret will reward you openly."[19]

[15] James Martin, *The Jesuit Guide to (Almost) Everything* (New York: Harper Collins, 2012), 19–20.
[16] Vincent, 13.
[17] Mt 5:21–30.
[18] Mt 6:1.
[19] Mt 6:5–6.

Remarkably, Jesus seems to suggest that privacy of a kind is instrumental to living an honest, spiritual life. But it is hard to imagine that he had anything like our notion of privacy in mind; it hardly would have been possible in his time and place. Ancient Galilee, especially for its poorest inhabitants who were the focus of Jesus' ministry, lacked an architecture befitting or suitable for privacy as we know it. In any case, there is a prevailing, even dominant social context for Jesus' teachings. Put simply: if you must be alone to purify your intentions, you will not be for long. Jesus presumes individuals who purify themselves in and for social interaction – not individuals exempt from it. The enduring debate for Christian thinkers must be put thus: is this purification of intent an exclusively mental practice and achievement? In which case, one might indeed prefer seclusion or isolation – for prayer, for example? Or is purification to be achieved in and through acts and interaction? The French Catholic philosopher Blaise Pascal endorses the latter in his famous essay "The Wager," where he discusses the wisdom of betting on the existence of God. It is indeed wise to do so, Pascal argues, even for those who do not believe; they should presume God exists, and then act like it, performing sacraments, rituals, and prayer. In the process, he concludes, this may bring them to faith, and at the very least tame their passions – which are the major obstacle to faith. They will be purified, and prepared for grace, through acts.

In another evocative passage in the Sermon on the Mount, Jesus says, "[When] you fast, do not be like the hypocrites, with a sad countenance ... when you fast, anoint your head and wash your face, so that you do not appear to me to be fasting, but to your Father who is in the secret place; and your Father who sees in secret will reward you openly."[20] This is a curious suggestion – God sees you in secret, no matter where you are. He has a secret window into your heart, where He can inspect you and judge you. This, too, strongly invokes the language of privacy, or so it will sound to our ears, but obviously, Jesus is not speaking of fasting in private, all alone and locked away. That is hardly the point. Rather, he means to say, present yourself authentically, earnestly, and resist worrying about the opinion of others. To rightly adjust your relationship to God, you must reject public opinion and affirmation. Echoing the Stoics, you must retreat from the common values, concerns, and prejudices of men. Jesus concludes the sermon by urging people to "lay up their treasures in heaven" – they may not "serve both God and mammon."[21]

The Reformation seems consequential to the development of privacy because "reflection on the mental inventory of the believer became more

---

[20] Mt 6:16–18.
[21] Mt 6:18–24.

important" during this period, thanks to the religious revolution at hand.[22] Such introspection will in turn demand seclusion. But again, talk of mental inventory invokes an older (much older) precedent in Christianity. There are few thinkers who undertook as important a mental inventory as St. Augustine, exemplified in his *Confessions*, written in the fifth century. Augustine looks back on his life, studying key events, enduring doubts, notable debates, and temptations, in order to understand how God's grace operated on him and his environment, ultimately bringing him to faith. The *Confessions* culminates with a long commentary on the wonders of memory, and the inner world in which individuals ought to immerse themselves: "The power of the memory is prodigious . . . It is a vast, immeasurable sanctuary . . . Although it is part of my Nature, I cannot understand all that I am ... [Men] go out and gaze in astonishment at high mountains, the huge waves of the sea, the broad reaches of rivers, the ocean that encircles the world, or the stars in their courses. But they pay no attention to themselves."[23] Retracing and collecting his memories enabled Augustine to consolidate the events of his life into a single narrative, leading from dissoluteness to grace – from a state of being lost among the many temptations of the world, to unity in and with God. And as he meditates on memory itself, he sees a window into, or extension of, the divine. The limitlessness of memory, this is the imprint of God on us; it is the mark of the infinite within. Augustine declares: "I have learnt to love you late, Beauty at once so ancient and so new! I have learnt to love you late! You were within me, and I was in the world outside myself. I searched for you outside myself and, disfigured as I was, I fell upon the lovely things of your creation. You were within me but I was not with you."[24] It is no coincidence that Luther, who also wished to draw the believer's focus inward, was originally an Augustinian priest.

In Jesus' teaching, interpreted by Augustine and passed on to Luther and Ignatius, it is easy to see how privacy, understood as seclusion or social isolation, can be inferred and anticipated. It would certainly seem that such privacy makes the task of spiritual purification that much easier, or possible at all. Aren't you better able to pray earnestly if no eyes are on you? Isn't it easier to fast in private, untempted by lures of the outside world? Again, I doubt that this was the intention of early Christian writers, since seclusion would have been a rare commodity – what's more, there is an undeniable social focus in the tradition. At the very least, it is reasonable to say that "[from] its inception,

[22]  Vincent, 14.
[23]  Augustine, *Confessions*, trans. R. S. Pine-Coffin (New York: Penguin, 1961), 216.
[24]  Augustine, 231.

Christianity has been torn by two apparently irreconcilable tendencies. It is an eminently personal religion, calling upon each person individually to convert, find faith and seek salvation … It is also a communal religion dependent on a church" – demanding charity, I might add.[25] The personalism of Christianity invokes an individual relationship with God; this relationship also demands a personal emptying, as some Christian thinkers have put it. How shall one achieve this emptying? Again, works and charity are instrumental, as is commitment to the common good. Scholars are coming to similar conclusions about the thought of St. Paul, which is an important revelation, since he is credited by the Protestant Reformation for elevating faith over works. In fact, Paul spoke prominently of *kenosis*, personal emptying, which he maintained could be achieved by, among other things, giving away most everything you own, and living in a community of similarly committed, sharing, charitable individuals. Aspirations for *kenosis* were expressed in the baptismal cry of early Christians: "No more Jew or Greek, slave or freeman, male or female!"[26] The aim, again, is to be an honest, pure, authentic person and believer before God, untainted and uncompromised by the social ties affixed you. In fact, you should shed your social affiliations altogether, and devote yourself to communal welfare. Paul's notion of *kenosis*, and the radical gender equality it invokes, was unacceptable in the broader Mediterranean world, which is why it was largely diminished by later editors, who added famously chauvinistic statements.[27] In any case, this serves to underscore the point that "a dialectical tension between personal and communal religion has shaped the entire history of Christianity," and it is easy to see how an emphasis on seclusion emerged.[28]

Puritanism, for example, came to link prayer with spatial privacy, which was in turn prefigured by the growing popularity of diary writing.[29] This latter phenomenon was effectively the product of growing literacy and the new spirituality combined. What better way to recount your mental inventory – so that you might never forget, evade, or deny it – than putting it on paper? The diary is a kind of private space all its own. It is for your own consumption after all – or the eyes of God – but it is no public document. Diary writing makes for a different kind of penance than Catholic confession. It is seemingly more honest. No one else is

[25] François Lebrun, "The Two Reformations: Communal Devotion and Personal Piety," in *A History of Private Life, Volume III*, trans. Arthur Goldhammer (Cambridge, MA: Harvard University Press, 1989), 69.

[26] Karen Armstrong, *St Paul: The Apostle We Love to Hate* (Boston: New Harvest, 2015), 40.

[27] Armstrong, 119.

[28] Lebrun, "The Two Reformations: Communal Devotion and Personal Piety," 70.

[29] Vincent, 13.

present to shame you or praise you for your thoughts and admissions. A recurring Catholic joke about confession, meanwhile, involves the penitent lying, or withholding key details from the priest – whom he may know personally, and, especially in a small parish, face on a daily basis. The penitent may not be so forthcoming in that case – or, like my family in rural Ireland, travel to a nearby town for confession, where they are unknown to the parish priest. Diary writing exemplified the Protestant emphasis on "the role of silent auditing as a means of engaging in the most profound form of spiritual communion."[30]

Christianity is an important resource for understanding the roots of privacy, and how we have come to conceive it and prize it today. But while privacy may have ancient roots, evident in some form in the Stoics and early Christians, it was not a significant political value or force until later. This is corrected in the early modern period. For, alongside the growing spiritual emphasis on privacy, a legal transformation was also underway: "As London grew, so did the legal rights of its residents. The ruling that 'the house of everyone is his castle' was set forth in 1604, and by 1700 it was . . . a hoary cliché."[31] This period also saw a significant transformation in the political landscape of England, where the power of the monarchy was diminished and increasingly balanced by Parliament. This realignment was not yet democratic; it still favored the aristocracy. But it was a period in which the language and sensibilities of democratic revolution developed and emerged. Claims to privacy protections grew in that context. In the 1760s, one politician, John Wilkes, invoked castle doctrine against the crown's "use of general warrants to mount a search for incriminating documents."[32] A few years later, the crown was fined for invading private homes in search of untaxed goods.[33] This is part of a broader political pattern emerging in eighteenth-century England. Privacy, as with other rights of the citizens, was not "invented in this period," but only "restated and extended as the power of the crown was challenged by an increasingly assertive urban society and as the continuing press of people and buildings demanded clearer regulation."[34]

Privacy has a special connection to democracy, or rather, it gains special significance and force as political power is democratized. As stated above, privacy was lauded as the protection for citizens over and against the king and his autocratic tendencies. Privacy became thus entwined with expressions of

[30]  Vincent, 15.
[31]  Vincent, 33.
[32]  Vincent, 33.
[33]  Vincent, 34.
[34]  Vincent, 34.

citizen power, outlining the essential ground in which democratic power takes root, and extends – namely, the home, where individuals are fortified, preserved, and protected.

In the nineteenth century, the bourgeoisie is instrumental in elevating privacy, enticing everyone else in the process. Privacy becomes synonymous with a kind of comfort and domestic security; and, historians argue, it focused on the family as a moral refuge amidst society at large. In France, this was necessitated by the Revolution, which upended the traditional structure of society, and sowed much chaos. "Domesticity," that is, private family life, "had a fundamental regulatory function" in society, providing much-needed stability.[35] Private family life was a necessary counterbalance to the individualism unleashed by the French Revolution, and the mob psychology that engulfed it, delivering the nation at turns to anarchy and despotism. The privacy of family life was also considered a needed protection against the harsh realities of industrialization, which produced cramped, inhospitable, smoke-filled cities. As the nineteenth century progressed, and concern for the living conditions of the working class grew, so did the recognition that "people needed warmth, cleanliness, and pure air. They also wanted privacy for their family and longed desperately for independence. They liked space in which to build and tinker. For all these reasons they dreamed of owning single-family homes," as exemplified by the bourgeoisie.[36] Increasingly, these erstwhile privileges of the wealthy urban class came to be seen as basic expectations – and rights – for all.

To be a proper human, respected and respectable, politically relevant and potent, entailed a private domain in which you could retreat, regroup, be nourished by family, and emerge confidently into the world. And the private retreat, gradually expected for all, was increasingly comfortable and well-appointed. Into the twentieth century, it was also expected that basic homes were "semi-detached ... with fenced gardens to the front and rear."[37] This came to be the model for much public housing in England. And innovations soon followed which greatly enhanced and reinforced the private realm, further solidifying people's expectations for privacy. This includes, of course, the car: people could now convey themselves and their family when and where they liked, insulated from undesirable bystanders and weather alike. At mid-century there was the television, which offered families the excuse to

[35] Michelle Perrot, "The Family Triumphant," in *A History of Private Life, Volume IV*, trans. Arthur Goldhammer (Cambridge, MA: Harvard University Press, 1990), 100.
[36] Roger-Henri Guerrand, "Private Spaces," in *A History of Private Life, Volume IV*, trans. Arthur Goldhammer (Cambridge, MA: Harvard University Press, 1990), 355.
[37] Vincent, 84.

find entertainment solely at home, and eschew the theater, pub, or town square. Families came to spend more time with themselves alone – traveling in the car, playing or lounging in their fenced-in garden, chuckling at TV shows, ensconced in their den. The Younger Report, which the British government commissioned in 1972 to review the state of privacy and make policy recommendations, was acutely aware of what these developments had wrought – quickly: "the modern middle-class family ... relatively sound-proofed in their semi-detached house, relatively unseen behind their privet hedge ... insulated in the family car ... are probably more private in the sense of being unnoticed in all their everyday doings than any sizeable section of the population in any other time or place."[38]

What this historical sketch serves to show, I hope, is that we have reached the pinnacle of privacy – which some now declare a universal right and expectation – quite recently and suddenly. In that light, it seems strange to declare assaults on privacy existential threats to human dignity, freedom, and social life. Did we only come close to achieving the latter for a short window of time in the mid to late twentieth century – halcyon days, when the suburban middle-class lifestyle was carved out, complete with attendant luxuries, and held up as a model for all humankind? And then, almost immediately, privacy was upended by digital technology? One thing that is clear, however, is that privacy, even when it was gained in modest amounts throughout history, was always threatened, it was always fragile. Arguably, this is its native state. Privacy is the product – and subject – of near constant conflict, and never seems to be enjoyed securely, for long. Surveying the campaigns over several centuries to carve out a protected state, it is easy to conclude that "the common thread connecting [them] was the sheer labor involved."[39] Are we still able for the requisite labor today?

The Younger Report claims that privacy was broadly achieved in the twentieth century as never before. At the same time, however, US historians will note that government, military, and economic expansion in this period was "accompanied, indeed made possible by regimes of documentation and the associated work of quantification and mapping."[40] The assaults on privacy in America were many – even while privacy was supposedly emerging and maturing as never before. Twentieth-century assaults included surveillance of the home population during World War I, public health initiatives that invaded and exposed the homes and lives of the poor, and a growing

---

[38]   Vincent, 120.
[39]   Vincent, 115.
[40]   Sarah Igo, *The Known Citizen* (Cambridge, MA: Harvard University Press, 2018), 59–60.

bureaucracy that sought to address a range of social ills, from retirement to unemployment to homeownership. Said bureaucracy was greatly expanded mid-century, starting with the New Deal, and the erection of the Social Security program, which assigned identifying numbers to all citizens – rendering everyone transparent to the government in the process. Many were worried about this program at the time, and issued dire warnings and criticisms that echo current concerns for privacy. And yet, "even if Americans temperamentally resisted regimentation as so many assumed, Social Security's enumeration effort came off with remarkable speed and efficiency."[41] In a now familiar pattern, it seems people's concerns for privacy – that is, regimentation and loss of freedom – could be appeased by important tradeoffs, in this case, a secure retirement. People quickly submitted to the new expectation that you would be tracked by the government and assigned an identifying number, if you hoped to gain legitimate employment. And should you lose your job, of course, "welfare payments hinged on individual visibility" to the government.[42] If anonymous, you were on your own. The poor have always been more liable to privacy invasions, be it from police or public health officials. But the US government also sought to claim more of their private lives in the process of expanding and extending assistance. This was the tendency of the 1960s era War on Poverty, which, in its "penchant for treatment, counseling, training, and rehabilitation programs meant that state agencies were tasked with probing even more deeply into the lives of the poor than previously."[43]

This evokes Foucault's account of "biopower." As governments sought to exert greater control over citizen populations – again, in an age of growing democratic sentiment – Foucault argues that they aimed to gain a presence in areas of our lives that were previously beyond political concern: healthcare, education, job stability, homeownership. In other words, basic life concerns. In one respect, this development looks eminently democratic: the government is expanding to meet the demands of the people, and, in many cases, extend the privileges of the few to the many. But this project entails that our government know us better, and thoroughly perhaps; and it greatly assists those with the ambition to control, manipulate, or oppress us. As the government expands to provide services that we soon take for granted, services that we presume any competent government can offer, privacy must be sacrificed. Can we enjoy expansive government services without sacrificing privacy, and making

[41] Igo, 83.
[42] Igo, 178.
[43] Igo, 179.

ourselves vulnerable? I suppose it depends on the integrity of those who govern, and the institutions over which they preside. Which again, seems to be a perennially fragile safeguard, and not one that will endure consistently or for long.

In the middle of the twentieth century, the US government decided that the suburban middle-class lifestyle was the appropriate model for all to pursue and enjoy (well, for white people at least). Accordingly, it favored construction and expansion of suburban communities, to the detriment of cities. Urban neighborhoods were condemned and razed to make room for highways, conveying commuters out of the city. The Federal Housing Administration offered assistance to white families fleeing the cities for detached homes, and relegated minorities to urban ghettos. Zoning laws were established that strictly segregated property use, and enforced neighborhoods of relatively uniform income levels in the process: industrial buildings here, commercial centers near the highway, residential neighborhoods safely removed from both. The latter were segregated according to income: apartments for immigrants and low-income families are located behind the commercial centers they serve; townhome communities for single professionals and young families lie behind them, providing a buffer for collections of three-bedroom ranchers – which in turn protect exclusive enclaves of "McMansions" on half-acre lots. Neighborhoods were, and still are, strenuously segregated in this way, in order to better preserve home value. Even while racial segregation was officially assailed mid-century, it persisted, and, together with class segregation, arguably expanded in the age of suburbanization.

At the heart of the suburban ideal, of course, is privacy. It is hard to imagine a built environment that prizes and protects privacy better, and announces it as a central value and aspiration. Families fled cramped urban quarters for detached homes, carefully distanced from their neighbors by lawns and picket fences. Suburban homes were equally removed from passing strangers: generous setbacks from the street were enforced, and front porches replaced by back yards; only a foreboding garage faced the street. When you consider that, on top of this, whole neighborhoods were already removed from commercial districts and communities of other income levels, suburbia is an impressive experiment in curating the personal experience. Which is to say, it suggests we are nearly manic in protecting ourselves and loved ones from unexpected, unanticipated, or unwanted encounters. Increasingly, as suburbia has matured and expanded, it has come to elevate privacy even more.

Single-family homes built today are 60 percent larger than in the 1970s, and with fewer residents per household, such that the "average amount of living space per person in a new home has almost doubled in just the last forty years."[44] Suburbanites are spoiled with private space. What do they do with it all? Once upon a time, homes had one to two rooms, used for a variety of purposes; new suburban homes, meanwhile, host a plethora of specialized rooms. Each child has his or her own bedroom, very often. There is a family room, of course, where everyone can convene for entertainment, like watching TV; a living room for entertaining guests, and a dining room to seat them on special occasions; and an informal breakfast nook for everyday family meals. Larger suburban homes sport exercise rooms, basement bars, and even private theaters. And though most people cannot afford these features, the homebuilding industry knows this model is still what they covet; the industry knows that extreme privacy and separation of uses – and gobs of personal space – is the ideal and goal. Environmentalist Bill McKibben recounts a visit to a homebuilders' convention, which showcased the "Ultimate Family Home." It essentially walls off family members from one another, and gives each his or her own wing of the house. This dream home offered a "personal playroom" attached to the boy's bedroom, outfitted with "its own 42-inch plasma TV"; the girl's bedroom, meanwhile, "had a secret mirrored door leading to a hideaway karaoke room."[45] "[We] call this the ultimate home for families who don't want anything to do with one another," one homebuilder quipped.[46]

Even while most people do not enjoy this level of comfort and extreme privacy, new homes trend in this direction. In the more popular Washington exurbs, where people flock for new, spacious homes on larger lots – and for less money – the gains for family privacy are obvious. Dining rooms and living rooms, where you might entertain guests (or God forbid, strangers), are near afterthoughts. They pale in size compared to gargantuan family quarters within, dominated by expansive kitchens and entertainment centers. Master bedrooms, where couples might retreat, are like hotel suites in some cases, with lofty ceilings, expansive walk-in closets, and spa-like bathrooms. These features are not unique to Maryland and Virginia, of course. They are the product of national homebuilders, who hawk their wares across the country, to clamoring demand. And our media – especially Hollywood – transmits this model of living worldwide, so that it is the standard that millions dream of, and hope to pursue.

[44] Mark Perry, "Today's new homes are 1000 square feet larger than in 1973, and the living space per person has doubled over last 40 years," Carpe Diem (blog), *AEIdeas*, February 26, 2014, www.aei.org/publication/todays-new-homes-are-1000-square-feet-larger-than-in-1973-and-the-living-space-per-person-has-doubled-over-last-40-years/.
[45] Bill McKibben, *Deep Economy* (New York: Times Books, 2007), 97.
[46] McKibben, 97.

Oddly enough, while the suburban landscape glorifies privacy as never before, it is the beneficiary of immense government support and expenditure – government that, as it expands its influence and reach, documents, measures, and quantifies us thoroughly and diligently. In short, the government has subsidized and enabled our flight to the suburbs (at no small cost), where we might hole up in private abodes. And there's more: ensconced in detached houses, protected from the outside world by fences and lawns and strict zoning laws, people have never had more privacy – even while, by all other markers, privacy is thoroughly routed. We happily enjoy the physical trappings of privacy, and build them up, weaving ourselves and our families in a veritable cocoon. But in the digital age, our lives are utterly transparent within – and we have made them transparent, assisting our many spies. Don't we know we are monitored in our suburban cocoons? Do we care? Is it too easy, behind our suburban walls and fences, to think we still have privacy? Does it all provide a sustaining illusion, convincing us that we still enjoy independence and quiet seclusion? Perhaps this illusion emboldens us to be careless about digital privacy, and repeatedly expose ourselves. At home, our privacy seems intact, secure. But it is not politically consequential, or powerful.

Perhaps we should call this something else entirely, like "privatism." Privatism is the focus on private, that is, personal goods, in contrast to – and inimical to – common concerns.[47] Is this all we want? Privatism over privacy? Our current situation suggests so. We are content to be surrounded by all our stuff, seated amidst creature comforts, unbothered by unwanted or unknown people – our interactions carefully managed. And Amazon anticipates our needs and desires before we do, urging us to feather our nest. In suburbia, we can lounge in our backyard patio, drink at our basement bar, watch movies in a home theater. But this all makes for a kind of social fragmentation and isolation that is politically troubling. To put a point on it: the atomism on display and evoked in our lived environment, this undermines democracy perhaps more severely than does the loss of privacy.

---

[47]   Patrick Deneen, *Why Liberalism Failed* (New Haven, CT: Yale University Press, 2018), 9.

# 6

## The Borderless, Vanishing Self

I have been arguing that privacy is on life support, and its prognosis looks dim. It is thoroughly besieged in the digital age, and the general population is perhaps its greatest enemy, happily surrendering it to indulge in all manner of conveniences and innovations. Critics and privacy advocates warn that this is a dire development; privacy is necessary for a free and fulfilled life. The digital tidal wave forces us to face a future where privacy may be nonexistent, or at least radically transformed, and diminished. I don't believe the proper solution is to urge people to start caring about privacy again, build stronger walls around their personal lives, so to speak, and block out spying eyes. This seems utterly impossible, and it is unreasonable or implausible to request this of people who are eager to tap into all that the digital economy has to offer. We must find a way to thrive despite this state of affairs.

But that discussion is easier to swallow if we understand something else about privacy: the prevailing concept thereof – the concept that dominates privacy theory, and much thinking about liberal democracy – is philosophically tenuous at best, untenable at worst. Privacy, as its advocates conceive it, may not be so essential to freedom after all. In fact, it betrays some disturbing illiberal tendencies, or points to illiberal consequences. And privacy theory is founded on a notion of the human subject that is dubious, to say the least. Which means that privacy may not in fact deliver the many virtues its advocates and defenders proclaim.

Recall one of the enduring arguments for privacy, inherited from the thought of John Stuart Mill: citizens require a protected personal space because, in democracies, the majority may turn tyrannical, and ignore and crush individual interests and concerns. A tyrannical majority, which other commentators also observed in nascent democracy, is especially dangerous because it "leaves fewer means of escape, penetrating much more deeply into the details of life and enslaving the soul itself."[1] The point is, it is easier for people to defy a single tyrant, at least spiritually, intellectually, emotionally. You may obey him outwardly, but remain resentful and independent within, sharing your disgust or scorn or spite with neighbors, and practicing minor acts of rebellion on the sly. When it is the masses who are tyrannical, however, that is a different proposition altogether. It is much harder to escape their pressure, which is now prevalent, and merciless. This tyrant is also fiercely strong because it has democratic power behind it – it is not dependent on a single person. To forestall the emergence of tyrannical masses, and preserve and protect the freedom of individuals, democracies have instituted the following principle: citizens must be permitted to think, say, and do whatever they wish, and pursue whatever makes them happy – no matter what the disapproving majority thinks – provided that they do not obstruct other individuals in their pursuits of happiness. This will be the essential formula and enduring mark of liberal democracy going forward, and the privacy of the individual is at its core. Consider Mill's words: "The only part of the conduct of any one, for which he is amenable to society, is that which concerns others. In the part which merely concerns himself, his independence is . . . absolute. Over himself, over his own body and mind, the individual is sovereign."[2] There is an inviolate domain where the individual is to be protected from society – indeed, society has no business there whatsoever. The individual has a right to cultivate his mind and body alone, in peace, and determine his own will, and voice.

And this cultivation can seem errant at times. It must take no particular form or path. In fact, liberty of conscience may include what society finds downright unsettling, offensive – dangerous.[3] But still, society may not venture into or legislate over that domain. Individuals must be allowed to think and say whatever they want, even if it is nasty. This right, and the domain of free speech and thought – the domain where our ideas bubble up – must be inviolate. This suggests that liberty of conscience is a delicate flower. It must be germinated in seclusion. It is not robust and resilient – certainly not before a tyrannical majority. In fact, and in general, a free conscience cannot easily suffer the jostling and congestion of neighbors who breathe down your neck, judge you, goad or pressure you with their eyes. The latter will deprive us of truly independent-minded citizens, which democracy requires. Or to put it otherwise, privacy – being left alone to think as you wish, wherever your thoughts

---

[1]  John Stuart Mill, *On Liberty* (Charleston, SC: Bibliobazaar, 2008), 14.
[2]  Mill, 19.
[3]  Mill, 21–2.

may lead – creates the proper cultural environment in which democracy flourishes and civilization advances.

When society seeks to legislate over people's private thoughts, no matter how noxious, it is not the censored individuals who primarily lose out, Mill argues, but society itself.[4] For, this has a chilling effect, and dissuades resident freethinkers, whoever they may be, from contributing to the general pool of ideas from which innovations come. And we cannot know where said contributions will come from – they may well come from the most unlikely source, the most unlikely group or individual. Even if the latter are threatening. We cannot anticipate how freedom and culture will advance. This has been borne out in recent history.

Civil rights expansions often start with ideas that the wider population finds heretical. Equal rights for women, African Americans or gays were initially perceived as preposterous or offensive. Now, for the most part, we take them for granted – at least, we take these rights claims for granted, though we may diverge on whether or how they are realized in practice. In any case, the lesson is: who knows what future freedom consists in? Who knows what it will encompass? Who knows where liberty will lead? Who knows how it will mature, evolve, expand? We ought not cut it short prematurely, as a tyrannical majority would like to do. Because we do not know what freedoms we may soon take for granted, we must not foreclose any idea, and shut down any freethinker. Who knows what will prove to be fruitful or momentous? We must do all that we can to nourish people's sense of security, in this regard, and make them feel free and safe to contemplate and experiment with ideas that are perhaps utterly mundane, or possibly combustible. "Only when we believe that nobody is watching us," one privacy advocate argues, "do we feel free . . . to truly test boundaries, to explore new ways of thinking and being, to explore what it means to be ourselves. For that reason, it is in the realm of privacy where creativity, dissent, and challenges to orthodoxy germinate . . . "[5]

You will note another suggestion here: artistic genius also relies on privacy. Artists are of course a popular target for social suspicion or contempt. They may be accused of glorifying what is lascivious, violent, or generally immoral. Plato recognizes the immense social and political power of their productions, which is why he recommends censoring their work, or banning them from the city outright. He works very hard to diminish the standing of art, dubbing it "mimesis," or imitation, which is a patently outrageous claim, in one respect: it hardly seems that artists ever aim to merely "imitate" or copy something. It is

---

[4] Mill, 42.
[5] Glenn Greenwald, *No Place to Hide* (New York: Picador, 2014), 174.

more accurate to say they seek to express or convey a scene as they imagine it, or, as in the case of ancient Athenian sculptors, represent an ideal human form, for example. But only a naïve onlooker – as Socrates so often pretended to be – would say that artists are imitators. Their work, their task, their mission is so much more than that. And that is precisely Plato's point, which he makes in his typical indirect fashion. Implicit in his critique is a grudging admission of art's power: artists are the creators of culture – the bedrock of morals. They breathe life into religion and patriotism, and stoke the fires of political courage. But their work, again, has unsettling origins – artists must be allowed to contemplate ideas and dabble in visions that may, at first glance, be abhorrent to the wider public. Who knows what iconic imagery or narrative might result, what art works emerge that are now the cornerstone of our culture, perhaps? As an example, take any of the banned books that are now widely reputed and revered classics.

This account of freedom evokes what the English philosopher Isaiah Berlin famously called "negative liberty." A strict boundary must be drawn between my mind, my personal life, and the influence of society. Personal freedom lies within that boundary, and is not to be defined, specified, or articulated – it may take whatever form you like, whatever form emerges. In fact, "the wider the area of noninterference the wider my freedom" – the more space for bold ideas to interact and collide, and in the glorious friction, produce new visions for liberty, or brave works of art.[6] There are two general problems with this account, however. For one thing, regarding the view that creativity demands such liberty, what are we to make of impressive art works and movements that emerged in societies that did not cherish, or even know, our standard of privacy? Can we rightly or justifiably say that contemporary American culture, where the freedom of thought is sacrosanct (at least in principle), indeed issues forth more examples of great artwork than earlier societies? This raises a debate I am not prepared to answer here – but I am inclined to say it is not liable to easy resolution, even by experts. It may not be resolved at all. Because it seems a preposterous suggestion, to argue that the oeuvre of American art outshines the classics, thanks to our personal freedoms, or otherwise. They are called classics for a reason – can their greatness ever be matched by future creators? But the point, one might say, is that privacy emboldens and invigorates the general sense of creativity. Setting aside the relative merit or beauty or power of the artistic productions, we can at least say that in contemporary democracies, where people may think and say whatever they wish – and know that they are

[6]  Isaiah Berlin, "Two Concepts of Liberty," in Henry Hardy (ed.), *Liberty* (New York: Oxford University Press, 2007), 170–1.

protected in so doing, even if their thoughts are explosive and controversial – people feel freer to create. They feel unleashed, and if our artwork does not (yet?) match the greatness of earlier productions, at least it exceeds it in terms of sheer output, and the joyful mania of our creative culture, which infects society at large with its courage and vivacity, and willingness to push boundaries. This is more plausible; except, I might point out, that creativity is so often inflamed or stoked in and by periods of constrained personal freedom. Much of the most impressive and powerful artistic works are born from conflict, political disquiet, resentment, resistance. As artists will aver, they are not so liable to document or depict periods of happiness, but personal challenges, lingering struggles, vexing trials, or outright tragedy.

As for the supposed political fruits of negative liberty, recall that American individualism and independent-mindedness, the trademark of our enduring democracy, took root in the rigid society of Puritan New England.[7] The Puritans themselves were fiercely independent and courageous; they were willing to leave Europe and enter a wilderness, so that they might worship as they saw fit. Their independence proved to be a precedent for future defectors from their society, spawning competitor colonies in New England. Similarly, our founding fathers who spoke of the universal equality of all men unwittingly set a precedent for future expansions of equal rights, which then had to be championed through great struggle. The point is, these brave ideas endorsed at the origins of American society, they were not delivered by privacy. They were conceived and realized in and through conflict, which emboldened the movements that championed these ideals. The conflict – the constraints against which champions of liberty and equality had to fight – gave their movements definition, and inner fire. This is not to say I would trade places with earlier generations, and struggle with constraints on personal freedom – nor is it to say we should tolerate such constraints today. Rather, it's hardly evident that noninterference is "a necessary condition for the growth of human genius," political or artistic.[8]

Civil Rights activists from the 1950s and 1960s had to persevere amidst terrible intimidation and outright violence. They were not able to cultivate their plans or arguments for desegregation in peace, but had to do so in secret, or under extreme stress and persecution. When African American soldiers returning from World War II "demanded that they be given at home the rights they had fought for overseas," many were

---

[7]  Berlin, 175.
[8]  Berlin, 175.

lynched.[9] The students who orchestrated sit-ins at segregated diners in the south were surrounded by angry, scornful youths and Ku Klux Klan members itching for violent confrontation.[10] The children that Martin Luther King recruited to protest in Birmingham in 1963 were repelled with water cannons and vicious police dogs. This did not stop them from persevering, and implementing King's "Jail no Bail" strategy, which clogged Birmingham jails for weeks. Bob Moses, who directed the voting registration efforts in Mississippi in the early 1960s, where African Americans were strictly denied the vote, was arrested by police intent on upholding the status quo; he was also subjected to vicious attack – his assailants acquitted by an all-white jury – and his life was threatened regularly.[11] Moses and his allies – some of whom were murdered – persisted nonetheless, in an unforgiving environment. The Freedom Riders, who dared to test the Supreme Court's mandate to deseg-regate buses and bus stations across the south, were literally terrorized, prompting federal intervention to preserve their safety.

The early labor movement also endured immense intimidation, or outright oppression. Labor organizers fought against powerful industrialists and their political allies to correct harsh conditions and meager pay endured by workers. Their efforts delivered many of the rights we take for granted today, including a minimum wage, worker safety regulations, eight-hour work days, and week-ends off. They were bullied throughout the process. In the Pennsylvania coal mines, labor organizers were falsely accused of perpetrating violence and terrorism as part of the Irish Molly Maguire gang, and executed.[12] When striking miners in Coeur D'Alene, Idaho, evicted scabs, and took prisoner the guards protecting the scabs, the governor "declared martial law," sent "both the state National Guard and federal soldiers," and sought "Gatling guns and small howitzers" to shell the miners.[13] The miners quickly surren-dered, but "[in] vicious reprisals carried out under the martial law decree, whole villages of strikers were rounded up, along with lawyers, bar owners, shopkeepers, even judges – anyone believed to have sympathized with the miners' union."[14] The city subsequently issued a ban on labor organizing in the mines. In the mid twentieth century, labor organizers faced stifling

---

[9]   Taylor Branch, *Parting the Waters: America in the King Years 1954–63* (New York: Simon and Schuster, 1988), 63.
[10]  Branch, 273.
[11]  Branch, 495–7.
[12]  Philip Dray, *There is Power in a Union* (New York: Anchor Books, 2010), 90.
[13]  Dray, 289–90.
[14]  Dray, 290.

persecution from the major auto manufacturers. General Motors ruled Flint, Michigan with an iron hand, crushing union activity. One worker complained that GM "so completely run this town and have it so well propagandized to their own good that one doesn't even talk here. You have no liberties at all. You couldn't even belong to a union and breathe it to a soul. That soul would probably be a spy."[15] But that did not stop the workers from orchestrating one of the most remarkable strikes in US history, when they decided to sit down in the factories, and subsequently occupied them for over a month in early 1937. The striking workers prevailed, securing a pay raise, and forcing GM to allow union organizing.[16] When labor organizers, emboldened by their success at Flint, decided to march on Dearborn and "hand union leaflets to workers" at the Ford plant, "Ford's private army … savagely beat them"; the city council subsequently "passed an ordinance making it illegal to pass out flyers within city limits," and in ensuing years, "Ford fired more than four thousand workers for unionism."[17]

In the early twentieth century, especially in the American West, labor organizers were routinely arrested for public speaking. Cities claimed that their speech amounted to agitation. San Diego was particularly inhospitable to labor organizing – and the San Diego Tribune urged that demonstrators "be shot down or hanged … "[18] Such statements emboldened vigilantes. They assaulted labor organizers traveling into town, and even kidnapped the editor of a rival newspaper, who was sympathetic to the cause of labor, and nearly beat him to death. Labor organizers were chastened by the violence in San Diego, and learned that "it was possible to outfox authorities where the rule of law prevailed, where established powers-that-be could be made to appear inadequate and forced to countenance their own hypocrisy; but where vigilantism went unchecked and police were inclined to look the other way or even collaborate, the odds became insurmountable."[19] The GM strike was buoyed, meanwhile, by support from the governor of Michigan, who was sympathetic to the labor movement, and sought to enforce labor laws that GM was ignoring. He enlisted the national guard, not to crush protestors as had happened in so many earlier strikes, but to protect them from GM's hired thugs. In other words, the governor had the power and the will to enforce rule of law – which he did. Labor organizing benefited once rule of law was upheld and respected.

[15] Erik Loomis, *A History of America in Ten Strikes* (New York: The New Press, 2018), 121.
[16] Loomis, 127–8.
[17] Loomis, 129.
[18] Dray, 304.
[19] Dray, 305.

Civil rights activists had a similar experience in this regard: as they prevailed upon authorities to respect rule of law, civil rights protests had more sway – they were protected in their activities – and they saw results. They could no longer be crushed out of hand. Activists persuaded authorities to respect rule of law after years of shaming them for their reprehensible treatment of nonviolent protestors, especially children.

The lesson is that the ability to organize securely in private, and speak, and explore controversial ideas, this is not so much the prerequisite for freedom, as it is the fruit of liberation movements. Which is to say, labor and civil rights activists gained the privacy to organize in peace and safety thanks to earlier efforts – and immense sacrifices – which prevailed upon authorities to respect rule of law, and live up to the ideals of liberty and equality upon which this nation was founded.

Simply put, society will not happily or willingly grant space and safety to controversial agents or organizations. Mill would have this protected by law; but as the labor and civil rights movements routinely discovered, it is too easy for the powerful to ignore rule of law. The individual right to privacy is impotent, if not impossible, in this setting. Rather, the civil rights and labor movements demonstrated the power of collective action and mass organizing, without the benefit or luxury of privacy, to force authorities to respect rule of law.

Returning to the idea that freedom involves or demands a zone of non-interference, it is problematic from another angle, too. What exactly constitutes interference? When am I interfered with? When is my personal life wrongly or overly intruded upon, and I am unduly influenced or pressured? The boundary between interference and noninterference, or between acceptable interference and the unacceptable kind, is terribly vague, and likely variable over time, place, and circumstance. Does the mere sight of something constitute interference? Must said image or advertisement then address me, somehow? Invite me? Seek to hijack my will, and urge me to make certain choices? How shall we be sure the latter is happening? Recall what Foucault points out about the coercion of surveillance, what makes it so devastatingly effective: it prompts me to ignore that I am manipulated; it plants the seed of censorship within, so that I spearhead it myself, and still feel free and self-determining.

In the digital age, marketers aim to interfere with us in ways that are hardly detectable, but highly consequential. Where is the border between mere advertisement, notifying us about certain goods and their benefits, and overt influence or manipulation? It seems impossible to pinpoint that transition, not least because people submit to so-called manipulation in varying ways. Some might submit wholly, some not at all. Some might be smitten by the mere glimpse of a product, while others will need a stronger dose of marketing – a repeated, intrusive, or subliminal dose. Some will obey marketers' silent directives perpetually, some only partially, or in fits and starts. This is because the decisive conditions for manipulation lie not necessarily in the nature and form of interference, the content of the advertisement and outreach, but in those who are advertised to. People may be more or less liable to manipulation as circumstances, their history, and their character allow. A group of researchers recently concluded, for example, that the "most important determinant of one's ability to resist persuasion is ... 'the ability to premeditate.' This means that people who harness self-awareness to think through the consequences of their actions are more disposed to chart their own course ... "[20]. Does noninterference prepare us to combat or withstand efforts at manipulation? Does it ensure that the nation is populated by strong-willed, independent-minded, resistant individuals? Better yet, does this form of freedom provide any personal – and civic – preparation at all? I will return to this concern presently, but the answer to all of these questions is "no."

This zone of noninterference is touted as the essential buffer protecting individuals from tyrannical interests without, and as the breeding ground for human genius within. But it is not necessarily incompatible with autocracy. "It is perfectly conceivable that a liberal-minded despot would allow his subjects a large measure of personal freedom," Berlin notes.[21] He points to so-called eighteenth-century "enlightened despots" as examples. Frederick the Great of Prussia and Joseph II of Austria permitted greater personal freedoms for their subjects, never surrendering their claim to absolute rule, or conceding political power to the masses. Indeed, Machiavelli would say, it is precisely necessary for an autocrat to permit his subjects a degree of personal space – for the sake of his own survival and success.

Machiavelli tells his apprentice prince that he must fear the populace; the people are a sleeping giant, far more dangerous than the selfish, scheming aristocrats who can be sidelined, manipulated, or simply slaughtered. Luckily, the prince can easily subdue and pacify the people, and even enlist their support, by nurturing their sense of presumed or desired personal freedom. He must allow and encourage his subjects to think they have a personal domain where they are sovereign – and which he is wise not to invade. It is better if he is feared than loved, but above all, the prince must avoid being hated, which is easy enough to do, so long as he follows this advice: "You will only be hated if you seize the property or the women of your subjects and citizens ... above all

[20] (Zuboff, 308)
[21] Berlin, 176.

else, keep your hands off other people's property; for men are quicker to forget the death of their father than the loss of their inheritance."[22]

It is not necessarily a sign of freedom – potent, consequential political freedom – that people are accorded zones of noninterference, where they may hoard possessions, or contemplate outrageous ideas. For Machiavelli, this is just as easily the condition of successful autocracy. The prince who urges his subjects to think they are free, and successfully imparts the notion that they are sovereigns at home, he will be able to do all manner of nasty things to advance his cause and expand power. Why? In his trademark cynicism, Machiavelli presumes that people are selfish at heart, and will want to focus on their own affairs, their own domains – especially if the reigning tyrant exhibits vicious cruelty on occasion. Why provoke his attention, if it is just as easy to busy myself with my own affairs. I will draw the line, of course, if he invades my personal domain – but such an invasion is unnecessary for the prince, and politically inefficient. It will prompt internal revolt, but the prince should be focused outward, subduing neighbors, solidifying and expanding his regime, so that he is resistant to the inevitable competition from like-minded rivals. Machiavelli sees little point in the total domination aspired to by twentieth-century tyrannies. And he would not have known the promise of surveillance, deemed so admirably efficient by Foucault. If he had known this, would Machiavelli have advised differently? I am not sure; he may well have. Though, again, Machiavelli's goal is not internal domination, but expansion, which the autocrat requires for enduring survival and glory. This agenda does not call for internal domination. In any case, the point remains: personal freedom of a kind – noninterference accorded the citizens – is not necessarily an impediment to the autocrat's designs. They may be compatible. As we will soon see, in the case of China, which assiduously monitors its citizenry, free speech is also perfectly tolerable, up to a point. Of itself, noninterference may not guarantee that citizens will be emboldened to stand up for their rights and liberty. Because, of itself, noninterference offers little in the way of potent political training for the people. It may be the breeding ground for controversial ideas that will bloom into civil rights gains – provided there are other key social and political ingredients at hand. Or it may prove an opportunity for people to turn inward.

In democracy, we have greater ambitions for personal freedom. We hope and plan for citizens to be autonomous. This is the positive notion of liberty, Berlin tells us, which "derives from the wish on the part of the individual to be

---

[22]  Niccolo Machiavelli, *The Prince*, trans. David Wootton (Indianapolis, IN: Hackett Publishing Co., 1995), 52.

his own master ... to be a subject, not an object; to be moved by reasons, by conscious purposes, which are my own, not by causes which affect me ... from outside."[23] According to its advocates, privacy is also critical to this notion of personal freedom. As Michael Lynch indicated earlier, controlling access to my mental states, this in itself amounts to a kind or form of autonomy; but it is also the key to later determining my path in life as I see fit. I must be left alone so that I may practice autonomy in my life, or be autonomous at all. Society poses the threat of heteronomy, which undermines the project of discerning my inner voice, or the law of reason that may help me be moral. But this aspiration to self-determination, it, too, may prove problematic.

In modern European intellectual history, where liberal democracy takes root, two accounts of individual autonomy were especially formative and influential. The Stoics described their psychotherapy as a process of combating, diminishing, or fending off heteronomy, the influence of the crowd, the weight of convention that plagues my soul with irrational fears and concerns. Society would have me join the race of acquisition, and recklessly pile up possessions that I must now worry about – externalities that are subject to random assaults of fate, which cause me great pain. "All the many and diverse cruelties that chance inflicts can never be so repulsed that many storms will not swoop down on those who spread their canvas wide," Seneca explains: "we must restrict our actions to a narrow compass so that Fortune's arrows may fall on empty space."[24] To achieve self-control, I must retreat – within. This may be moral free-dom, but it is difficult to translate into political liberty, at least broadly. The Stoics produced some citizens of uncommon courage and indepen-dence who proved to be a pain for those in power; and they celebrated such individuals. But they are few – because this inward retreat is hard, unappetizing, and politically isolating if it lacks the imperative for duty, which, I have argued, later Stoic admirers lost or ignored. In general, Stoicism is plagued by a larger paradox: it is eminently democratic in one sense, profoundly elitist in another. All that moral freedom requires is reason, which everyone possesses; the problem is, few, if any can elevate their rational capacity to the degree the Stoics envision and admire. This is made clear by their saying, "the wise man is happy even on the rack." That is an impressive degree of tranquility and emotional independence – but who can achieve it? For that reason, the Stoics added, "the wise man

[23] Berlin, 178.
[24] Seneca, "On the Tranquillity of Mind," in *Dialogues and Essays*, trans. John Davie (New York: Oxford University Press, 2007), 127.

is rare as the phoenix." Since the phoenix is a mythical creature, it leads one to wonder if Stoic self-control is possible at all – or just another myth?

The other prominent tradition of autonomy is liable to similar criticisms that it is unrealistic and overly demanding. Immanuel Kant held that rational autonomy is the defining feature of morality.[25] I am moral to the extent that I give law to myself; moral law is discerned by reason, through a process of universalizability. Which is to say, if I determine that a particular course of action can be universalized – if I determine that it ought to be carried out all the time and in every case, such that I am not making an exception of myself – then that is the morally acceptable and commendable thing to do. By contrast, if I seek to accommodate notions of personal happiness or pleasure in my moral thinking and outlook, this is the path to doom: I will make an exception for myself in certain cases, to ensure my happiness. I believe this account resonates with us, and speaks to a popular understanding of morality. We tend to identify morality with altruism; the morally appropriate course of action calls on me to ignore or sacrifice my personal desires, hopes, and intentions. If we make room for the latter, even on occasion, Kant worries, who knows what immorality we may soon be capable of, and justify? By that same stroke, however, this account of morality is also excessively aloof and cold. A truly moral person must, if asked, affirm that he takes no joy or pleasure in moral deeds – a perverse turn of events, one philosopher noted, if you are visiting a sick friend.[26] You visit him out of duty, which results from universalizing; you may not visit because he brings you joy. Suddenly, this seems alien to moral thinking. Whither empathy, which often proves a reliable moral moti- vator? Kant will have none of it; feelings are notoriously liable to influence and manipulation – they are the doorway to heteronomy. Only reason can make me free and independent.

This account of self-determination is also lofty – perhaps excessively so. Kant proceeded to talk of a "kingdom of ends," a moral realm where everyone treats one another as an end in himself, not a means to some other end. Everyone is recognized as bearing dignity because of their rational autonomy, or capacity for it. Though Kant did not mean to invoke a literal earthly regime, one can be forgiven for hearing utopian strains. And, Berlin believes, this is the ultimate failing of positive liberty, too. Accounts of freedom fleshed out in terms of self-determination too often lead to unreasonable demands and

---

[25] See Immanuel Kant, *Grounding for the Metaphysics of Morals*, trans. James Ellington (Indianapolis, IN: Hackett Publishing Co., 1993).
[26] See Michael Stocker, "The Schizophrenia of Modern Ethical Theories," *Journal of Philosophy*, 73/14 (1976), 453–66.

expectations – and prove tyrannical. On one hand, he sees an inevitable elitism: some will be rational – likely few – while the masses muddle through; and the former will look down on the latter, confident that they alone can and should rule. It leads to a "despotism ... by the best or the wisest."[27] And, I would argue, this is evident in the technocratic tendencies of many democracies – actual and nominal democracies alike. Our founding fathers, for example, intended that the republic would be ruled by wealthy, educated people, who were best equipped to think of the common good of the nation. A century later, federal agencies were charged with caring for our forests and food supply, and were populated by specially educated, trained, and objective individuals – who were eventually replaced with pliable, inexpert directors, thanks to the influence of corporate lobbies. Communist regimes, which assiduously strove to so elevate the will of the people and realize a strict egalitarianism, took popular rule out of the picture altogether, assembling a despotism of experts. But Berlin chiefly takes issue with the cruelty evinced by regimes committed to utopian dreams or designs. Utopianism is violent – and it is founded on unrealizable ideals, which ignore the "crooked timber" out of which humanity is made – timber that may not be straightened without breaking.[28]

The notion of freedom as individual self-determination risks being idealistic, or, at least, not wholly realistic. Can I ever be sure I've attained it? Can I ever be certain my decisions are properly, exclusively my own, influenced or imparted by no one else? It's a high bar – can I ever be confident I am sufficiently rational to exercise autonomy? Contemplating all this, furthermore, we are soon led to considerations beyond the self. Which is to say, if I would be self-determining, this requires no small degree of external input and preparation, paradoxically. If I would practice and fulfill the autonomy that privacy makes possible, I must be trained for it, with considerable guidance and support. An autonomous individual who takes full advantage of the privacy accorded him by society requires an environment that likewise nourishes his capacity for self-rule.

This points to a larger problem underlying privacy theory: it presumes a notion of the self that is philosophically suspect, if not altogether discredited.[29] It presumes a notion of the self that is simple, self-reliant, and self-contained. If left to my own devices, I can be a source of creative genius

[27] Berlin, 200.
[28] Berlin, 216.
[29] See Julie E. Cohen, *Configuring the Networked Self: Law, Code, and the Play of Everyday Practice* (New Haven, CT: Yale University Press, 2012), 128.

and incisive political dissent. What will upend or prematurely kill my potential is if I am tampered with, swayed, culturally and politically colonized. I –
myself and alone – am the source of all that is authentic. To put it otherwise, if
I am beset by opinions, beliefs, or prejudices foisted on me from without, they
can be purged to expose "an autonomous core" within, "an essential self
identifiable after the residue of influence has been subtracted."[30]

This is certainly reminiscent of Emerson and Thoreau's vision, which so
inspired Justice Douglas' momentous defense of privacy. "Nothing is at last
sacred but the integrity of your own mind," Emerson declares.[31] I am my
own authority on the most crucial matters. A pure, honest, gleaming me
awaits – I only need to discover it or tap into it. And when I do, I will understand that "no law can be sacred to me but that of my nature ... [The] only
right is what is after my constitution."[32] Thoreau puts the Emersonian conviction to the test at Walden Pond, wrapping himself in the benevolent folds of
nature – or so he imagines them. Consider how he justifies the urge to set off
walking in the wilds: "Here is this vast, savage, howling mother of ours, Nature,
lying all around, with such beauty, and such affection for her children ... and
yet we are so early weaned from her breast to society, to that culture which is
exclusively an interaction of man on man."[33] We are "so early weaned" from
the truth, taught to spurn and disrespect it, in thrall to the dissimulating and
deceitful voices of men.

Emerson and Thoreau seek to elevate the virtue of self-sufficiency that has
been revered in American culture ever since, especially our libertarian odes to
independence and personal responsibility. I need for little, and those essential
needs I can easily satisfy myself – provided that I am clear-eyed about what
they are. This is the task at hand. I only have to immerse myself in proximate
nature, connect with my primal mother, and my essential self will emerge
clearly, whose precepts I may confidently obey. This means I must also sever
ties to society and human culture in essential ways, and understand that they
are inessential to my well-being, and often troublesome. However, this
account ignores all that goes into the making of me – the making of
a sensible, capable, and, yes, otherwise self-reliant individual. I bear the
indelible imprint of others even as I march off alone into the woods, perhaps
bent on discovering some truer, more essential self. The path I take, the state in
which I uncover and hail that truer self, this is influenced by forces around me.

[30]   Julie E. Cohen, "What Privacy Is For," *Harvard Law Review*, 126/127 (2013), 1906.
[31]   Ralph Waldo Emerson, "Self-Reliance," in *Nature and Selected Essays* (New York: Penguin
       Books, 1982), 178.
[32]   Emerson, "Self-Reliance," 179.
[33]   Henry David Thoreau, "Walking," in *Nature/Walking* (Boston: Beacon Press, 1991), 110.

How can I ever recognize the voice of authenticity when I am only always accustomed to hearing the words of men? How will I know I have alighted upon this voice, and pick it out of the encompassing din? It is more honest to recognize my debt to others, and the perennial frailty of my condition – how I am reliant on external forces, and utterly at the mercy of many. And there can be no other way.

The seventeenth-century Dutch philosopher Spinoza deplored the propensity of man to consider himself a "kingdom within a kingdom," that is, insulated and isolated from the laws of nature.[34] We like to think we are creatures apart; we alone are free and self-determining, and are favored creations of God – a God who loves each of us so intimately, that "He knows the number of hairs on my head," to cite a well-worn medieval saying. Spinoza rejected all that, complaining that much of it – implicated in superstition – incites anxiety, fear, anger, and violence. We should rather recognize how we are so intimately part of nature. This is therapeutic, and closer to the truth. If I contemplate and study my situation carefully and honestly, Spinoza maintained, I will admit that my borders are porous, vague, and variable.

Feared for his heresy – atheism in the eyes of many – Spinoza described the human subject as a mode of the one substance, God or Nature, conceived under the attributes of thought and matter. To be human is to be but a momentary momentary apparition on the face of God/Nature, a fleeting accumulation of material and ideal (or intellectual) components, soon to disperse again. And the conditions of my assemblage, brief persistence, and dispersal are determined by forces beyond my control. It is folly to think I have sway over the most essential facts of my existence. The best I can hope for, echoing the Stoics, is to determine how I shall think about my fate. For, Spinoza argued, I have the power to derive intellectual joy from understanding my fate, and nature at large. To put it otherwise, paradoxically, I may become free – free from mental anguish – so far as I see myself determined by surrounding forces, and understand the nature and extent of that chain of forces.

One might take issue with Spinoza's extreme emphasis on external determination, which would dispense with free choice and action. But his larger point remains: we must understand we are part of nature, and all that that implies. It is our perennial temptation to think otherwise, to consider ourselves unique and apart – isolated, alone, solely in charge of our destiny. I pose Spinoza's account as a contrast with Emerson and Thoreau, though they, too, urge us to flee to our nature – our mother. And yet, they remain conspicuously

---

[34] See Baruch Spinoza, *Ethics*, trans. Samuel Shirley (Indianapolis, IN: Hackett Publishing Co., 1992), 102.

anthropocentric: nature is where I may discover the true me; it is where I am purified and elevated. It is where the discrete and unique sphere of my autonomous self becomes apparent. Isolated from the society of men, "I" emerge. Spinoza contends that nature teaches otherwise, if we appraise it and our situation frankly. For one thing, nature is hardly so benevolent as Thoreau imagines, but is mindlessly cruel – or merciless, and mechanical. It tells me, furthermore, that my borders are blurred. I cannot see where I begin or where I end – if I really look, and understand. My nature bleeds into others, who likewise bleed into me.

Privacy theory presumes a notion of the human subject that smacks of what René Girard calls the "Romantic Lie," the claim that I am or can be independent and utterly self-determining, and owe my essence to nothing and no one else. There is an "authentic self" I must uncover. In this Romantic Lie, "the hero wants something, and it is really 'he' who wants it – unaffected by others, as if he were not also a slave to public opinion and the approbation of friends and family"; rather, there is "an inevitable third in these transactions – the one who modeled the desire, who taught us to have it."[35] Desire is mimetic, Girard insists. It is hubristic and needlessly false to ignore this fact, and entertain the proposition that I am self-forming, or terribly unique. But such is the inheritance of Modern philosophy, that school of philosophy dominant from the Renaissance to the Enlightenment, when human rational capacity was elevated and admired, and predicted to have vast (perhaps even unlimited) potential. For Descartes, this meant we might ultimately understand nature completely, and thereby control it. And politically, modern thinkers dreamt of producing states founded on such encompassing knowledge of human affairs – a political science, if you will – that they could resist internal and external demise, at least for a very long time. This period also offered dreams of the independent individualistic citizen that became familiar to so much democratic theory. And indeed, as I will take up later, democracy seems unthinkable without autonomous subjects who make up their minds on their own, and independently deliver political judgment. How could the state capture and convey popular will otherwise? Modern philosophy's account of the independent, autonomous subject has been roundly disputed by later thinkers, but it was already suspect in the eyes of some contemporaries, as Spinoza reveals. In any case, this view of the subject endures.

Lynch's defense of privacy, visited in Chapter 2, conspicuously draws on modern subjectivity – Girard's Romantic Lie. I require "privileged access to my mental states," Lynch argues, so I may be able to make autonomous

[35] Cynthia Haven, *Evolution of Desire* (East Lansing, MI: Michigan State Press, 2018), 91.

decisions, and act as a unique individual. In fact, my human dignity, my very personhood, demands that this privileged access is respected and preserved. We must wonder about "privileged access to my mental states." What is that exactly, and why is it so important? What constitutes said privilege, and what exactly might indicate or determine that it is challenged, endangered, or altogether missing? Furthermore, what count as my "mental states," and what make them "mine" exactly? How can I verify their provenance or own-ership with any neatness or clarity? Any close examination of my mental states – my emotions, convictions, or beliefs about the world – reveals that they extend beyond myself, start from without, and encompass others. I may inherit key opinions and outlooks from family and friends, for example; or they play a formative role in the opinions and outlooks I come to hold, on a constant basis. At best, such opinions are a collaborative product. My convictions about the world – known facts, if you will – are confirmed and contributed to by others, a vast inheritance really. I don't embrace them, much less discern them, in a vacuum. Even my memories, in many cases, are not my own, but are verified by others, or wholly imported, and of course shared with others. They are never wholly "mine," as far as I can tell.

As a case in point, if you try to recall your childhood home, or bedroom, the image you conjure is forged in large part by contributions from parents, siblings, friends. They tell you what your home was like; they tell you what was in your bedroom – the posters and pictures on your wall, for example, your toys, your pet, your favorite blanket. Perhaps you see a photograph and recall your room and all its contents with greater confidence. Most of our memories have this structure: they are collaborative products, whether we admit it or not. Our memories are elusive, as is our very consciousness of what's going on around us.

It is populated, for example, by what Leibniz called "*petites perceptions*," those partial sensations that inhabit the corner of your eye, and are ignored until brought to your attention.[36] Is it warm right now as you read this book? Do you hear birds chirping outside, or cars rushing by? These are *petites perceptions* which fall into focus as I alert you to them. It is not correct to say you don't perceive them – nor is it accurate to say you are wholly aware of them. *Petites perceptions* inhabit some middle ground, and indicate that the outline of consciousness fades into ambiguity. Freud had something like *petites perceptions* in mind when he spoke of the "preconscious," referring to perceptions before they enter your consciousness, and which you are not

[36]  See G. W. Leibniz, *New Essays on Human Understanding*, trans. Jonathan Bennett and Peter Remnant (Cambridge, UK: Cambridge University Press, 1996).

self-consciously aware of.[37] Traumatic incidents pass directly from the pre-conscious to the unconscious through the act of repression, he argues, and psychoanalysis is the process of helping people recall trauma, hauling it into view by the self-conscious ego. Freud elevates the role of analyst in this regard, but everyone plays a similar if lesser role in the lives of others, helping them recall events and experiences that may have been neglected, lost, ignored, or forgotten for whatever reason.

The notion that I have a neatly circumscribed collection of mental states to draw on – states I uniquely own or access – which in turn inspires a unique course of action, is dubious. I share mental states with many others, and have no monopoly on them, as far as I can tell. Perspective will provide my thoughts and recollections with some distinctness: my partial memory of an event is marked by how, when, and where I witnessed it, from my perch in society, or the universe; this can and should be supplemented by the partial memories of other people, also determined by perspectival particularities. But when my point of view is supplemented in this manner, I inherit their mental states, at least in some degree – and they inherit mine, if the exchange is mutual. Or to put it otherwise, and bluntly, if I forget a certain experience or event, and then recall it with the help of a friend, part of my mental state is now his too, and there is an odd detour, or circuitous path to the contents of my mind – which, in a way, lay outside my very mind. This starts to sound messy, and complicates the supposed roots of autonomy. How can I know when a decision is properly mine, drawing on resources that I own or determine or claim? What if the ideas or opinions at the root of my decisions come from elsewhere – when can I be said to take ownership of them? What is the autonomous stage or moment in this process? Is it when they are combined by me to make a unique decision? Is that it? Can I be sure I am the one authoring this combination, and it is not prepackaged, anticipated, or prompted in some way? Kant runs into a similar problem in his moral theory: he says the measure of a moral agent is his will or intention, which must be purely rational, and autonomous in that regard. From the outside, however, we can never know those intentions and ascertain their purity; any moral agent may be conflicted, and equally obliged by passions to deliver pleasure and happiness. It is problematic to determine this from the inside, too – to ascertain the purity of my intentions. My rational, conscious mind is hardly so transparent and self-evident as some imagine; much of me is and remains inscrutable, stretching out of view, into the murky depths and tangled roots of the self. The nature, origin, and integrity

---

[37]  See Sigmund Freud, "The Ego and the Id," in Peter Gay (ed.), *The Freud Reader* (New York: W.W. Norton and Company, 1995), 628–658.

of my intentions, I am afraid, will never be completely clear. Sometimes their complexity is illuminated over time, through many experiences, and upon much reflection.

Some will continue to insist that "we all instinctively understand that the private realm is where we can act, think, speak, write, experiment and choose how to be away from the judgmental eyes of others. Privacy is a core condition of being a free person."[38] But who is to say, when alone, that "I choose how to be"? Who is to say "I" am choosing at all? And who can be sure that being alone bars or restricts outside influence? As Martin Heidegger noted, "being-with" others is constitutive of my being as such; I only come to know myself in relation to others in the world – and I know the world thanks to their imprint.[39] In that respect, being alone is just another way of being-with: I continue to conceive of myself and operate in relation to, or in comparison with others – though they are not physically present. I cannot simply deliver or remove myself from this fact of my existence, even for a period of time. It is doubly misleading to suppose that this imagined removal is the condition for personal freedom and potent political action. It is hard to see how mere removal, a space of noninterference, makes me autonomous or politically demanding and effective. It seems guilty of a kind of magical thinking, that autonomy and political will miraculously appear if I am simply consigned a private realm – if I am just left alone. To the extent that I am socially created and disposed, this theory risks alienating me from, and certainly ignoring, the sources of my influence and nature, sources that make me the distinctive person that I am, such as it is. How can I be sure that the voices in my head are trustworthy? How can I be sure of their precise origin, and direction?

It's hard to imagine or understand how we ever escape the influence of others. Even when I retreat into a private domain, away from spying eyes, they continue to move me. In essential ways, I am formed in and by the company of others – which disposes me to act and think in certain ways. Ways that may later be called "autonomous." It is always a supposition, and a dubious one at that, that I act alone, of my own resources and direction – that mine is the only authentic voice that can light the path ahead. Thus, it seems less urgent to claim that we need privacy to be free and independent thinkers – are we ever? What would that be? What would that look like? In any case, collective action

---

[38] Greenwald, 172.
[39] See Martin Heidegger, *Being and Time*, trans. John McQuarrie and Edward Robinson (New York: Harper & Row Publishers, 1962), 149–53.

seems more politically consequential in advancing the bounds of freedom. And it requires a kind of civic preparation that noninterference or privacy of itself cannot muster. In fact, the emphasis on individual privacy may be disempowering, drawing us away from a political wellspring that is more robust, more nourishing.

# 7

## Autonomy and Political Freedom

The political state is a free-willed creation of reflective individual citizens. Such is the directive issued by Modern philosophy, and which we take for granted in liberal democracy. According to Social Contract theory, articulated principally by Hobbes, Locke, and Rousseau, humans leave a state of nature to create and enter the political sphere, which they willingly, intelligently inaugurate through a mutual "contract." Living independently in a state of nature, while perhaps preferable in some respects, is ultimately unsustainable. For humans to effectively pursue and achieve personal ends, and find fulfillment, whatever shape that may take, they must sacrifice absolute freedom in nature, to live together in security. The salient point for the discussion at hand is that, as Social Contract theory has it, individuals conceive of their goals prior to or independently of the political community. The polis is reduced to a mere platform, if you will, a stage that permits or enables us to pursue what we want, in relative peace and harmony.

Could such a transaction ever take place, critics wondered? Where in the world or in human history did people ever come together in this manner and, shaking hands, agree to set aside their natural freedoms willingly, lucidly? It seems improbable, to say the least. But whether this was a historical occurrence is beside the point. Social Contract theory means to say that this notion of rational agreement and mutual sacrifice of unlimited rights grounds political legitimacy. That political state is legitimate to the extent that citizens approve of its existence, and they express their consent – often implicitly – because the state allows and enables them to pursue their goals. When or if the state fails in this regard – if the government has been hijacked by an autocrat, for example, who serves only his own interest or desires – citizens may rebel. A Social Contract suggests that contracting members can withdraw their approval, disband the state, or exchange the ruling regime for one that honors the popular will.

A curious feature of Social Contract theory is that it tends to conceive of individuals alone and independent in nature, unaffiliated with anyone else – like a family. Family structures might be the most natural or logical basis for understanding how nascent communities really formed. But Rousseau, for example, conceives men spurning family life in a state of nature, periodically colluding with members of the opposite sex, to satisfy their urges, then bounding off at once; the lure of independence is so strong. This independence carries through to the political state: a legitimate polity honors, preserves, and channels it. Thus, it is presumed, citizens make decisions primarily with a view to individual gain, with a view to restricted interests and concerns, and not with the broader community in mind. In contemporary democracies, people will affirm that they are looking out for their family – but that is where affiliation stops. I have argued that it halts with the immediate family, and the extended family is largely cut off. Such affiliation does not of course bleed into the larger community. Your neighbors are not considered relations of any kind. Political life is put forth as a functional relationship. You may land next to whomever as your neighbor, it does not matter. He may remain a perfect stranger; your only responsibility to him, and he to you, is to not get in each other's way. That is the sum of your mutual obligation.

Social Contract theory has imparted to liberal democracy a foundational fiction: humans are individuals above all, unconnected to and ultimately uninterested in others in a fundamental moral or political sense. Democratic citizens are essentially "placeless" and "homeless" in this regard.[1] This is the vision of the French Revolution, which considered Rousseau a prominent influence: regional markers of difference and allegiance are washed away, in strict service to enforcing equality. After the Revolution, people were no longer Provençal or Norman or Gascon – or Protestant or Catholic – but French, united by a shared language, and certain ideological commitments, but no longer religion and community. This ignores the extent to which we are formed and disposed by our regional differences, and religious and cultural affiliations. Liberal democracy conceives citizens as atomistic individuals, responsible for their own values and destiny – who will reason and vote accordingly.

Privacy theory is heavily implicated in this account: I require privacy – I must be untainted by social influence – to clear the way for personal decision making. I can only discover my authentic will and ascertain my unique destiny if left alone in crucial ways. And, my native and inherent freedom is intact so

---

[1]   Patrick Deneen, *Why Liberalism Failed* (New Haven, CT: Yale University Press, 2018), 77.

long as privacy is preserved. Privacy is that purifying element that allows citizens to exercise consent, and be free in the state.

Some philosophers have sought to offer an updated version of autonomy that takes into account the many sources of the self – a "relational autonomy." We are social beings first and foremost, and "develop the competency for autonomy through social interaction with other persons. These developments take place in a context of values, meanings and modes of self-reflection that cannot exist except as constituted by social practices."[2] My social setting and formative cultural traditions supply the values and experiences that will shape and guide me if or when I am self-determining at all. And my ability to be self-determining, which involves no small degree of rational acuity and honest self-appraisal, is formed through interacting with others. In my social life, I may come to understand which values resonate, which guide me effectively, or not. I may then decide to alter or dispense with certain values inherited from my cultural background or religion – in favor of others that better reflect inner convictions, as they occur to me through social interaction. Autonomy is displayed in this act, this choice. I come to take ownership of my life-orienting values, the particular combination thereof that meets and coexists in my personal life.

Alternately, we might say that an individual exercises autonomy when he recognizes and embraces a narrative for his life, which develops and evolves over time. An autonomous individual endorses a narrative that incorporates and manifests value commitments, and then ensures as best he can that future choices – personal or social – do not overly alienate him from that perceived narrative. This, too, requires "basic competence in one's ability to reflect critically and to make one's desires effective under favorable conditions."[3] Favorable conditions for individual self-reflection include government support, ironically – the services and protections that uphold society and the economy, and afford us time and energy to reflect. We are again faced with the paradox that citizen autonomy, which should decide the government at hand and stand in oppositional relationship to it if it turns authoritarian, likewise relies on strong government just to be realized and fulfilled – or mustered in the first place. We must hope that government is sage and benign enough to produce individuals who can choose it and challenge it. Reflective citizens require an education system that fosters critical thinking skills and civic habits, and a free press that makes us

---

[2] Marilyn Friedman, "Autonomy, Social Disruption and Women," in Catriona McKenzie and Natalie Stoljar (eds.), *Relational Autonomy* (New York: Oxford University Press, 2000), 40.
[3] John Christman, *The Politics of Persons* (New York: Cambridge University Press, 2009), 242.

aware of real political choices at hand.[4] For a democracy, and the kind of citizens many presume for it, much depends on government munificence. Privacy, one could argue, is also a favorable condition for necessary self-reflection, of course, and it, too, is reliant on government munificence. Privacy is a right that must be protected and preserved. But will citizens know how to use it effectively – to reflect incisively, for example, on the narrative of their lives, their essential values, and then make relevant, consistent choices?

Prevailing notions of privacy side step the question of what preparation and training we require for substantive self-reflection. Too often, little or no account is given for how autonomy or free thinking – the kind that pushes political boundaries and advances civil liberties – is supposed to emerge from mere privacy. As I argued in the previous chapter, it is almost a magical creation: just give people time and space, and, yes, they may come up with plenty of crazy, possibly offensive and combustible ideas – but such is the raw material of political freedom. Free individuals, taken together, can be trusted to mold it all into shape eventually. This view is reminiscent of Adam Smith's Invisible Hand: just as free individuals pursuing their own economic gain will, indirectly and unwittingly, advance the common welfare in the process, so their unfettered speculation and experimentation will advance and expand liberty. I suspect that privacy advocates will say that, ideally, people would be trained to use privacy wisely; specifically, they would agree that people should be well prepared to deploy a critical mind when given time and space alone. But that is not the emphasis of privacy theory – and that is a lingering problem. Privacy tends to be conceived, articulated, and advocated in its negative form, and its positive form is undetermined – or merely hoped for. Will individuals be autonomous in a political sense, if given time and space to reflect – if left alone? Will they be consequential, powerful political actors? Privacy may just as easily prove illiberal; free, private individuals can be politically sidelined. They may sideline themselves. Free, private individuals can be enamored by and engrossed in private concerns, to the detriment of common concerns that demand collective action. Free, private individuals – urged to protect their private freedom, by themselves, as in GDPR – can be isolated against much greater powers, corporate and governmental, and easily subdued, managed, or chased into a state of helpless resignation.

In one respect, it is understandable why privacy theory has little to say when it comes to defining or prompting the substantive reflection that one might engage in in private. It is a creature of liberal democracy,

4   Christman, 242–3.

which is the political effort to accommodate diversity – diversity of faith, cultural background, moral conviction, sexual orientation. Liberal democracy accommodates said diversity chiefly by claiming an official agnosticism or indifference regarding it all, cleansing politics of such concerns. It effectively lifts politics above the fray, by reducing it to a merely functional relationship entered into by contracting individuals who, at least nominally, reflect on their personal concerns and interests. Citizens are to maintain a kind of official indifference towards one another, towards what drives their passions and makes them unique and different; and they are to tolerate people's eccentric pursuits or shocking indulgences, so long as they do not cause undue harm. In this context, in this regime, privacy may produce anything at all. That is the inevitable result of a society that is free in this manner – and that is its iterated aspiration. But there is no guarantee it produces free citizens.

Free thought and speech are among the most highlighted and cherished rights in liberal democracy. But, free thought and speech, consigned to individual citizens, may not be worth much, though they are often enough to satiate the masses, and let them think liberty is safe and secure. There is much more to civic freedom. Democratic citizens are not necessarily prepared by unrestricted speech as such; quite the opposite may occur. They may become preoccupied, uncohesive, defiantly individualistic, striking out on paths of their own, insulting others along the way. Untamed speech can drive people apart, as we see online. In the cacophony of the digital universe, we discover that free speech has arrived at a very undemocratic conclusion – or rather, it has contributed to a state of affairs that undermines and threatens democratic function and coexistence. Seeking out sympathetic souls, feeling free to issue unbridled invectives, digital citizens migrate to echo chambers where they grow hardened towards one another, alienated. Needless to say, they dare not communicate across the divide, though this is supposed to be the essence of democracy, which the Internet was supposed to enhance. Left to their own devices, isolated in private spaces – alone in the basement, before the computer – people are driven apart. And nothing could suit autocracy better.

Freedom is an active enterprise, as opposed to a negative space in which individuals can operate. Better to think of liberty as a project that citizens must practice, uphold, and defend, perhaps constantly. The belief that we are free simply when we are unrestricted in our thoughts and words "blurs recognition of our central need to possess conceptions which are used as tools of directed inquiry and which are tested, rectified and caused to grow in actual use," John Dewey writes. "No man and no mind was ever emancipated merely by being left alone ... "[5] It is serious business learning the "tools of directed inquiry" in a democracy – tools, I might add, that are impactful, and which effectively mobilize communities. We cannot trust or hope that individuals will magically develop such tools – or maintain them – alone, on their own. It takes time and experience for people to learn which tools work best, and how they can be imparted. No single individual can be expected to gain such knowledge in his lifetime. It is learned and perfected over many generations, through a community. Similarly, no single individual on his own, lacking such tools and training – inherited, developed, and flexed in a community – can be expected to engage in accurate, concerted self-reflection, and perform an accurate judgment of reality.

The Chinese government is famous for its efforts to censor parts of the Internet for the home audience – "The Great Firewall," it's called. But it turns out, China is engaged in less censorship than is commonly perceived. Rather, it is instructive to see what its government chooses to censor, and what it does not – and the techniques it employs. Researchers found that "Chinese government censors were not suppressing criticism of the state or the Communist party," but only "posts that had any potential to encourage collective action" – for or against the state, oddly enough.[6] In a way, this makes sense; the Chinese government should not suppress criticism, so much as hear it and understand it – in the right way, that is, or under the right circumstances. To be specific, the Chinese government is happy to understand criticism, so long as it is not threatening – yet. The regime benefits from hearing criticism, and allows it to circulate, because it provides the government with a "feedback mechanism to foster rebalancing."[7] That is, the Chinese government, which gives citizens little opportunity to lodge official complaints, gains needed insights into its weakness and strengths, and the various trends and factions among the general population, from online banter. Authoritarian regimes typically lack such insight, which often proves to be a crucial blind spot. What's more, the persistence of online criticism lends a modest degree of democratic legitimacy to the Chinese state. People feel they at least have some freedom to complain – which is a relief in itself. That may assuage the populace for a time in the absence of real democracy.

Then there is the Chinese regime's "50 Cent Party," a veritable army of online commentators so named because they are paid 50 cents for each online post, and are expected to be prolific in their emissions.[8] While this shadowy,

---

[5]  John Dewey, *The Public and Its Problems* (University Park, PA: The Pennsylvania State University Press, 2012), 132.
[6]  Zeynep Tufekci, *Twitter and Tear Gas* (New Haven, CT: Yale University Press, 2017), 235.
[7]  Tufekci, *Twitter and Tear Gas*, 235.
[8]  Tufekci, *Twitter and Tear Gas*, 237.

unofficial arm of the Chinese government has been known for some years, most believed it was principally charged with issuing comments in support of the regime, or targeting government critics. Apparently, that is not so. Researchers studying the 50 Cent Party's handiwork noticed, by contrast, that its minions are busy blurting out all manner of distractions online, to confuse the people, obscure the truth, and disarm government opponents by dispersing and undermining would-be allies and sympathizers. They tend to "post at high volume during critical junctures, such as anniversaries and sensitive events, but not about topics that are sensitive and critical."[9] They aim to divert people's attention from real political concerns, and possibilities. The result is that the Chinese government effectively mucks up social media, which is then unable to serve the political purposes many had hoped for, like informing the public, illuminating the truth independently of biased news outlets, and consolidating support of parties that communicate and represent the will of the people.

These forces deployed by China – and, as we learned in the 2016 election, by Russia, too – and a host of numerous agents and entities all over the world, have greatly harmed the ability of the digital universe to operate as a public square. Much of the disinformation, we have learned, is aimed at raising hostilities, making certain parties more hardened in their views, and intolerant of the opposition or any who disagree with them. This poisons the well of democracy. Voters start to wonder: who knows what to believe anymore? It's such a mess out there. And why should I even try to engage other people if confusion and vitriol await?

How can we, from our private perches – no matter if they are inviolate – deal with the onslaught of organized efforts at confusion and disinformation? How can each of us alone, of our own devices and acuity, deal with the 50 Cent Party, and its imitators, which abound? We cannot. In this sense, privacy is politically problematic: autocratic regimes are happy to see us retreat into our private cells, isolated, fragmented, at each other's throats, perhaps. And the privacy that people typically want, as I have argued – the privacy to enjoy their possessions and family in the quiet of their own homes, no matter who is watching and why – is illusory and politically inconsequential. We can be too easily satisfied with the semblance of privacy, while the powers that be dominate our lives in other ways.

It is important to note what the Chinese government abhors above all, and looks to foreclose in online activity: the possibility that people might organize in public – for or against the government, mind you. Why does the regime wish to

---

[9] Tufekci, *Twitter and Tear Gas*, 237.

prevent even favorable demonstrations or mass organizations? One observer summed up the thinking thus: "Once people learn to mobilize, even if they do so to support us, who knows what they will try next?"[10] Organizing and mobilizing, this is real political power, and the Chinese autocrats know it. When the people assemble in public, and build common bonds, discover the thrill and possibilities of expressing their will, this is trouble. More than any nation, China knows the impressive power of popular assembly – nonviolent power, I might add. Consider one iconic image the government bars from the Internet at home: the man staring down a line of tanks at the Tiananmen Square protests in 1989. He did not do this alone, of course, though visuals can be deceiving. He was emboldened by masses of protestors accompanying him, just out of the picture; this one man, facing a line of tanks, epitomizes the power of confident assembly. And the Chinese government wants to see no repeat of that.

There is reason to suspect that privacy theory is implicated in certain misconceptions about the nature and proper course of democracy – such as the view that it is primarily a mass of unaffiliated individuals who need their space in order to act and behave as political creatures. As several theorists and commentators have argued, democracy unwittingly took an illiberal turn insofar as it elevated the concerns and interests of individual citizens above all else, and wiped away vestiges of earlier ties and foundations – and the need for them. It seems progressive to assert that the individual citizen is a bearer of universal, immutable rights that government must recognize, honor, and protect. It seems progressive to dispense with conventional and irrational markers of place and faith, which are in fact negotiable, fluid, and fleeting – especially when we likewise elevate the rational individual capable of reflection. He can tell us what he wants; he is able to determine clearly and confidently what makes him happy, what makes for personal fulfillment. In service to the latter, as Tocqueville predicted in his dispatches from the early American republic, democratic citizens will empower and expand the government to serve their personal interests – to secure their personal path forward, and do as they please, independently and individually, responsible to no one else.[11] This issues forth a growing bureaucracy, and expansive government powers designed to meet the growing number of popular needs, and satisfy a growing number of perceived or declared rights. I do not wish to dispute said rights, which may include the right to an education, the right to housing, or

---

[10]   Tufekci, *Twitter and Tear Gas*, 235.
[11]   See Alexis de Tocqueville, *Democracy in America*, ed. Richard Hefner (New York: Penguin Books, 1984), 290–5.

the right to healthcare. I only wish to point out that an immense power disparity emerges when government grows and individuals largely stand alone and unaffiliated before it – no matter the privacy, or personal buffer they have before said behemoth.

Privacy is of little use in this context – amidst this power disparity. To that extent, the emphasis on privacy, the insistence on recovering it or protecting it, may redirect us from resources that inform and sustain the coordination and exercise of popular power. According to John Dewey, these resources are supplied by associations – individuals are not counted on to come upon or develop democratic skills on their own. Associations channel the will of the people far more effectively and consistently than if the latter are a mass of unaffiliated individuals. Thus, Dewey argues, democracy is properly conceived as a collection of associations.[12] They provide crucial nourishment for the political orientation and mobilization of citizens, the "methods and instrumentalities" mentioned above. Associations are the testing ground for democratic skills, where they are learned and imparted, helping overcome the resignation of individual citizens. At the very least, associations embolden citizens to take part in political action at all.

It is a mistake to view democracy solely or even principally in terms of government, or measure it in terms of bureaucratic function, citizen protections, or the trappings of elections. As we have seen too often, it is not hard for regimes to orchestrate some semblance of democracy, the illusion of popular support. In the United States, which we tout as the oldest, largest democracy on earth, barely half the population takes part in elections – in a good year. Presidents rise to power with a minority of the popular vote, and millions are denied a ballot through various legal hoops. In many ways, the United States is a democracy in name only – where government initiatives are enabled or stymied by powerful special interests and industry lobbies – but the citizens are largely persuaded their interests are preserved, and do not overly object to the political decline. In truth, however, "the idea of democracy is a wider and fuller idea than can be exemplified in the state even at its best. To be realized, [democracy] must affect all modes of human association, the family, the school, industry, religion ... [Governmental] institutions are but a mechanism for securing to an idea channels of effective operation."[13]

Democracy is properly organic; it is not artificially, self-consciously imposed from above – indeed, history repeatedly tells us this is not likely or possible, though we try it over and over again. There is a tendency to view

[12] Dewey, 92.
[13] Dewey, 119.

democracy as an ideal form of government, delivered to a rational people, or a people ready and secretly yearning for rational self-direction. But reason may have little to do with it. When it is forceful or impactful, democracy surges forth from associations that are not necessarily laboratories of rational reflection; they are not carefully constructed workshops where individuals are each allotted their own space to arrive at genius, on their own time and pace. Rather, associations tap into democratic instincts, and train democratic habits. "Regarded as an idea, democracy is not an alternative to other principles of associated life. It is the idea of community life itself," Dewey tells us.[14] Which means, we all have a predisposition for democracy, to the extent that any of us are members of a community. Taking part in communal life conveys basic and crucial democratic lessons: I learn how to recognize the will of my neighbors, and, if it conflicts with my own, negotiate. There will necessarily be give and take. I must be instinctually disposed to making the necessary sacrifices of communal life; reason will not reliably do this – reason too easily finds excuses against personal sacrifice. "Only when we start from a community as a fact, grasp the fact in thought so as to clarify and enhance its constituent elements, can we reach an idea of democracy which is not utopian," but realistic, and actual.[15]

Democratic tendencies, a democratic outlook, an appreciation of democratic function, this is all nurtured in associations; each is community writ small. Democracy is reliably prepared for when practiced, nourished, and taught in the family, the school, the church, social clubs, or professional or political advocacy groups. This is not to say that each association is democratic in itself, in its own governing structure. As a father, I will attest that the family ought never be democratic, where children have equal say with parents (in that case, my four kids would regularly outvote me, and we would have chicken fingers for dinner every night). Having been a middle-school teacher, subjected to the mischievous impulses of preteens skewed by raging hormones, I will adamantly say the same for the classroom. The point, rather, is that democratic citizens are made and formed in these associations, where they learn to be part of a community of others with similar natures, desires, and interests. In these associations, even if they are not democratic through and through, democratic instincts can be sown by debates over the political landscape, for example, which enlighten and inspire potential or future voters, and impart appreciation for civic values – rooted in a milieu, I might add, that can be a touchstone for future political motivation, guidance, and reflection.

[14] Dewey, 122.
[15] Dewey, 122.

Dewey, for his part, was deeply interested in the democratic nourishment and preparation provided by schools. Schools are of special concern not principally because of the information passed on there, though civics and history lessons are important for young citizens to learn, so that they may be informed voters. But the mere transfer of information can take place anywhere, in any setting – at home, with your parents for example. Schools serve a different purpose: they enable students to develop skills and habits that are essential to being democratic citizens. They provide a venue where citizens from a young age may come into contact with people from very different backgrounds and traditions, learn to talk to them, coexist with them, and negotiate conflicts as they arise – as they invariably do. In other words, the school offers the opportunity to form a community.

It is a further misconception about democracy that individual citizens are primarily motivated by a rational grasp and sober assessment of their personal needs and interests. As we see too often in modern democracies, much to the consternation of analysts and critics, individuals do not always–or even regularly– vote according to self-interest, but are driven by other aspirations and affinities. American political scientists, for example, have long struggled to understand why white working-class voters migrate to the Republican party, which dismantles labor unions and progressive policies (like healthcare reform) that would boost working-class welfare. Republican leadership reliably promotes the interests of the wealthy, often at the expense of the working class – by, among other things, giving tax cuts to the wealthy, and cutting social programs. Democrats strive to make this evident, noting the growing wealth gap, the most severe inequality we have seen in almost a century, and the demise of social mobility for vast portions of the population. This has largely failed; the white working class has apparently found something else to rally around. That would be group identification, which proves more powerful in stirring voters than calls to reason.

I find the notion persuasive, that "the criteria of the political, its *differentia specifica* (i.e., defining feature) is the friend/enemy discrimination. It [*sic*] deals with the formation of a 'we' as opposed to a 'they' and is always concerned with collective forms of identification."[16] This is a major blind spot of liberal democracy, which insists on viewing citizens as reflective individuals who best know their personal interest, lucidly pursue it, and support abstract institutions that enable their way of life – like rule of law. Demagogues find it too easy to rally people against rule of law, or cause them to ignore when it is broached; they only need to stoke nationalist sentiments, or fan the flames of class resentment and racial spite. We ought not run away

[16] Chantal Mouffe, *On the Political* (New York: Routledge, 2005), 16.

from this fact of political motivation. We ought not simply try to ignore this natural tendency of ours – to group identification – but take advantage of it. Because, evidently, group identification operates through people anyway. Associations may channel group identification in positive ways, ways that are constructive for democracy.

Associations prepare people politically by instilling habits. We cannot count on people to take part in politics prompted or guided by self-reflection, just as we cannot expect they will rationally vote their personal interest. Citizens must be disposed to participate politically; they must be programmed, if you will, to consider or prioritize the interests of a community, as opposed to individual, selfish interests. The temptation to associate with a group will overtake them soon enough, as I have argued, but the task is to make sure the source of this temptation agrees with democracy. Citizens must first develop an instinctual appreciation of or devotion to democratic institutions.

Besides family and school, what might salient associations be? To be specific, what associations might train and nourish democratic habits and values, the building blocks of electoral power? What associations effectively channel popular will, allowing it to exert an impact on the polis? Churches and religious organizations are natural options. They galvanize voters regularly and impressively. This notion may prove anathema to proponents of liberal democracy, which is defiantly secular; it aims to look beyond the religious affiliations of citizens and, crucially, urges that citizens do the same with respect to one another. Born in the Enlightenment, liberal democracy tends to view religion as unforgivably irrational. Religion is beset by much superstition, and has a long, sorry track record of inciting violence. What's more, religion is often authoritarian in character, but we are supposed to be contemplating associations that impart democratic values and instincts. Regarding the relative irrationality of religion, I will say this: it will be difficult if not impossible to transcend or depart the irrationalities endemic to group affiliation and identification. In the following chapter, I will consider how this irreducible irrationality and the destructive potential of group interaction might be mitigated or handled. As for the other charge, even religions of an authoritarian bent dispense crucial democratic lessons to the faithful, teaching them to coordinate and have their will known and heard. Some religious groups, like the Quakers, are democratic through and through, rejecting authoritarianism inside and outside the church. And many have been instrumental in championing civil rights gains, expanding the bounds of political liberty – even, from time to time, the stubbornly authoritarian Catholic Church. Religious organizations are not necessarily anti- or un-democratic. They are critical in forming and directing individuals personally and socially.

In the civil rights movement, for example, churches played an essential role encouraging, inspiring, and organizing protestors. Religion may be essential to how a person makes sense of his life and existence. To that extent, liberal democracy is also misguided in how it seeks to weed out signs of religious affiliation, making society suitably secular – think of the ban on the hijab in France, or Quebec's flirtation with outlawing the wearing of crucifixes.

Returning to the labor movement, the unions played a key role channeling worker demands, and power. Workers realized early on that, so long as they were unorganized and unaffiliated, they could not negotiate or challenge powerful employers. They needed to comprise a proper body – with political power – and organization. Early labor protests were less successful when they were spontaneous. In those cases, it was too easy for employers to cast the protesting workers as violent anarchists and saboteurs – and greet them with violence. Over time, this state of affairs did not suit employers either; they did not come off well in the press. Industrialists soon determined it was best if they could negotiate with an official body that represented worker demands, and presented them in orderly fashion.[17] The unions that were charged with this task, they were not wholly democratic, of course. They had vested leadership, charged with making key political decisions, trained in the art of negotiation, and knowledgeable of the broader labor landscape. Workers who were engaged in the fight, they empowered such leadership. And important gains were made in the name of liberty and equality.

Local political assemblies, neighborhood governance bodies – town-hall meetings – may also count as powerful democratic associations. As many will attest today, local politics in America is widely ignored or disrespected; the soap opera in Washington garners all the attention. But the United States has a proud history of local governance, where citizens engaged in democratic assembly regularly and passionately, so much so that Tocqueville remarked how power was so very decentralized in America.[18] He was deeply impressed by town meetings, for example, where citizens from all walks of life contributed to policy decisions that bore on the community as a whole.[19] Clearly, he noted, the process was invigorating for its participants, who were emboldened to weigh in on all manner of issues. This gave people a sense of ownership over the process, which sustained their continued interest and participation. For anyone concerned about the undue influence or power of religious associations, local governance groups might offer a compelling secular alternative.

[17] Philip Dray, *There is Power in a Union* (New York: Anchor Books, 2010), 116.
[18] Tocqueville, 62.
[19] Tocqueville, 108.

But attendance at local town-hall meetings is poor, and Tocqueville would not see today anything like he had witnessed. Why? Many find participation in local politics utterly uninteresting – an endless procession of dull discussions over school construction, sewer lines, traffic stops. That will put one to sleep after a long day at work, and long drive home. We are more likely to show up if the proposed school sits next to our backyard and threatens our peace and quiet – and parking. Though enamored by the vitality of our local politics, Tocqueville was sure it would not last. America was too commercially driven, in his view; sooner or later, people would be too tempted to focus on private gain, and gradually exclude common concerns.[20] And yet, even for those few who might be open to local participation today, they are often not aware of the possibilities or avenues for participation – because said avenues are not proximate or readily evident. Communities today are not designed to prioritize easy political association of neighbors and ordinary citizens.

The architecture of suburbia urges us to focus on private concerns, detach ourselves from one another, and retreat to backyard oases. This layout has undermined socializing of various sorts, beyond the political. Once upon a time, neighbors might convene at corner bars, public markets, or town squares. Now such convening takes effort – you have to get in your car, back it out of the garage, and travel a few miles for a public encounter. And once upon a time, many Americans were members of fraternal clubs – like the Elks, the Knights of Columbus, or the Rotary Club – which were also a front for a bar, but offered venues for political action. Easy association with neighbors – or anyone – is made much harder in America today. Our built environment matches the aspirations and outlook of liberal democracy where we are all detached individuals, focused primarily on ourselves – inclined to associate only with effort and deliberation.

Our tendency to affiliate with associations, which might ground, channel, and mobilize political action, has been assaulted in another respect: politics has come to be dominated by, if not identified with, economic concerns. Democratic politicians attain success when they speak to and address so-called "pocketbook issues," like taxes or the price of gas. And politicians are increasingly expected to take a greater role in the economy at large, and help fend off recessions, or right the ship after financial turbulence – making sure everyone's retirement accounts are safe and sound, and, hopefully, on the rise. In one respect, however, none of this is properly political, especially if we hew closely to etymological signification. "Political" refers to matters pertaining to the "polis," matters debated and considered there, by the citizens at large (in

---

[20]  Tocqueville, 293.

ancient Greece, admittedly, this was a restricted portion of the population). "Economics" comes from the Greek word "oikos," which means household, and invokes the functional duties and tasks that keep the household running – matters pertaining to the satisfaction of needs and desires, matters pertaining to the business of survival. Hannah Arendt observes that none of this is distinctly or uniquely human.[21] To the extent that economics is preoccupied with satisfying human needs and desires – never asking about their nature or quality – and promoting mere survival or physical flourishing, economics is devoted to concerns and features of human existence that we share with the animals. And, concerned as it is with economics, politics is expected to be functional; it addresses universal, basic human needs.

This sounds again like the inheritance of liberal democracy, which seeks to ignore or transcend controversial issues like morality and faith, and focus instead on universal, basic needs. But this is also the inheritance of the nation-state, imparted by the French Revolution, and which overlaps with the idea of liberal democracy, though not completely. Liberal democracy is one species of nation-state, of which there are other chilling, illiberal incarnations, like Soviet Russia and Maoist China. In many ways, critics like Arendt argue, the illiberal – totalitarian – incarnations were prepared for by the same conditions essential to liberal democracy; thus, they are surprising relations. The French Revolution produced the nation-state, a relatively homogeneous, expansive, and immensely powerful political creation such as the world had never seen. Citizens are washed of regional and religious markers of difference, and reduced to the status of atomistic individuals before an all-powerful central state – all-powerful because it is vested with addressing the egalitarian impulses and demands of the revolution. The state must wade into economics – become preoccupied with it – to ensure that basic needs are met, that people enjoy a certain standard of living, and that wealth is more evenly distributed.

This view of politics gave rise to Marx's prediction of the "withering away of the state," drawn in turn from Saint Simon, the early French socialist, who envisioned a day when the "government of persons" might be replaced by the "administration of things."[22] Devoted as it is to function – consumed with the distribution of wealth, in the name of greater equality – there would be less to debate, politically. Economics purports to be a science, after all, and when the formula for wealth distribution, or the healthy function of the market, is discovered or decided, we are delivered of the need for further deliberation.

[21] Hannah Arendt, *The Human Condition* (Chicago: University of Chicago Press, 1958), 38–49.
[22] Arendt, *Human Condition*, 60.

The secular state only needs to understand welfare in material terms, not vague speculative or moral terms.

This development has grave political consequences. Defined by functional concerns, politics will now be the domain of experts, social scientists, technocrats – a de facto oligarchy. The new oligarchs, seeing themselves as scientists of a kind, with a pretense to unimpeachable objectivity, will issue the right policies for us, without our input, or at least, little of it. This political universe, it should be clear, is less than hospitable to democracy, though the nation-state is the common foundation or platform for democracy today. On matters of special significance, like happiness or the afterlife, the oligarchs will leave us alone; we can, and should, contemplate or express such matters primarily in the privacy of our own homes. The latter are no longer considered viable or relevant political concerns. They are unforgivably messy, inconclusive, and divisive.

Personal differences, especially of belief and morals – cultivated, articulated, and propagated in associations – are deemed an affront to peaceable political society, where matters are to be decided rationally or scientifically. The liberal democracy that emerges emphasizes and enforces equality in key respects, and strives towards conformity – in public. If you must indulge in unique behavior, if you must express real difference, and group affiliation – or religious faith – do so carefully, and discreetly. It's best if you indulge the latter in private. Freedom is consigned to the private realm, according to this scheme, and individualism is forged and celebrated in private. Because, in privacy alone, real uniqueness – which might rankle or offend – is tolerated. In public, by contrast, differences are downplayed or muted, and conflict diminished, and hopefully resolved through compromise, or a willingness to conceal cultural and personal differences that might prove offensive. Arendt explains that in classical times, by contrast, "the public realm ... was permeated by a fiercely agonal spirit, where everybody had constantly to distinguish himself from all others, to show through unique deeds or achievements that he was the best of all. The public realm ... was reserved for individuality; it was the only place where men could show who they really and inexchangeably were."[23]

This is a compelling suggestion, if contrary to our sensibilities today: the public realm is where individuals are made, announced – where individual uniqueness is displayed, expressed, and enacted. Arendt indicates that individuals sought to assert themselves and stand out as individuals; accommodating Dewey, I might say rather that individuals, understood as a confluence of

---

[23]  Arendt, *Human Condition*, 41.

social currents, produced and emboldened by group affiliation, emerge as such in public – not private.

Liberal democracy affirms that we should indeed be bold, creative, and unique individuals, but largely in private, so that we do not disturb or upset others. The public realm is expected to be a place of relative unity – homogeneity – and harmony, and when it is not, as in the current partisan atmosphere in the United States, people bemoan a kind of political failure. It seems we have never been more politically divided than in the age of Trump; Americans from different parties so rarely see eye to eye, and are instinctively offended by one another's views. To maintain unity in the public realm, or at least a sense of decorum, it is best not to say anything of substance, anything that smacks of real convictions that shape and direct you as a person. Such discussion is reserved for special occasions, or special forums, and special audiences. Like the blogosphere, where we issue incendiary remarks to like-minded peers, and become more fixed in our views, more intolerant of others – where we drift further from political foes, and grow hostile to them, until they are quite nearly "evil." And how can you expect to work democratically with entities or agents that are evil?

There is something nonsensical in the notion that I discover, exercise, or express individual differences in private – alone in my basement, undisturbed, unpro- voked, unchallenged – untouched by essential orienting and grounding forces. If there is no audience to witness, affirm, and respond to said differences, no group that provides key real-time insight into how I should understand, embrace, and exercise these differences, what does individualism mean, or matter? In public, where associations meet and interact, and sometimes collide, this is where individual differences are claimed and performed, properly speaking.

What of autonomy in this context? What is it, if, as I have been arguing, we must reconsider the role of individual agency in shaping oneself? Does the notion of relational autonomy offer some kind of bridge to conceiving a free society without privacy, as it is commonly understood and defended? Does relational autonomy offer a sufficiently nuanced account of personal and political freedom? Unfortunately, it seems this notion still clings to an untenable account of privacy. For, its proponents emphasize the role of reflection, the kind that implies privacy as a state where I am "let alone" in some essential fashion, to cogitate, and arrive at unique decisions rationally, which I embrace and recognize as my own, alongside or in response to the traditions that formed me. I may pause, somehow and somewhere, and decide which essential values speak to me, which do not, and choose the right combination to guide my personal life choices.

Who is to say, however, if my decisions post-reflection are so independent and self-driven and self-conscious after all? Do they really depart from the tradition I reject, for example? Do I really attain that needed space, where I distance myself sufficiently, or at all, from my formative tradition? To what extent are my decisions merely a reaction to that tradition, a reaction that is largely instinctual, irrational, angry, prompted by unrecognized trauma? Alternately, to what extent are my "reflective" decisions imbued by the tradition I depart from, and still marked by it in key respects? When is a rebellion like this ever truly or properly "mine"?

To their credit, philosophers who posit relational autonomy are fully aware of the conceptual difficulties – difficulties we may never fully escape or iron out. But, they argue, we must posit autonomy nonetheless, because democracy demands it. Autonomy is an essential "cultural ideal," which "creates a supportive climate for personal scrutiny of traditions, standards and authoritative commands."[24] We must tell people they are autonomous, or that autonomy exists and is worth pursuing, because we cannot have a free society without it. The notion of autonomy informs people that they can and should choose how to live their lives as they see fit, and make demands of government, acting and thinking as democratic citizens. Alternately, we might say that "autonomy does not refer to an ideal of an independent and self-generated life ... [but] is simply the status marker for citizens participating in collective deliberations whose legitimacy constitutes just manifestations of political power."[25] Indeed, how can we understand or imagine citizen deliberation without presumed autonomy? Isn't it a prerequisite for listening to others, heeding them, respecting them? It certainly alters my calculations if I think of them otherwise – as programmed, witless automatons, for example. I cannot take political interlocutors seriously if I do not think they know what they want or say what they mean.

The political fruits of autonomy, understood in this way, are valuable, and I am not sure I would like to do without them. We must, however, resist the metaphysical suggestions of autonomy, namely, that we are each of us a self-creation. We must resist the temptation to think of ourselves, as Spinoza put it, as a "kingdom within a kingdom." This is philosophically dishonest, and, I have been arguing, politically troubling insofar as it fragments us into a sea of atomistic individuals, while political power depends on us recognizing crucial bonds and relations. Perhaps the troubling aspects of autonomy can be tempered if we connect it with an older tradition.

In Classical and early Christian thought, autonomy was understood as a kind of self-control, a discipline of desires and passions, which "forestalled

---

[24]  Friedman, 43.
[25]  Christman, 208.

tyranny, within the polity and the individual soul ... Classical and Christian political thought was self-admittedly more 'art' than 'science': it relied extensively on the fortunate appearance of inspiring founding figures and statesmen who could uphold political and social self-reinforcing virtuous cycles. A signal hallmark of modernity was the rejection of this long-standing view of politics."[26] This invokes the Aristotelian view of self-control – which, against the Stoics, rejects any impossible standard of self-control. Happiness, Aristotle maintains, is dependent on health and wealth; one requires a degree of both to be happy. Penury and ill health cannot be overcome in this regard. The Stoics of course disagreed – they held out the promise that a "wise man can be happy even on the rack." One can overcome his physical ailments and shortcomings, no matter how severe, and defeat the passions. But moral self-control is more art than science, Aristotle contends, with relative degrees of success, which can be periodic, variable, subjective, and fleeting. And character is central to moral calculations. Virtue is a matter of displaying and practicing a rather consistent character over time, and in different situations. Specific virtues may vary; what it means to be courageous over time may change with the setting. But the person of moral character, he generally knows what it means to be virtuous in different situations. This person displays "practical wisdom," which requires considerable experience and practice. And it is dependent on important resources, supplied by the community at large. Character is founded on habits, so you had better make sure people are instilled with good habits. For that reason, Aristotle insists, ethics ultimately gives way to politics; it is impossible to pull the two apart, they are so deeply intertwined and imply one another.

For the Greeks, furthermore – and this is a view famously articulated by Plato – desire is tyrannical. If you do not work to limit it and discipline the soul, desire will take over. And it is insatiable. Thus, the soul at the mercy of desire, Plato maintains, endures a kind of slavery. If you would be free, you must discipline the passions of the soul; you must nourish and fortify the rational part of the soul, through philosophy, to keep the passions in check. Plato also insists that the kind of city one inhabits is essential for imparting good moral training. The polis must hail certain virtues, and promote them in the citizens: wisdom, courage, temperance (or moderation), and justice.[27] These will become what the later Aristotelian philosopher Thomas Aquinas calls the Cardinal Virtues, though he spoke of *practical* wisdom, or prudence,

[26] Deneen, 23–4.
[27] See Plato, *Republic*, trans. G. M. A. Grube (Indianapolis, IN: Hackett Publishing Co., 1992), 103.

instead, which he specified as the proper judgment regarding human behavior and action.[28]

Accordingly, the pre-modern view of liberty "was not doing as one wished, but was choosing the right and virtuous course"; it was "the condition achieved by self-rule, over one's appetites and over the longing for political dominion."[29] By contrast, a negative freedom is dominant in liberal democracy, where you may do as you wish, whatever occurs to you or gives fulfillment – who cares about the shape of your soul? You are free to indulge your desires so long as you don't harm others. Liberal democracy has long been the unwitting beneficiary of religious and moral traditions that inculcate character training, political theorist Patrick Deneen reveals, thereby preventing a wholesale surrender to tyrannical desires.[30] But as it steadily chips away at those traditions, largely in service to professed secularism, and agnosticism regarding moral character, liberal democracy has no inner resources to stymie moral decline. I believe this has major implications for our critique of privacy.

So long as privacy is principally defended as a negative good – so long as it is defended as the right to be left alone, so I can figure out my thoughts, opinions, tastes, what might come of it? What can we hope or expect that privacy will nurture in people? What kind of people can we expect it will produce? I have argued that liberal democracy is prone to a kind of magical thinking: let people think, say, and do whatever they like; political liberty will emerge from the chaos. We may not define or constrain the behavior of free individuals, as far as possible. I submit that the kind of privacy we see online – and yes, it is illusory, for we are spied on from many angles – evinces a troubling eruption of tyrannical passions. Just the sense that we are alone and unwatched, or anonymous – just the simulation of this state – prompts us to indulge sometimes dark passions. Like trolling, where people insult, demean, and stalk victims online, often doing great damage, inflicting personal harm, or trauma. Or the booming pornography industry, expanding to accommodate a steady stream of fetishes. Or the rabid partisanship that plagues digital communications: people feel free to let loose, emit offensive tirades, and indulge deep prejudices. Less dark, perhaps, but equally consequential, we have seen impressive greed unleashed in the digital age, where consumers are easily tempted by online hawkers, and easily purchase all manner of goods. As a result, consumer spending has doubled in America since only 2002, putting

[28]   See Thomas Aquinas, *A Summary of Philosophy*, trans. Richard Regan (Indianapolis, IN: Hackett Publishing Co., 2003), 167.

[29]   Deneen, 100.

[30]   Deneen, 82–90.

many in debt, or making their financial situations worse – and producing nearly 70 percent more waste over the same period.[31] Greed, lust, even sadism, this is what many have opted for in their digital freedom and its simulated privacy. Perhaps it is because these indulgences are so enticing and readily available, and the driving passions so tyrannical, that we find it easy to overlook the tenuous state of privacy and its purported benefits.

Self-control, as Aristotle and Plato conceived it, links one to a community or association; it grounds one in a communal setting and support, because that is where self-control is articulated and guided, and strength replenished. We cannot discipline the passions alone, on our own. Left to our own devices, desire mushrooms, and dominates – and politically, divides. Accordingly, Aristotle remarks that the man who would live alone is either a beast or a god – he succumbs to his passions wholly, or is miraculously resistant to them.[32]

Damningly, Deneen says that liberal democracy is closer to a "res idiotica" than a "res publica."[33] In the res idiotica, citizens are urged to worry about their personal concerns – such is the etymological root of "idiotic" (idiom refers to what is one's own). In the res idiotica, citizens are concerned less with the common good, or with collective interests and aims, which might truly lend political force, and turn instead to an increasingly omnipotent government to satisfy their needs and desires. The end result may be a state where we are each immersed in or preoccupied with tantalizing, tyrannical desires, such that we hardly care or know about machinations of power above and beyond.

For its advocates, privacy is a major, if not principal, countermeasure to centralized power and threats of autocracy. The private realm is where defiant individualism resides, and unorthodox ideas are born and cultivated, before they burst onto the public scene to challenge those in power. I favor Dewey's view that mobilized "publics," comprised of active and perhaps competing associations, stand "in a supportive relationship to the state and its representative institutions" – or, if the state resists democratic input, adopt an "oppositional role, and build power external to the state."[34] The associations, and the mobilized publics they create, predate or live independently of the state. They are expressions and movements of democratic power, which the state is supposed to

---

[31] Alena Samuels, "Online shopping is making us accumulate more garbage," *The Atlantic*, August 21, 2018, www.theatlantic.com/technology/archive/2018/08/online-shopping-and-accumulation-of-junk/567985/.

[32] Aristotle, *Politics*, trans. C. D. C. Reeve (Indianapolis, IN: Hackett Publishing Co., 1998), 5.

[33] Deneen, 173.

[34] Melvin Rogers, "Introduction" to John Dewey, *The Public and Its Problems* (University Park, PA: The Pennsylvania State University Press, 2012), 24.

address, channel, and observe. In any democracy worthy of the name, these publics must be reckoned with; they are the font of democratic power, and the corrective for democratic government – which we cannot hope will arise from within the regime itself. These publics, which occasionally throttle the government from without, as it were, and snap it into line, they are "the essence of democracy's radical character," as Dewey sees it.[35] Arbitrary power is not principally defended against and democracy preserved by individuals whose privacy is inviolate, but by mobilized masses, animated by democratically infused and committed associations – which have a viable space to converge, and act. That is not the private, but the public realm.

---

[35]   Rogers, "Introduction," 29.

# 8

## Powerful Publics

People have long sought out the public realm because of a desire for transcendence. The ancient Greeks sought it out because they wanted more than the *oikos*, or the family home, had to offer. Accordingly, the private realm was long deemed "privative" in some essential way – it deprived us of what it means to be uniquely or distinctly human.[1] In Classical times, the *oikos* was the realm of function and hierarchy. It was hierarchical because of the task at hand, the business of survival. But things were otherwise in the public realm, where men were free – for those lucky enough to be citizens, that is.[2] When they entered the public realm, the realm of politics where freedom was exercised, people were released somewhat, or temporarily, from the tyranny of necessity, and could entertain higher matters and higher concerns – uniquely human concerns.

Necessity entails or demands a kind of violence. We must subdue the earth, scratch at it, corral and butcher the animals to make a living; we must fell trees or hew rocks to construct shelters, which will then rebuff assaults of sun, wind, cold. For the Greeks, the public realm is free of such violence. It is where matters are handled and problems negotiated through *lexis* and *praxis*, speech and action.[3] Citizens reason with one another, and seek to persuade or impress their peers. This involves some presumption of equality as well.

In Athens, the *agora* was the public space in question, today a collection of touristy restaurants and souvenir stands, commonly understood or translated as "marketplace." But it was much more than that. The agora was a place where citizens convened and interacted, and political discussions took place, for anyone to hear. Commerce was carried on there, too, but that was not its

---

[1] Hannah Arendt, *The Human Condition* (Chicago: University of Chicago Press, 1958), 38.
[2] Arendt, *Human Condition*, 30.
[3] Arendt, *Human Condition*, 25.

defining feature, Arendt argues. Citizens principally went there for other goods. They went there because they wanted "something of their own or something they had in common with others to be more permanent than their earthly lives ... The polis was ... their guarantee against the futility of individual life, the space protected against futility and reserved for the relative permanence if not immortality of mortals."[4] Functional concerns, sating the demands of necessity, none of this has the character of permanence. Desires come and go; you toil to satisfy them, only to see them return in similar fashion, with similar urgency. We seek to escape this treadmill of desire, even if only temporarily and periodically.

Humans are the species that hankers after the immortal. Our flight to the public realm exemplifies this yearning. Or it did for much of our history. How did the Greeks and Romans hope to attain immortality in public? They sought virtue; they sought glory. They aimed to elevate themselves through great deeds, so that their reputation and their name might live on. And the public realm was *agonal*, riven by contest and competition, as people sought to outdo one another in acts of virtue, acts that might distinguish them, and endure. Classical philosophers were fond of citing noteworthy figures as moral exemplars; their life story, the virtuous character they displayed, this was the principal lesson carried on for posterity. In the public realm, and in public memory, people sought to distinguish themselves as noble individuals. And there was no comparable opportunity foreseen for the private realm, where endeavors were consigned to oblivion, sooner rather than later.

The public realm has been greatly diminished today. In its place we have "society," this new hybrid, "which is neither private nor public," and is the product of the nation-state.[5] In elevating equality, the nation-state urges that we fit in – we are less free to stand out. Glory is disrespected, and has become a wholly alien value. Glory, we think, is the obsession of narcissists and egomaniacs – actors and politicians at their worst or most comical; or it is the goal of the warrior class. But it is no widely esteemed virtue. Immortality is not a properly public goal at all anymore. Religious allegiances and metaphysical aspirations are private matters. Society blurs the border between public and private concerns, confusing the former for the latter, and elevating the business of survival – economics. It is in this context, over and against the conforming oppression of society, Arendt claims, that privacy takes on its modern form, as sheltering our intimate

---

4   Arendt, *Human Condition*, 55.
5   Arendt, *Human Condition*, 28.

lives.[6] Privacy is now seen as a refuge, and no longer the vital complement to the public realm.

Surveying the American landscape, it is apparent that the public realm is hardly so vibrant as it once was, as it was intended to be and designed. Formerly proud public spaces can be found in town centers across the country, at once busy crossroads, or before government buildings, but are now rarely populated, and routinely bypassed. I think of the courthouse square in my hometown, occupied only by lunching office workers on weekdays. The rest of the time, it is empty and silent. It was, however, constructed and laid out with great care – with bold aspirations and ideals in mind, evident in the solid edifice at its heart, which has easily weathered the years, its granite pillars sculpted to evoke classical times and republican values. The dreary office buildings that have cropped up around it since the 1960s hardly measure up. They convey mere functionality. They are designed to announce little more than the business conveyed within: here you can secure a mortgage, buy insurance, or apply for a government permit. Could these services be elevated? Sure, but that is largely the domain of branding today, that form of marketing alchemy which seeks to identify products and services with enduring values – such that certain values eclipse the products or services in question. Nike, for example, is so much more than a shoe; rather, Nike is a message, a feeling, an emboldening spirit – "Just do it!" And insurance is more than a bet to hedge against future losses, damages, or death; it is a testament to your prudence and wisdom – offered by a good neighbor or friend (who is in fact an inscrutable, multinational firm). The marketing industry understands the human yearning for transcendence very well.

We used to design public places with these expansive values in mind. We used to design spaces that laid claim to permanence, often by linking us with a nurturing past and inspiring tradition, and indirectly invoking the next millennium, where our progeny will likewise endure. It is hard to say what constitutes the premiere public space in America today, but I would nominate the shopping mall, because this is so often where people converge in our culture, or where they go in order to feel like they are out "in public," among a crowd. And the mall certainly seems public; it behaves like a public space in conspicuous ways, or it looks like one. But in many ways, it is not. The mall is made sufficiently welcoming and innocuous, its hard edges smoothed over, so that it does not disturb or distract us from the task at hand: shopping. My local mall has sought to discourage visits from unruly teenagers, who often come from the inner city, and unnerve suburbanites. This policy renders the mall

---

[6]   Arendt, *Human Condition*, 38.

more homogeneous, less threatening. In that respect, the mall has become an extension of the private realm, where shoppers look to be surrounded by their own kind.

Lately, the mall is undergoing an interesting – and telling – transition. In many cases, enclosed malls are being repurposed as open-air "lifestyle centers," which, through various design features, seek to evoke older public spaces that were not so wholly devoted to commercial concerns. Lifestyle centers align stores along a quaint "main street" layout, exuding loads of charm – but surrounded by a sea of parking. Brick sidewalks, wrought iron benches, and lampposts are de rigueur; fountains are a popular feature, as is abundant topiary. One area lifestyle center even touts a fire pit, with the grave of a favorite sportscaster beneath – encircled by a Wegman's grocery store, California Pizza Kitchen, and Dick's Sporting Goods. Storefronts are easily remade for a revolving procession of retailers, who seem to replace one another with regularity, as trends and tastes change. I have often found the final resting place of this poor sportscaster a bit odd, if not offensive – for him. He is installed in a veritable temple to materialism, which caters to fleeting desires, and is perennially reshaped according to consumer whims and economic forces. Despite cursory efforts to the contrary, the lifestyle center makes little pretense of permanence; in all other ways, it militates against it. Not to mention the fact that his resting place is hardly so final. He will likely be moved (I wonder when *his* lease is up?); malls hardly last a few decades before they need to be radically remodeled or redesigned – or retired.

The mall – or lifestyle center – remains a private space, despite nominal gestures attesting otherwise. You can't engage in political protests there. You can't really assemble socially, or for long, as teenagers routinely discover. You can't throw a party there, or have a picnic. You can't hold a rally at the mall. Speech and assembly are tolerated at the pleasure of the mall owners, and their all-important tenants. The modern mall strives to purge difference – real difference, the kind that matters, and which might be alarming or distracting. It diminishes the chance for unmediated, unplanned encounters with strangers. Similarly, it forbids confrontation with jarring transcendent claims or aspirations, which might inspire a person to think about something other than shopping, and maybe even feel a bit guilty about his materialist indulgences.

With design features straight out of imagined 1950s small-town America, lifestyle centers aim to be charming. For Arendt, this is a key give away: charming spaces are not properly public. The public realm cannot tolerate charm "because it is unable to harbor the irrelevant."[7] Spaces that exude

---

[7]   Arendt, *Human Condition*, 52.

charm are not intended to inspire; they are not designed to remind us that we are mortal, that our life on earth is short, that we should strive to make a name for ourselves that will endure, here or in heaven. Charming spaces are largely intended to comfort us, and make us feel safe. They will not challenge us – charm is not compatible with deep questioning, moral challenges, or personal confrontation. Real public spaces, whose meaningfulness endures, or at least lingers, issue bold claims about human nature, social history, or political destiny. They may remind us how and where we are falling short in attaining lofty goals. They may remind us of goals that are perennially pursued, but perhaps never achieved – because they are ideals.

Charm is an apt term for attempts to insert seemingly public spaces in otherwise private domains. Like the tidy "pocket parks" you find in newer suburban and exurban residential developments, often arranged around the retention pond, where neighbors can walk their dog, or sun themselves on a bench, watch the kids play on a jungle gym – but never meet any real neighbors. That is unacceptable, when one treks home after a long day at work. Confrontation with difference – even if it is only perceived or imagined confrontation – is out of the question. We'd rather close the door. And tune in to a news station that reaffirms our worldview.

We have designed our lived environment to mirror the demands and expectations of liberal democracy, where real personal differences are not welcome in the public domain, but must be kept out of view as far as possible. This insistence is politically debilitating: we do not grow accustomed to talking to one another and bridging or negotiating differences, learning a shared language, identifying and honoring common goals and values. In this setting, where easy socializing is made rare – socializing with strangers and neighbors alike, mind you – we lose a common world, which democracy requires. We lose a shared view, understanding, or account of reality.

This again evokes our current political plight, where people are marooned in digital bubbles, and are more divided than ever, it seems. Media critics and political commentators long for a day when we had a shared view of the world, and could at least agree on basic facts – like if our president had orchestrated a spy operation against the opposition party (viz. Watergate). In the age of Trump, his partisan faithful denied evidence that his campaign colluded with Russian operatives, or at least benefited from their efforts, and instead denounced it all as so much "fake news." It is a vast conspiracy, they insisted, rooted in elaborate lies – the drumbeat of a liberal press, bent on taking down the president. Our political parties are so resistant to one another, they no longer agree on what constitutes reality. This extends to the realm of science, too: half the population believes that scientists' evidence-based claims about climate change are just opinion, rooted in prejudice, and serving specific, predetermined political aims.

This is not to say that opposing parties should ever fully agree. I don't mean to give the impression that the public realm is a shared space where we all can be brought to agreement most or even some of the time. Yes, there ought to be agreement on some basic facts and foundational values. More importantly, however, citizens must respect one another, though not necessarily in a friendly, sympathetic way. Still, they must be open to one another, at least minimally – but even this is increasingly foreclosed in our current political landscape. Citizens must see one another as human beings, engaged in similar struggles, beset by similar prejudices and passions, sometimes prone to discontent and conflict – *not* as irredeemably evil or alien entities. This basic openness, this ability to identify with one another, even grudgingly, is achieved and sustained through common and perpetual interaction, which a truly public realm provides for – and which, of its nature, is hardly harmonious or peaceful. In fact, precisely because the public realm is inherently uncomfortable, challenging and raucous, and because our reigning political ideology insists on harmony and homogeneity, people are inclined to flee it.

Philosopher John Rawls offered an influential update on Social Contract theory when he posited a thought experiment dubbed the "veil of ignorance." If members of society ignored their personal differences – differences of gender, income, class, talent, race, ethnicity, etc. – and conceived of what rights should be elevated or secured, and how resources should be allocated, there would be considerable agreement among all of them, Rawls maintained. His thought experiment was also a goal: we should strive to inhabit the kind of society where citizens rationally transcend their differences, whereupon there will be little dispute over the conditions and requirements of a fair playing field, and everyone has equal opportunity to get ahead and thrive. This vision seeks to bracket or diminish the role of passions in making key political decisions and arrangements, but Chantal Mouffe believes this is a major oversight or omission, characteristic of democracy more broadly. The "consensual approach" to politics, as she dubs it, is overly abstract and impracticable, and damaging to democracy.[8]

Politics must allow for, entertain, or host conflicts of difference. When they are ruled out or barred, and distinguishing features ignored or thrust underground, the conflicts risk morphing into something worse. In short, Mouffe argues, when agonism is not permitted, it leads to antagonism. We cannot hope or choose to "ignore the affective dimension mobilized by collective

---

[8]   Chantal Mouffe, *On the Political* (New York: Routledge, 2005), 4.

identifications and to imagine that those supposedly archaic 'passions' are bound to disappear with the advance of individualism and the progress of rationality."⁹ For proponents of liberal democracy, and its resident citizens, the prejudices and animosities inherent in or suggested by "archaic passions" are terrifying indeed. Many cannot bear to tolerate or allow them, for fear of the divisions they will sow, dooming coexistence, or destroying society altogether.

But politics can and should be understood as the means by which persistent and enduring conflicts are managed, not forbidden or banned outright; to that extent, such conflicts are properly or more effectively channeled, and tamed. The differences that spark conflict must not be simply brushed away, concealed in the private realm, as is the tendency in liberal democracy. We must provide a forum and opportunity for them to be aired and exposed – and clash. "Political questions are not mere technical questions to be solved by experts," but must be entertained – frustratingly – by citizens who are inexpert, partial, and possibly prejudiced.¹⁰ Political questions – unlike economic questions – are precisely those that resist solution, or resolution. They will and must be left open, hashed over again and again. We must learn to live with them as such, and the enduring tension or turmoil they impart.

Political projects and claims that truly motivate people, along fault lines of group identification and association, are inherently hegemonic: they tend towards a universalist worldview or agenda that resists compromise.¹¹ Like it or not, that is the native tendency of politics that energizes citizens, driving them to debate, assemble, and vote. We ought not deny it, or shrink from this fact, but accept and accommodate it. Compromise is not a gripping political goal or promise. It does not enthrall voters. Which is why, Mouffe thinks, political participation has declined in some democracies.¹² I think she's right. In the United States, the political party that has shown more appetite for compromise – the Democrats – routinely struggles to drive sympathetic voters to the polls, though demographics indicate the party should be ascendant, if not dominant. Democrats also fail to motivate their base with regularity, though the GOP does not seem to share this problem, or not to the same degree. I think this has a lot to do with each party's respective "call to action."

Consider, for example, the gun debate: Democrats plead for "common sense" regulations – like universal background checks on gun sales, which

⁹   Mouffe, *On the Political*, 6.
¹⁰  Mouffe, *On the Political*, 10.
¹¹  Mouffe, *On the Political*, 3.
¹²  Mouffe, *On the Political*, 24.

are indeed eminently sensible – but have been rebuffed, even while most Americans say they favor gun control measures. The problem is, voters sympathetic to gun control are not consistently motivated to support gun control candidates – or vote at all. Gun rights supporters, meanwhile, vote with regularity, and elect candidates who favor increasingly radical measures, like Permitless Carry, or easier access to armor-piercing bullets and silencers. Are political arguments for expansive gun rights irrational? Of course they are; they are reckless, too. The NRA insists we need all these semi-automatic rifles in order to resist tyrannical government, also to protect our basic freedoms of speech, assembly, and religion. The gun lobby maintains that we are not recognizably free at all, or in any respect, unless we are able to buy very powerful guns, and preferably carry them in public. Precisely because these arguments are bold, precisely because they invoke ideals and uncompromising visions for society, they inspire voters – even those who might be sympathetic to individual gun control measures, as many conservatives are. The NRA has succeeded in linking the gun debate to the broader culture wars. For their part, the Democrats wield sensible, scientific studies from the public health community, and urge modest measures that will make it harder for some people to access guns – and they have largely failed to mobilize effective support for gun control (though the tide may be changing since the 2018 election).

I might offer a similar diagnosis of the healthcare debate. President Obama went a long way to assuage Republican wariness on healthcare reform, even adopting a model that had been cooked up by a conservative think tank, and first enacted by Mitt Romney when he was Republican governor of Massachusetts.[13] Obamacare is essentially a market-based reform of the healthcare industry, where citizens are forced to buy insurance, thereby expanding and diversifying the risk pool, enabling insurers to lower prices on premiums. For a variety of reasons, the reforms intended by Obamacare have struggled to achieve success. Indeed, Republicans have thrown up some debilitating roadblocks, like disbanding the "mandate" that people buy health insurance, the economic linchpin of the law. Republicans succeeded in marshaling opposition to Obamacare by claiming, among other things, that it was a first step to socialism, and our greater liberty was imperiled. Democrats scoffed at the patent absurdity of these claims, made the economic case for Obamacare reforms – and found themselves punished in the polls.

---

[13]  Avik Roy, "How the Heritage Foundation, a conservative think tank, promoted the Individual Mandate," *Forbes.com*, October 20, 2011, www.forbes.com/sites/theapothecary/2011/10/20/how-a-conservative-think-tank-invented-the-individual-mandate/#47b89fe26187.

Hegemonic visions and claims impress voters and mobilize them. Politics must allow for contestation between such visions – we need not insist that we compromise, make peace, stop arguing, and find common ground (though politicians can and should do this behind the closed doors of Congress). In fact, it is dangerous if contestation between competing hegemonic visions does not occur, or is not allowed, and one hegemonic view is simply elevated, while the other is vilified for being too dangerous, intolerant, or regressive. And some people are silenced as a result, their views hustled off into the private realm. Yes, some political views and projects – and hegemonic visions – are morally troubling, even objectionable. But we must, as far as possible, allow every viewpoint and political vision the freedom to be heard and announce itself fully, to campaign and compete, within certain limits. I realize that this has long been held out as the official or purported mission of liberal democracy, with its professed tolerance. But it has done a poor job – thanks to inherent shortcomings and innate limitations.

This view of politics, as allowing and managing inevitable conflict, accepts Freud's claim – shared by Schopenhauer and Nietzsche, among others – that we are compelled by powerful innate aggressive drives that cannot easily be denied. When repressed, Freud argued, these drives issue harmful symptoms, personally, culturally, politically; they don't go away simply by being repressed. How, he asked, does civilization deal with aggressive – and erotic – drives that are of their nature asocial? The answer is that civilization fosters "communal bonds through the mobilization of the libidinal instincts of love ... A collective identity, a 'we' is the result of a libidinal investment, but this necessarily implies the determination of a 'they'."[14] My erotic urges find relief or satisfaction when I bind myself to a group; my aggressive urges find outlet when the group I identify with is pitted against others. The group will bond more tightly, and occasion more libidinal investment, to the extent that it sees itself locked in competition with others. Paradoxically, this outlook, behavior, or propensity diminishes and defuses the possibility of greater violence breaking out. I might add that, just being allowed to vent, just being allowed to voice frustration, hostility, and anger, and gain some recognition, helps satisfy some welled-up aggression. Democratic institutions are uniquely outfitted to permit the contestation of individuals driven by these instincts, and effectively channel it – if we let them operate as they should. One thing, however, is clear: socially threatening hatred or animosity does not go away simply by being banned, banished, or ignored. It

[14] Mouffe, *On the Political*, 25–6.

only risks coming back in newer, perhaps more troubling, ways, which we are unprepared to handle, address, or contemplate.

In the summer of 2017, Americans looked on in horror as white supremacists staged a large and dramatic march in Charlottesville, Virginia. Among other things, the rally was organized to protest the removal of a statue of Confederate general Robert E. Lee. White supremacists paraded through the iconic campus of the University of Virginia, which Thomas Jefferson had designed with Enlightenment values in mind, carrying torches and chanting that Jews "would not replace us." They were confronted by mobs of angry and alarmed counterprotestors; violence ensued, and a woman was killed when a white supremacist drove his car into a crowd of opponents. And then President Trump caused outrage when he said both sides were to blame for the violence – and there were "many good people on both sides" of the protest.

Many were appalled by the brazen display from white supremacists, who were supposed to be sufficiently shamed into silence, and consigned to the dustbin of history – but were instead emboldened by the Trump era, and the president's penchant for inciting racial hostilities and suspicions. Bigots from across the spectrum were coming out of the woodwork, speaking out on various media. And this is not a uniquely American phenomenon. Liberal democracies around the world – many which lamented our ugly history of racism – are seeing a troubling surge in hate groups. In the United States, it has been stunning to see white supremacists emerge in such public fashion, when, only recently, they were anathema. On *Saturday Night Live*, comedian Michael Che summed up the exasperation of many: "Nazis, Confederates – what's with all these old timey threats making comebacks? What's next? Vikings? Polio?"[15] Clearly, bigotry was more prevalent and entrenched than many had assumed. Many are perplexed by the stubborn persistence and bizarre return of racist sentiments linked to historic injustices and atrocities. We cannot hope, however, that such hatred will vanish merely by being censored or kept in private. This is likely to produce the opposite result, and racism will burst out in sickening and unanticipated displays of violence, and we won't know what to do about it, or how to respond.

Indeed, the United States has seen a rise in violence perpetrated by far-right extremists, such as white supremacists. Since 9–11 they are responsible for more

---

[15]    Michael Che, quoted by Elizabeth Blair, "Saturday Night Live stops accepting jokes from freelancers," *NPR*, September 14, 2017, www.npr.org/2017/09/14/551047820/saturday-night-live-stops-accepting-jokes-from-freelancers.

acts of domestic terrorism than are Muslim extremists.[16] And 2017 was marred by other combustible protests, where white supremacists were confronted by anti-fascist counterprotestors, and violence ensued, such as the so-called "Battle of Berkeley." Many of the counterprotests and violent confrontations occurred on college campuses when noted bigots and white supremacists were scheduled to deliver talks. "This is what public demonstration looks like in an era when white nationalism isn't on the fringes, but on the inside of the political mainstream," one law enforcement expert explained. And yet, he noted, "there was an unending stream of violent themed chatter and an almost choreographed exchange of web threats between antagonists across wide geographic expanses."[17] In other words, the violence was presaged online – whipped up, prepared for, exacerbated by escalating rhetoric that bigots felt comfortable spewing from their private bunkers. Digital media allow for or enable easy escalation. And it seems a stretch to say white nationalists are "on the inside of the political mainstream." Yes, they have been emboldened by the Trump presidency; but many of the Charlottesville protestors have seen fit to go underground.[18] Thus, they do not feel wholly encouraged to enter and populate the public realm, which, I would argue, might help defuse their simmering resentment; they still feel sufficiently rejected, shamed – ironically, even persecuted, they say. So long as they feel they are not tolerated and not listened to, this provides an easy argument for bypassing the political realm and opting for violence.

If white supremacists anticipated a violent response on university campuses, it was because they noticed an increasingly prominent – and, for some, alarming – cultural trend taking place: college students are intolerant of views that they deem hurtful to some, views that make for a hostile learning environment. They favor "stopping and punishing offensive speech by faculty and students" alike, and target perceived "microaggressions" in an effort to create "safe spaces."[19] The result has been what some from within liberal academia itself have assailed as a new form of censorship. The phenomenon is not limited to universities of course. Many outside academia endorse a similar approach to hateful worldviews when they emerge in public. Shall we tolerate them? Shall we allow them to present themselves in all their glory,

---

[16]  Janet Reitman, "U.S. law enforcement failed to see the threat of white nationalism. Now they don't know how to stop it," *New York Times*, November 3, 2018, www.nytimes.com/2018/11/03/magazine/FBI-charlottesville-white-nationalism-far-right.html.

[17]  Reitman, "U.S. law enforcement failed to see the threat of white nationalism."

[18]  Reitman, "U.S. law enforcement failed to see the threat of white nationalism."

[19]  Erwin Chemerinsky, Howard Gillman, *Free Speech on Campus* (New Haven, CT: Yale University Press, 2017), 10.

blare their message, and solicit followers? Shouldn't we shut them down preemptively? Shame them into nonexistence? Because so many Americans already assume that silencing hate is the proper approach, they were traumatized by the election of Donald Trump.

Harvard professors postponed exams and assignments the day after the 2016 election, to accommodate students who felt blindsided by the news.[20] Professors across the country gave up on planned lectures (myself included) and instead devoted class time to a kind of group therapy, helping students process the news that the electorate had just rewarded a candidate who flirted, sometimes openly, with bigotry. What did this say about our country? What did it say about a nation that had seemingly evolved on the issue of race, twice electing an African American president with a Muslim name? At the University of Pennsylvania, Trump's alma mater, a "breathing space" was organized for devastated students, which included "cuddling with cats and a puppy, coloring and crafting, and snacks such as tea and chocolate."[21] Many colleges also offered counseling services to students devastated by the election results. Such responses elicited conservative scorn, and complaints about liberal "snowflakes" who were too easily wounded.

The widespread trauma was foreshadowed by students' refusal to tolerate or contemplate the very existence of the Trump candidacy, and all that it represented. At Emory University, students were irate when, during the presidential campaign, they found the words "Trump 2016" scrawled on sidewalks around campus.[22] The university president granted one angry student group a hearing, after it had marched on his house in protest. He subsequently released a statement saying that students were reacting to perceived intimidation in the slogan chalked around campus. That is an accurate assessment; intimidation was Trump's calling card. And yet, it is strange to protest the mere presence of the Republican candidate's name on campus – in the middle of an election. Do students expect to be protected from reality outside their campus bubble, when that reality is harsh and unbecoming? Students demand safe spaces where views they deem offensive – no matter how trivial, or even if they were never meant to cause offense – are shut out, and they are neatly insulated

[20]  Hannah Natanson, "Professors postpone exams after Trump's win," *The Harvard Crimson*, November 11, 2016, www.thecrimson.com/article/2016/11/10/professors-classes-post-election/.

[21]  Jennifer Kabbany, "Ivy League university hosts post-election 'breathing space': Puppy cuddling, coloring, chocolate," *The College Fix*, November 10, 2016, www.thecollegefix.com/ivy-league-university-hosts-post-election-breathing-space-puppy-cuddling-coloring-chocolate/.

[22]  Susan Svriuga, "Someone wrote 'Trump 2016' on Emory's campus in chalk. Some Students said they no longer felt safe," *Washington Post*, March 24, 2016, www.washingtonpost.com/news/grade-point/wp/2016/03/24/someone-wrote-trump-2016-on-emorys-campus-in-chalk-some-students-said-they-no-longer-feel-safe/?utm_term=.ae045a1579c8.

from what is potentially upsetting or disturbing. This seems to be poor preparation for the outside world, where students will not be protected from rudeness or bigotry by accommodating university administrators. Some critics have argued that this hypervigilance against microaggressions and perceived offenses is downright pathological, making students prone to a kind of "emotional reasoning" that compounds anxiety.[23] In any case, the students at Emory and elsewhere wished to silence talk of Trump and associated bigotry, but their insistence did nothing to make it all go away. Instead, these incidents suggest that young adults – future citizens, mind you – are increasingly unable and unprepared for life in the public realm, and would rather inhabit some expanded private realm where they need not be confronted or challenged with disconcerting views.

In liberal democracies, it was long taken as gospel truth that politicians are not to be tolerated if they so much as breathe a hint of bias or prejudice. That was considered an immediate disqualifier. Romney's 2012 presidential campaign was supposedly doomed because he suggested that half of Americans don't want to work, and expect to be taken care of by the other half of the population, the hardworking, conservative half. People were up in arms over this, as well as his insensitivity towards women, evident in the claim that he had "binders full" of their names from past networking, and for future cabinet appointments. In hindsight, Romney was simply too awkward or timid to pull this off, and his infractions are laughably minor compared to Trump, who dispensed with any pretense of politeness from the start, declaring among other things that Mexican immigrants are criminals. Many presumed that Trump's campaign would immediately flame out, but it turns out that millions of Americans appreciated his inflammatory rhetoric, and his willingness to say it. Finally, many thought, here is someone willing to say what we think, but have been shamed into silence. The closet racists had not been converted or chastened at all, it turned out; they were only waiting for someone like Trump to express their lingering prejudices – and they admired him all the more for his courage to speak out. In their intolerance, their unwillingness to contemplate or hear any racist notions or suggestions, liberals were largely unprepared for a threat like Trump – who has since issued grave attacks on democracy.

When students in Athens, Georgia, protested Trump's campaign, one of his supporters taunted them with a sign that said "No Safe Spaces"; another man

[23] Greg Lukianoff and Jonathan Haidt, "The coddling of the American mind," *The Atlantic*, September 2015, www.theatlantic.com/magazine/archive/2015/09/the-coddling-of-the-american-mind/399356/.

sported a poster with the word "Deplorable," and a big arrow pointing to himself.[24] This invoked Hillary Clinton's controversial claim that many Trump supporters were a "basket of deplorables," referencing, in her mind, the neo-Nazis and Ku Klux Klan members that openly endorsed him. Apparently, her comments misfired, and many Trump supporters felt it was evidence of liberal elite scorn for them and their views – views that many on the left felt should not even be uttered. Trump supporters indicated they were tired of being silenced and shunned. They were tired of being looked down upon. This was their revenge.

"No Safe Spaces" aptly rebuts the outrage of liberal college students. We do favors to no one by erecting Safe Spaces – least of all the students themselves. The notion runs counter to the very nature of politics, where, as Mouffe argued, hegemonic positions ought to compete, out in the open. I admit it is a tricky proposition. Many worry that in giving a platform to neo-Nazis, we normalize or legitimize them – we enable them to expand their ranks, and advance politically. Intolerance, many think, is the key to handling them, the only way. But I would argue that it is preferable to hear enduring racist views, learn how noxious they are, understand how they evolve, where they are held, who holds them. One journalist warns that "the genius of the new far right . . . has been their steadfast determination to blend into the larger fabric of society to such an extent that perhaps the only way you might see them as a problem is if you actually want to see them at all."[25] She complains how they have figured out a way to fit in – largely by concealing their hate-filled views, or smoothing their edges, repackaging them in a way that makes them sound somewhat mundane or innocuous. One extremist she interviews stated his views "so laconically you might forget that he actually believes in the concept of a white ethnostate."[26]

White supremacists strive to fit in or lay low; but we ought to encourage them to stand out, and state their differences – as we all should. Racist views can be addressed better this way, I wager, and potential violence preempted, prepared for, or defused. Encourage the white supremacists to express hegemonic views – in hegemonic terms – and in the marketplace of ideas, compete. Don't urge them to hide. Let them spew their venom – short of inciting violence. The border between hate and incitement is vague, and we

---

[24] Associated Press Photo, "Supporters of Donald Trump hold signs taunting anti-Trump student protesters Nov. 9 in downtown Athens, Georgia," November 9, 2016, www.bostonglobe.com /opinion/2016/12/12/get-real-campus-liberals-and-prepare-battle-trump/vhrcjrohWHTOuXO K3dk1FI/story.html.

[25] Reitman, "U.S. law enforcement failed to see the threat of white nationalism."

[26] Reitman, "U.S. law enforcement failed to see the threat of white nationalism."

may not always get it right. But we have too assiduously chastened perceived hate and offense, and the Trump phenomenon proves that this approach does not work. Released from the shadows, in the company of opponents, or the minorities they revile, extremists might finally feel ashamed – which they can too easily avoid if left alone, banished to the private realm, where they encounter sympathetic peers online.

To be sure, American democracy fares better in this regard. In their insistence on establishing tolerant, harmonious societies, European democracies have gone so far as to make some extremist speech illegal, banning anti-Semitism or Holocaust denial, for example. More recently, Europeans have grown uneasy with the Muslim minorities in their midst, especially when they opt for more conservative expressions of the faith – expressions that ancestors had long shed, in many cases. Clearly, European Muslims, who choose to wear the hijab while their parents and grandparents did not, are reacting to perceived disrespect or outright hostility from the white majority. They are urged to fit in; they are urged to dispense with views on women and gays that are insufficiently tolerant. And if you are deemed intolerant, UK Prime Minister Tony Blair had this contradictory message for you: "Our tolerance is part of what makes Britain Britain. So conform to it, or don't come here."[27] In the urging to fit in, Muslims hear another message: don't stand out – it would be better if you were less visible altogether; you must reject or conceal parts of your tradition, culture, and faith that make you distressingly different. And there is the additional unspoken claim, which many Muslims know from experience: even if you do all you can to "fit in" or "lay low," there is no guarantee Europe will accept you – because of your skin color, faith, and last name. Upon reflection, it is no wonder that many Muslims react the way they do, and seek to reconnect with former traditions and practices – practices that do precisely the opposite of what Mr. Blair demanded. The tolerance of European liberal democracies hardly seems so tolerant at all.

But I have been arguing that this is inherent to liberal democracy itself, and even the US branch is not immune to similar pitfalls. For, of its nature, liberal democracy demands that real difference and uniqueness is consigned to the private realm, where it cannot disturb or offend, while the public realm must be peaceful and homogeneous – and hardly so public after all. What kind of public realm is this, when people are asked or urged not to show who they most truly are, and what they most passionately believe, for fear that it might be

---

[27]   Quoted by Will Woodward, "Radical Muslims must integrate, says Blair," *The Guardian*, December 9, 2006, www.theguardian.com/uk/2006/dec/09/religion.immigrationandpublic services.

upsetting to some? We cannot really expect that politics will take place there, or that democracy is advanced under such conditions or stipulations. When parties or movements or political groups are censored in public, officially or unofficially, this makes for a situation such as ours today, where opponents increasingly see one another as intrinsically, irredeemably evil. And you cannot try to talk to, much less coexist with, people who are evil.

The public realm is inherently rough and tumble – when it is allowed to be properly public. Too many citizens in modern democracies are wary of such tumult, or they are unaccustomed to it, and prefer to retreat to the serene security of the private realm. Or they are persuaded that tumult and conflict is unnatural, and unbecoming the political sphere. Under such circumstances, when you lack a vibrant and diverse public realm, you likewise lose active, open democratic citizens, citizens who understand implicitly what it means to be political, and coexist, and negotiate, with the opposition. At home, in private, people try to interact politically in the digital agora; but, increasingly, we see that such interaction is vitriolic. And the vitriol infects and disables democracy more broadly.

Some will contend that there are prominent examples to the contrary, where the digital commons served admirably as a new public realm, and digital communications assisted and enlivened notable political demonstrations. What shall we make of these? And what do they suggest the digital agora portends for us as citizens?

At Tahrir Square in Cairo, social media was a favored tool of the demonstrators who amassed there in 2011, and ultimately brought down the long-standing dictator Hosni Mubarak. Social media was also lauded for helping organize and publicize the Occupy Wall Street movement in New York, when young protestors camped at Zuccotti Park for several weeks, drawing attention to growing inequality in America, and the rise of the 1 percent. And again, social media played a crucial role in assisting the loud and tumultuous protests in Istanbul in 2013, when activists sought to halt government plans to develop Gezi Park; these protests came to express a host of complaints against growing autocracy in Turkey.

For the most part, these movements, which earned awe and admiration early on, failed, in some ways spectacularly. Not long after deposing Mubarak, and engaging in a messy experiment with democracy, Egypt reverted to stifling autocratic rule. We might credit the Occupy movement with bringing the narrative of the 99 percent to a wider consciousness, but it did not see favored policies enacted. In fact, Americans saw fit to put Republicans in charge, who arguably made inequality worse, thanks to massive tax cuts for the wealthy, attacks on Obamacare, and deregulatory favors for the Wall Street banks. As for Turkey, the Gezi Park demonstrations hardly slowed emergent autocratic rule; President Erdogan became more entrenched, and more bent on curtailing civil rights. The Black Lives Matter movement in the United States was hailed for its use of social media to bring much-needed attention to excessive and unwarranted police violence against African Americans. The Trump phenomenon constitutes a certain rebuke to the claims and hopes of racial activists.

What went wrong with these "networked movements," as digital media scholar Zeynep Tufekci calls them?[28] Why did they fail to bring about desired or championed causes? It seems that essential features of these networked movements, which from one angle looked to be unique strengths, defeated their political viability. On one hand, networked movements are marked by a strong degree of horizontalism.[29] They have been radically democratic, and often leaderless.[30] Digital technology is the reason for this: demonstrators could communicate with one another directly, and with masses of people immediately; they could also bypass or hide from the powers-that-be. Networked movements require and involve no top-down communication, where there is a single point or person or office serving as gatekeeper, from which information proceeds, and official statements or positions are disseminated. The radical democracy of these movements has been thrilling to members who rarely or never encountered anything like this before. Needless to say, it emboldened precisely those protestors campaigning against autocratic regimes.

Lack of leadership, bolstered by digital communications, proved to be a key liability for networked movements. At Gezi Park, the Turkish government took control of the protest narrative, when protestors, clinging to the radically democratic nature of the movement, were unwilling to nominate lead negotiators. The government went ahead and selected what it considered apt representatives of the movement, but the protestors were incensed. They felt that chosen parties "did not necessarily represent them – they had not elected them and often were not open to electing or delegating power, especially decision-making power, to anyone."[31] It seems demonstrators were unaccustomed to this, and were indignant at the request. Digital communications, of their nature, had not prepared the protestors to anoint or defer to leaders. To the contrary, digital organization, where anyone and everyone can voice their

---

[28]  Zeynep Tufekci, *Twitter and Tear Gas* (New Haven, CT: Yale University Press, 2017), xxx.
[29]  Tufekci, *Twitter and Tear Gas*, xvi.
[30]  The Black Lives Matter movement may be a notable exception here, since it involved a few feature spokespersons.
[31]  Tufekci, *Twitter and Tear Gas*, 72.

opinions immediately, and rise above the din, fosters the notion that protest does not need representative or enlightened leaders.

What's more, "modern networked movements can scale up quickly and take care of all sorts of logistical tasks without building any substantial organizational capacity before the first protest or march."[32] They can emerge seemingly overnight, expand rapidly, and garner huge amounts of media attention. Due to shallow roots, however, they cannot endure. By contrast, the US civil rights movement had a longer, contested history of preparing and organizing. Civil rights protestors had to take great care in constructing an "infrastructure for logistics," which was largely laid in place before major demonstrations – because of the inevitable challenges they anticipated, protesting in the racist South.[33] Networked movements, lacking history, trials, and experience, are liable to "tactical freeze" in the face of reactions that invariably follow initial success.[34] They are unable and unprepared to adapt, reinvent themselves if need be, and carry on the fight, perhaps in totally different ways; they are too easily disbanded and dispersed by powerful opponents that wish to do them in.

Political liberty requires that we constantly improve "the methods and conditions of debate, discussion and persuasion," which in turn "depends essentially upon freeing and perfecting the processes of inquiry and of dissemination of their conclusions."[35] Digital communications fare best on this latter point. It is hard to think of a better medium for disseminating information than the Internet, which has unleashed a tsunami of data. But so far, digital communications fall short with respect to other ingredients of democracy – "improving conditions of debate and discussion," for example, or "perfecting processes of inquiry." Digital media have enabled massive amounts of information to circumnavigate the globe in the blink of an eye, but we tend to engage limited amounts of it, which is understandable given the absurd abundance of data. We migrate to parts of the Internet or blogosphere that sound familiar, and this only serves to harden or limit our perspective, instead of broadening it, and softening our point of view.

Following Dewey, I agree that deliberation is the essence of democracy, the critical practice and talent of democratic citizens. It implies a kind of reflection, but is necessarily social, and distinct, for example, from contemplation. Quite simply, deliberation refers to the reflection carried out in and by a community. Citizens must be trained for it, the habits of deliberation

[32]  Tufekci, *Twitter and Tear Gas*, 70.
[33]  Tufekci, *Twitter and Tear Gas*, 70.
[34]  Tufekci, *Twitter and Tear Gas*, xvi.
[35]  John Dewey, *The Public and Its Problems* (University Park, PA: The Pennsylvania State University Press, 2012), 155.

engrained and imparted in a social setting. And it is unclear that this practice can be carried out remotely, as in digital communications. "A community must always remain a matter of face-to-face intercourse," Dewey insists.[36] Why? Why can we not muster a digital "community," properly speaking? Why do digital media (thus far) fail to produce community, in the democratically significant sense of the word? Why prioritize face-to-face interaction and communication?

For one thing, it is harder to hide from people when you must confront them personally and physically. When addressing people to their face, in protest or persuasion, you must force yourself to be open to them, even in some small way. Just to speak, just to address or appeal to them – and, you hope, speak effectively – you must enter into or adopt their perspective or worldview, even briefly, or in part. Learning or trying to speak in a way that others, who are sometimes quite different from you, can understand, this is a practice that necessarily builds empathy. For, it requires that we truly listen to them, which means taking in the nuances of communication that can only fully be transmitted in person. At the very least, this stands a better chance of producing grudging respect and acknowledgement of the others' humanity – which is too easily ignored online, where you can drop verbal bombs and walk away.

As they stand now, digital media make it too easy to speak thoughtlessly, carelessly, roughly, offensively. You are less apt to do so when your interlocutor, your enemy or victim, stands before you, and looks into your eyes – and may react violently to perceived offense. Or you must deal with the physical ramifications of seeing him insulted and demeaned. Confucius was very concerned about the art of speaking: it requires foresight and careful consideration of the setting, your company, and rational goals, he said. How you speak, and how you prepare to speak – if you prepare at all – are critical to the development of character.[37] In short, Confucius argued, the way you learn to speak to others, even instinctively, will inform the character you embrace, and exude. It impacts how you see and navigate the world. Speech determines the kind of social creature you will be, how you will coexist with others, and draw nourishment from them. When our training is diminished in this regard, and we are less accustomed to addressing diverse parties and interests, and building relationships that might endure through many trials and tribulations, we are diminished as citizens, and the community suffers in turn.

---

[36] Dewey, 156.

[37] See, for example, Analect 2:18 in Confucius, *Analects*, trans. Edward Slingerland (Indianapolis, IN: Hackett Publishing Co., 2003), 13–14.

Digital organization, much less individual privacy, does not intimidate illiberal regimes. But networked movements reveal that many people are hungry to assemble and exercise democratic power – in public. Such movements may figure out how to build upon digital structures in a more sustainable fashion. Until that day, however, they ought to recognize where power is reliably found and cultivated – and how change proceeds arduously, slowly, and through sometimes painful conflict and cooperation. Digital organization, and any private dissent, must be matched by displays of popular power, preferably over long periods of time, engrained in community traditions, in the public sphere. There can be no better substitute or alternative.

# Conclusion

Many are worried for the fate and future of privacy, and rightly so. It is impossible to get anything done these days without leaving telltale digital trails, which eager spies scoop up. And it turns out you don't have to divulge much for companies to learn a lot about you. Our digital monitors are busy figuring out how to plumb our intimate depths on the basis of seemingly innocuous and mundane details – details that we hardly give a thought to. What's more, some companies, like Facebook, aim to compile profiles of you even if you are a relative troglodyte, and engage in little or no digital commerce at all. If you do all you can and should to protect your privacy, even making the ultimate sacrifice of foregoing digital communications altogether, this may not be enough. Facebook will simply learn about you from your neighbors, friends, and family, who invoke you, or imply your existence.

Scholars, activists, and legislators champion regulations that might better protect the privacy of consumers and citizens in the digital age. On one hand, they would like to constrain the mammoth technology firms; on the other, they hope to empower individual consumers to better care for their privacy. The former entails that we require corporations to be more careful in handling and managing the personal information of consumers, and also to be less aggressive, greedy, and reckless in monetizing every single piece of consumer data. I am skeptical about constraining the Facebooks and Googles of the world in this fashion. The genie is already out of the bottle: these corporations have immense power to monitor us, analyze and understand us, predict and perhaps influence our behavior. Is it reasonable to expect that they will simply stow it away and leave it dormant? For how long? Can we count on them to be good citizens, and resist the temptation to deploy this power? For that matter, do we know all the power these firms have, now and in the near future, so that we may regulate effectively and consistently for the global marketplace? Some of our spies will skirt if not avoid the law, and use surveillance and data analysis tools anyway. Even if you doubt the efficacy of corporate efforts to monitor and understand us, their bold ambitions have been laid bare; with the tantalizing prospect of influencing consumers, they will surely hone methods of data collection and analysis. Some of the firms in question are among the richest, most powerful companies on earth, indeed, in history. In the United States, they have effectively resisted regulation, and will continue to fight it. Thanks to their intense lobbying, we may never have the chance to constrain them sufficiently or fully, or in ways that keep up with the swift pace of innovation.

I am also dubious about regulations that would empower individual consumers to better protect their privacy. Central to this new surveillance economy is the willingness, even eagerness of consumers to sacrifice their privacy in return for bountiful convenience. Why should we have much confidence that they will take it upon themselves to resist this sacrifice, at least in great numbers? This would require a kind of mass conversion, where people come to understand and appreciate the value of privacy anew. Many theorists and philosophers are busy defining and defending privacy, but I am unsure how their efforts are supposed to inspire the mass conversion that is needed – even something more modest. For example, I don't see how people are to be swayed by arguments that free speech depends on privacy when, in the age of social media, speech of all kinds, temperaments, and perspectives flows freely – indeed, too freely. Social media have effectively, and for better or for worse, made people feel freer than ever as expressive individuals – and as autonomous agents, too, navigating the economy and daily life in superior fashion, getting what they want precisely when they want it, how, when, and where. I admit this sense of personal freedom and autonomy is incomplete, if not illusory. It does not amount to political liberty and power that is consequential or effective. But these are the challenges that privacy's apologists are up against in their effort to rally support for this embattled institution, and make regulations work. I am not optimistic that privacy advocates can overcome these challenges any time soon – or soon enough. Digital technology evolves at lightning speed, and offers consumers countless new temptations in exchange for their personal information. As I sought to show with looming medical innovations, surveillance – of a very intimate kind – is a central feature, such that the innovations, which will be in high demand, are unthinkable without it. Surveillance is soon to be, if not already, deeply embedded in our daily life and expectations.

The battle for political liberty requires that we open other fronts. To combat the behemoths that aim to manipulate us on the basis of data collection, and, as best they can, turn us into mindless automatons or brand devotees, we must do more than protect the negative space of individual freedom. Rather, we must recommit to the values, virtues, norms, and habits of democratic life, in order to produce citizens and individuals who can better withstand the efforts of manipulation and control.

My main task here has been to consider the prospects for political freedom when privacy is endangered if not extinct – which the digital age promises. Specifically, I wanted to see if or how democracy might survive in these straits, since critics claim that privacy is absolutely necessary for democracy to function. Many people today do not know how, or cannot be bothered, to act the part of democratic citizens, but for reasons unrelated to lost or threatened privacy. Many Americans are not inclined to act politically; they do not care to take part in politics, such as Tocqueville saw in the early republic, by actively and routinely contributing to public deliberation on policy matters. This seems utterly uninteresting to people today; or it is simply out of the realm of imagination. The democratic deliberation of early American townships is hopelessly remote, and never occurs to us as a viable option to fit into our weekly or monthly routines. Instead, we have opted to act politically through proxies, that is, elected officials. And, as the *Federalist Papers* indicate, this governing model was meant precisely to limit the impact, influence, and political activity of ordinary citizens. Their desires and demands would be taken up and channeled, also molded and edited, by representatives who hailed from elite circles. This was Hamilton and Madison's intention. Jefferson knew it, and objected. Late in life, Jefferson wrote how our model of government would not sustain broad democratic interest and activity among the people.[1] And he was right.

Digital media have contributed to political ignorance and impotence. By which I mean, as digital participants, we do not learn how to be and act as political creatures. Rather, we learn to act principally as private individuals, in a virtual public realm – where it turns out we are not so private. It is a curious state of affairs, and I can't help but be reminded of Plato's "Myth of Gyges" from the *Republic*. Glaucon tells Socrates this myth to make the point that people are only concerned to appear just; in truth, they want to commit injustice. They would rather indulge their vices without suffering public opprobrium. And Gyges' ring, which in Glaucon's telling renders invisible the shepherd who discovers it, launches its possessor on a path of sin. With

---

[1] See for example Thomas Jefferson, "Letter to Samuel Kercheval, July 12, 1816," accessed at *The Online Library of Liberty, Liberty Fund. org*, http://oll.libertyfund.org/title/808/88342; and "Letter to Thomas Cartwright, June 5, 1824," accessed at *The Electronic Text Center*, University of Virginia Library, http://etext.lib.virginia.edu/etcbin/toccer-new2?id=JefLett.sg m&images=images/modeng&data=/texts/english/modeng/parsed&tag=public&part= 276&division=div1.

this, Plato offers a compelling thought experiment: if you could make yourself invisible on occasion, what would you do? How would this impact your behavior? Would you use your newfound power to work for the common good? Wouldn't you rather be inclined to indulge your wildest desires, since there is no risk of social disdain or judgment? Fantasizing about the prospect of invisibility leads us to contemplate dastardly deeds.

Online, many of us behave as if we had found Gyges' ring. We act and speak as if no one is watching, or no one is looking directly at us – or no one knows our identity. And of course, none of that is the case, though it feels otherwise. Everything we do is watched – intently – and catalogued, and analyzed; and then that information is used in ways we hardly anticipate or understand – or like. The mediated nature of digital platforms makes it easy for us to ignore or forget the impact of our digital trails.

It also makes it easy to ignore the impact and influence of our words. For all the show of free speech online, we do not become more politically empowered in the process, because, for the most part, we are not properly political at all in this medium. Liberated as seemingly invisible individuals, free to do and say what we like, we do not build common bonds, but are driven apart – and often drive one another apart, through incendiary, divisive, careless speech. As we see in the case of recent networked movements, we have not yet learned how to exercise and accumulate political power online, or at least translate it into consequential political action in public, and in history. That may change, but so far, digital media have done a better job of enabling autocrats and weakening democracy.

Though many worry for our privacy (and many do not), the health and vitality of our public life is a greater concern for political freedom. In the public realm, this is where we understand how to be political creatures; it is where we act the part of citizens. And the totalitarian states that Hannah Arendt describes, which conquered the private lives of their subjects in the aim of total domination, began by invading the public realm, and under-mining public life. They could only conquer the private realm by first destroy-ing the framework and architecture of public assembly and organization. As Arendt tells it, totalitarian regimes were prepared for by the nation-state, which undermined existing communities and communal identification, and instead highlighted the role of citizens as atomistic, autonomous individuals before the central government.

In its current state, the digital agora is a poor substitute for public spaces that have been emptied, degraded, or dismantled. In short, digital media prove to be no public space at all, because they do not nurture us as effective political actors. The latter entails that we have the facility and means for reaching out to other citizens, no matter how different they may be, and coordinating our abilities and powers. It entails that we are trained and nurtured in the habit of organizing, and that we are provided spaces where we can reach out to diverse individuals and communities, communicate fully – as responsible, visible human beings, in all our complexity – and flex our muscles in coordinated political bodies. Tellingly, John Dewey refers to said bodies as "publics," and they are the key to exerting power in a democracy, both because they transmit democratic talents and dispositions, also because they allow us to contest massive institutions and interests who wish to abuse or control us.

Luckily, unless otherwise tampered with, society offers the chance for these "publics" to emerge organically from a variety of natural, preexisting associations. Social Contract theory would have us believe the individual is the basic element of society, the building block, if you will. Society is formed when individuals, after independent reflection, decide to contract together. I suspect, rather, that we are social through and through. We are socially disposed, and socially active and involved long before we get to decide on it. We are each of us part of a miniature association called the family. And each family, even before we vote on it, is already plugged in to other larger associations: schools, churches, ethnic or social clubs, political parties, unions, neighborhoods. These associations naturally shape us. If designed or disposed accordingly, they inform how we should operate in a democracy. Being part of an association, even short of having an equal vote, is already a democratic practice in a way. For, it requires that we learn to live with and listen to people who are different from us, and oppose our interests on occasion. Coexisting in a democracy requires that we learn to negotiate life with diverse peoples – and not opt for violence to get what we want.

For these and other reasons, there is a lot riding on the way we design, construct and sustain our lived environment, with a view to whom we will encounter and engage with on a regular basis. Traditionally, Americans have done too good a job segregating society, either racially or along class lines. We are too often successful in avoiding those who are different or threatening. Digital media are notably – and conspicuously – guilty on this count. We hardly need encounter anyone unusual or challenging online; it is, or can be, a perfectly curated milieu, purified of anything disconcerting or controversial, which might expand or modify our perspective, and teach empathy.

Part of being a public creature is encountering and enduring competition from our peers, neighbors, and fellow citizens. In liberal democracies, we tend to think the public realm should be relatively conflict-free and given to rational compromise, but that is too much to expect of an engaged, involved demos. A conflict-free public realm is better designed for a detached, sedated populace, who hand over political decision making to experts, technocrats, or a ruling class. A democracy worthy of the name requires that people are invested in policy-making decisions, and in the elevation and pursuit of guiding ideals. None of this is the subject for peaceful, detached discussions. Political and moral ideals, which are at stake, speak to and invoke our emotions. They earn our support, or better yet our devotion, by stoking emotional attachment. This is a stubborn fact about political life that we would do well to acknowledge and account for. There is little use in ignoring it.

To that extent, the liberal democratic model, which features and elevates privacy, is problematic. According to this model, the public realm is supposed to be transactional and orderly. It demands a kind of homogeneity, or, better yet, it can't really handle sustained or significant heterogeneity. What is unique, controversial, distinctive, and divisive ought, in liberal democracy, to be shunted to the private realm, where no one needs to contend with it. Do not offend: that is the public mantra. Be tolerant. Thus, liberal democracy would reduce us to economic actors, because that is our least controversial incarnation.

Perversely, this strenuous effort for tolerance spells its reverse: we are intolerant of multi-dimensional human persons when they appear, in all their foibles and all their glory. We are less prepared to deal with humans who exude unruly emotions, superstitions, or prejudices. We instinctively seek to shut them up and shut them out. This is no way of learning to live together. It is a kind of fantasyland – or, better yet, a virtual reality, such as we find online (and, increasingly, on college campuses), where we can seek out our own, and avoid anything uncomfortable or unexpected. This is no preparation for life in the real world, the sometimes unpleasant world outside our four walls. And it is no preparation for life in a real democracy, which bears rude surprises from time to time – like the resurgence of white nationalism. We need to find a better way to receive and tolerate public input of all kinds – we need to find a better way to receive and interact with human beings, in their real, stubborn, and sometimes vexing diversity.

"All thinking, strictly speaking, is done in solitude," Arendt writes, "and is a dialogue between me and myself."[2] As such, solitary thinking is the condition of, as much as it is conditioned by, social engagement. It is produced and shaped through interacting with others. I learn how to carry out the dialogue of thought through said interactions. That is where I learn how to ask questions; that is where I discover how questions operate on people, when they are

---

[2]    Hannah Arendt, *Origins of Totalitarianism* (New York: Houghton Miflin Harcourt Publishing Co., 1994), 476.

effective, and when they are not. That is where I learn to give useful or deceitful responses – and perhaps understand better when and how I lie to myself. And the discursive nature of thought disposes me in turn to be a social actor. It enables me to have and hold conversations with others – it prepares me to speak and listen, confidently or openly, as the case may be. It prepares me to address others so that I can extract reasonable, productive responses, not simply cause offense or spark conflict.

Social interactions anchor and animate thought. I must regularly return to the outside world for my inner dialogue to be grounded, and confirmed, so that I may have confidence in its veracity, pertinence, relevance, and import. Otherwise, I am unmoored, floating to oblivion. "The banality of evil," which totalitarian regimes prompt us to abide or abet, "is the inability to hear another voice, the inability to have a dialogue either with oneself, or the imagination to have a dialogue with the world."[3] Totalitarian regimes sever our social connections, and, in this way, doom the project of thought – our sanity, our very humanity.

To the extent that we have privacy or anything that approaches it, like the solitude conducive to thought, it relies on public action, interaction, and sustenance. The personal space that privacy advocates aim to preserve and protect is the inherent by-product of effective democracy, where moral and political attention is focused on the public realm, and the power that is generated there. And what we do in that personal space, the reflection and growth that occurs there, is informed and nourished by public power. We citizens will secure our privacy, such as it is, when we empower ourselves by combining forces and energies, channeling our strength, and expressing our will to any who would subdue or control us.

---

[3] Lyndsey Stonebridge, interview by Krista Tippett, "Thinking and friendship in dark times: Hannah Arendt for now," *The On Being Project* (podcast), May 18, 2017, https://onbeing.org/programs/lyndsey-stonebridge-thinking-and-friendship-in-dark-times-hannah-arendt-for-now-may2017/.

# Index